CW00959276

ONLY IN
COLOGNE

Duncan J. D. Smith

ONLY IN
COLOGNE

A Guide to Unique Locations,
Hidden Corners and Unusual Objects

Photographs by
Duncan J. D. Smith

**The
Urban
Explorer**

To the memory of my father Trevor,
who first inspired me to track down unusual locations,
I dedicate this book with love

Above: Detail of a gravestone in the Old Kalk Cemetery (Alter Kalker Friedhof) (see no. 48)

Page 2: Late Gothic storage buildings (Stapelhäuser) on Fischmarkt with the Church of St. Martin the Great (Gross-St.-Martin-Kirche) behind (see no. 36)

Contents

Introduction   8

City Centre (West Bank):
Innenstadt North (Borough 1) (Altstadt-Nord, Neustadt-Nord)

1   The Ruins of Colonia Agrippinensis   11
2   The Father of Modern Perfume   14
3   The Fountains of Cologne   17
4   The Invention of the Stumbling Stone   19
5   Excavating the Goldsmiths' Quarter   21
6   Churches in Ruins   23
7   An Unusual Statue for a Prussian King   25
8   The Most Popular Theatre in Germany   28
9   Private Passions Made Public   30
10 A Medieval Sense of Humour!   32
11 Cathedral Curiosities   34
12 Walking the Roman Walls   37
13 A Descent into Cologne's Crypts   40
14 The Birthplace of Electronic Music   43
15 A Shrine to Cutlery   45
16 Where Voices of Dissent are Still Loud   47
17 Street Names and House Numbers   50
18 The Horse Heads of Richmodstrasse   52
19 The Fascinating History of Money   55
20 Panama Hats and a Good Cup of Tea   57
21 How Cologne Might Have Looked   60
22 The Horrors of Klingelpütz   63
23 In the Footsteps of Pilgrims   66
24 The Sinking of the *Cöln*   68
25 The Underground Chandelier   70
26 A Pioneer of Post-War Modernism   73
27 Cologne's Original Skyscraper   76
28 The World's Greatest Heap of Debris   79
29 A Car in Concrete   81

City Centre (West Bank):
Innenstadt South (Borough 1) (Altstadt-Süd, Neustadt-Süd)

30 The World in a Museum   83
31 A Dozen Romanesque Churches   86
32 Don't Forget the Mustard   88
33 Casanova and the Chapel of Misery   91
34 Silver Screen Cologne   93

35 Portals to the Past   96
36 Hotel Secrets, Secret Hotels   98
37 Europe's First Art Hotel   101
38 The Sound of Chinese Bells   104
39 Homage to a Water Reservoir   107

City Centre (East Bank):
Innenstadt (Borough 1) (Deutz)

40 The Last of the Swing Bridges   110
41 Is That Really a Church?   113
42 A Road under the Rhine   116
43 The World's First Engine Factory   119
44 An Award Winning Petrol Station   121

Eastern Suburbs:
Porz (Borough 7)
Kalk (Borough 8)
Mülheim (Borough 9)

45 On the River at Zündorf   123
46 Wild in the Country   126
47 At the Temple of the Afghan Hindus   128
48 On God's Green Acres   130
49 From Brewery to Beer Glass   133
50 The Real Home of the Suspended Railway   136
51 The Heart of Turkish Cologne   139
52 Where Robber Barons Once Held Court   142
53 A Home For Old Trams   145
54 Cologne's Earliest Inhabitants   148
55 A Prussian Optical Telegraph Station   150
56 An Unexpected Japanese Garden   152

Northwest Suburbs:
Ehrenfeld (Borough 4)
Nippes (Borough 5)
Chorweiler (Borough 6)

57 On the Trail of Rare Creatures   154
58 Palm Trees and Giant Water Lilies   157
59 Old Railroads on the Rhine   160
60 Bunker World   162
61 The Forty Millionth Ford is a Fiesta   165
62 A Curious Lake   168
63 A Taste of the Country   171

64 Where the Red Baron Learned to Fly   173
65 The Jewish Stones Speak   176
66 In Search of the Real Cologne   179
67 Memorials to Human Suffering   182
68 A Lighthouse Far From the Sea   185
69 Rock Climbing in the City   187
70 A *Jugendstil* Bathing Temple   189
71 The European Capital of Carnival   192

Southwest Suburbs:
Rodenkirchen (Borough 2)
Lindenthal (Borough 3)

72 A Hidden Roman Tomb   195
73 Historic Housing Estates   197
74 A Kidnapping in Lindenthal   200
75 Adenauer the Innovator   202
76 How Hitler Became Chancellor   205
77 Napoleon's Cemetery   208
78 The University Coal Mine   210
79 From Cemetery to Market Hall   212
80 Controversy at the Martin Luther House   215
81 Building Towers for Bismarck   217
82 Once Germany's Largest Fortress   219
83 The Legend of Bishop Maternus   221
84 Gunpowder, Candles and Art   224

Appendices

Opening Times   227
Bibliography   230
Acknowledgements   231
Imprint   232

Introduction

> "In Köhln, a town of monks and bones
> And pavements fang'd with murderous stones"
>
> Cologne, Samuel Taylor Coleridge (1828)

Cologne (Köln in German; Kölle, in Cologne's Kölsch dialect) might only be Germany's fourth largest city – and overlooked by some visitors in favour of Berlin, Hamburg and Munich – yet it remains the country's most historic. The words of the English poet Samuel Taylor Coleridge (1772–1834) capture well Cologne's rich and storied past. Located strategically on the banks of the Rhine it was here two thousand years ago that the Romans founded their northernmost colony, which gave rise to the city's name.

The location was economically important, too, explaining Cologne's later transformation into a Frankish power base, and the accession of its wealthy merchants to the Hanseatic League. As *Sancta Colonia*, Germany's largest medieval town boasted an enviable array of Romanesque churches, with holy relics guaranteeing the city's position as a major pilgrimage centre.

In 1475 the Holy Roman Emperor Frederick III (1452–1493)* conferred the status of Free Imperial City upon Cologne, a status it retained until the arrival of Napoleon's forces in 1794. From 1815 until the end of the First World War Cologne was under Prussian administration, and became a heavily fortified bulwark against France. After the Second World War, during which much of the city centre was destroyed, Cologne became the largest city in the German Federal State of North Rhine-Westphalia (though not its capital); it has subsequently reinvented itself as the region's major service, cultural, and media centre.

Cologne's long history is all pervading and prompts many of the recommendations proffered by the relatively few mainstream guidebooks. The undemanding visitor thus gains easy access to a broad array of museums, galleries, restaurants, and noteworthy buildings. However, there is much more to Cologne than meets the eye, and this guidebook has been written for those independent travellers wishing to discover something more of the place for themselves. It only takes a few minutes of planning, and a glance at a good street map**, to get off the beaten track and discover a very different Cologne.

Based on personal experience walking through the city's nine boroughs *(Stadtbezirke)* the author points the explorer in a new and unusual direction. This is the Cologne of Roman ruins and religious relics; forgotten fortresses and unexpected sanctuaries; abandoned cemeteries and little-known museums; atmospheric crypts and individual shops; not to mention the city's superb nineteenth century sewer system and an artificial coal mine beneath the university, both of which can now be visited. Cologne is also a city with a turbulent past, its poignant Jewish history and numerous memorials to the victims of Nazi aggression still bearing grim witness to terrible times.

As might be expected, many of these unusual historic locations are located in Cologne's former walled town *(Altstadt)* on the west bank of the Rhine, and Deutz on the east. It was in this central borough that the history of Cologne began. A similar number of locations, however, lie beyond these well-trodden areas, in the boroughs of Ehrenfeld, Nippes and Chorweiler to the northwest, and in Rodenkirchen and Lindenthal to the southwest. Further hidden corners await discovery across the river in the eastern boroughs of Porz, Kalk and Mülheim.

Using Cologne's far-reaching light rail network *(Stadtbahn)*, which includes both overground tram routes and subways *(U-Bahn)*, as well as the city's extensive bus and cycle routes, the explorer can quickly reach all the locations described – and that's without detracting whatsoever from the sense of personal discovery that each of these places has to offer. Indeed, directions have been kept to a minimum so as to leave the visitor free to find their own particular path. Whether searching for the relics of Saint Ursula and her virgins, tracking down where the Red Baron learned to fly, gazing up at Cologne's original skyscraper, staying at the world's first art hotel, or exploring the city's Turkish Quarter, it is hoped that the explorer will experience a sense of having made the discovery for themselves.

Duncan J. D. Smith, Cologne & Vienna

* The dates given after the names of Germany's various monarchs are the actual years they reigned for, whereas those given after important non-royal personalities relate to their birth and death.

** Most street maps of Cologne cover the city centre and surroundings; the excellent Falk Stadtplan Extra covers all nine boroughs and shows rail, Stadtbahn and bus routes. (Borough names and numbers are given beneath each chapter title, with district names in brackets for the *Innenstadt* only. At the end of each chapter there is a selection of other locations within walking distance. An alphabetical list of opening times appears at the back of the book.)

A pile of Roman pots displayed in Cologne's Romano-Germanic Museum (Römisch-Germanisches Museum) on Roncalliplatz

1 The Ruins of Colonia Agrippinensis

Innenstadt (Altstadt-Nord) (Borough 1), a tour of Roman remains
beginning in the basement of C&A at Schildergasse 60–68
Stadtbahn 1, 7, 9 Heumarkt; Bus 132
(From 2015: Nord-Süd-Stadtbahn Rathaus)

The story of Cologne really begins with the Romans. Between 58 and 51 BC the legions of Julius Caesar (100–44 BC) conquered that part of Western Europe known to them as Gaul. During the campaign they depopulated the left bank of the Rhine – the eastern border *(Limes)* between Gaul and tribal Germania – so as to accommodate the re-settlement of a Roman-friendly Germanic tribe from the right bank called the Ubii. This occurred in 38 BC when the Roman General Marcus Vipsanius Agrippa (c. 63–12 BC) established a legionary camp known as Oppidum Ubiorum, on the site of what is today modern Cologne. In 50 AD, at the behest of Agrippina the Younger (16–59 AD), the wife of Emperor Claudius (10 BC–54 AD), the settlement was re-established as a high status city *(Colonia)*, to be known henceforth as Colonia Claudia Ara Agrippinensium (CCAA for short). By 90 AD it had become the capital of the Roman province of Germania Inferior.

In its heyday, Colonia Agrippinensis was a mirror of Rome in the provinces. Like the Eternal City it had an imperial altar (hence *Ara*), a *Capitolium* in which the Capitoline Gods were worshipped, a grid street plan, and a protective wall (see nos. 12 & 13). Two thousand years later and elements of the layout can still be made out in the landscape of the modern city. Hohe Strasse, for instance, which was the first completely pedestrianised street in Germany, follows the course of the Roman *Cardo Maximus* (the main north-south street in a Roman settlement). Similarly, Schildergasse lies over the *Decumanus Maximus* (the main east-west street), where at number 60–68 a great chunk of the Roman Forum can be found opposite the public toilets in the basement of C&A!

Beneath modern Cologne there are numerous tantalising fragments of the Roman past: a Roman exercise hall *(Palaestra)*, open air pool *(Natatio)* and warehouse complex *(Horrea)* beneath the Church of St. Martin the Great (Gross-St.-Martin-Kirche) at Gross St. Martin 9; the *Capitolium* beneath the Church of Saint Maria im Kapitol (St.-Maria-im-Capitol-Kirche) at Kasinostrasse 6 (Altstadt-Süd); and a

The impressive ruins of the Roman Praetorium

cemetery of Roman stone sarcophagi beneath the Church of St. Severin (St.-Severins-Kirche) on Severinskirchplatz (see no. 13).

To make sense of it all head to the Romano-Germanic Museum (Römisch-Germanisches Museum) at Roncalliplatz 4 (Altstadt-Nord) (the remains of a paved street leading to the former Roman harbour were unearthed during the museum's construction and removed to its south side). This excellent museum contains not only impressive large-scale sculpture, including a former city gate and a fifteen metre-high mausoleum, but also objects from everyday life, including leather sandals, oil lamps, thimbles, glassware, brooches, children's toys, a lady's hand mirror, weighing scales, and bronze writing implements.

After visiting the museum head underground once again, this time to experience the most impressive of Cologne's subterranean Roman remains. The *Praetorium* was the seat of the governor of Germania Inferior and what's left of it can be reached by a staircase at Kleine Budengasse 2 (Altstadt-Nord). A series of walkways, squeezed in between Roman ground level and a modern concrete roof, give access not only to the ruins but also to the Roman sewer (Römischer Abwasserkanal) that once drained the building. Measuring 2.5 metres high and 1.22 metres wide the sewer was in use until the Roman withdrawal from the Rhineland during the fifth century, and it can be walked for several hundred metres.

This stone-built sewer beneath Kleine Budengasse once drained the Praetorium

The eventual fate of the *Praetorium* represents the fate of the Romans in the Rhineland. Between 260 and 274, when the Franks and Alamanni threatened Roman control in Gaul, it became the imperial residence of the renegade Gallic Empire. When the area was reconquered by Rome, Emperor Constantine I (272–337) rebuilt the *Praetorium* and constructed the first permanent bridge across the Rhine, to a bridgehead fort called Divitia (now Deutz). This failed to prevent the Franks from sacking the town in 355 and 388, and in 455 Colonia Agrippinensis became the capital of the Frankish sub-group, the Ripuarians. By this time the Roman army had withdrawn permanently from the Rhineland, and the *Praetorium* was occupied subsequently by the Merovingian and Carolingian Franks. The building was eventually destroyed by an earthquake sometime in the mid-eighth century.

Other places of interest nearby: 2, 3, 6, 14, 16, 18

2 The Father of Modern Perfume

Innenstadt (Altstadt-Nord) (Borough 1), the Farina House Perfume
Museum (Duftmuseum im Farina-Haus) at Obenmarspforten 21
opposite Gülichplatz
Stadtbahn 1, 7, 9 Heumarkt; Bus 132
(From 2015: Nord-Süd-Stadtbahn Rathaus)

"I have discovered a scent that reminds me of a spring morning in Italy,
of mountain narcissus, orange blossom just after the rain. It gives me
great refreshment, strengthens my senses and imagination." With
these words the twenty three year old Italian *parfumeur* Giovanni Maria Farina (1685–1766) described his elation at having created *Original
Eau de Cologne (Original Kölnisch Wasser)*, which he named in honour of
his adopted home on the Rhine. The distinctive perfume is still being
produced by the same family, and sold from the same place at Obenmarspforten 21 (Altstadt-Nord), which is now home to the fascinating
Farina House Perfume Museum (Duftmuseum im Farina-Haus). Few
other products in the world have been so connected with the name of a
city for so long.

Giovanni Maria Farina first arrived in Cologne in 1706. In 1709 his
brother Giovanni Battista established a business at the corner of Unter
Goldschmied and Gross Budengasse selling "French Goods" such as
silks, wigs, feathers, belts, and buckles. There was a lucrative market
for fine trappings during the Late Baroque (Rococo) period in Cologne,
and Giovanni Maria was invited to join the venture with his perfume.
It is interesting to note that despite being foreigners in Cologne the
Farina brothers enjoyed civil rights as Catholics. Their not being en-
titled to join a trade guild actually worked in their favour, since they
could trade across several fields and beyond the boundaries of the local
community, which was crucial since the real market for luxury goods
lay in the princely societies outside Cologne.

In 1714 Giovanni Maria became a citizen of Cologne as Johann Maria Farina, and in 1723 the business was moved to its present-day site
on Obenmarspforten (today's neo-Baroque premises were erected in
1897–1899). Johann Maria designed the sales room himself, which he
believed should be worthy of the refined clientele who were expected
as customers, and who would act as emissaries for his perfume in the
wider world.

Farina was well versed in the art of the *aromatiseur*, that is the pro-

An original perfume
bottle in the Farina
House Perfume
Museum (Duftmuseum
im Farina-Haus) on
Obenmarspforten

cess of distilling pure alcohol from quality wines, ethanol being the
superlative carrier of fragrances extracted from blossoms and fruits.
But what made his perfume unique was his expert use of pure essences
hitherto unknown in Europe, such as bergamot, lime, grapefruit, and
bitter orange *(neroli)*, sourced from their region of origin. The labori-
ous process of *enfleurage* by which essence is extracted from the plant
is illustrated in the Perfume Museum today. Farina's *Original Eau de
Cologne*, with its top note of citrus borne by evaporating alcohol, en-
raptured those who wore it, creating an aura about them of the far-off
Mediterranean. The real stroke of genius was that the middle and base
notes of the perfume, in combination with the skin, produced an individual aroma for each user.

Another innovation at the time was Farina's ability to maintain exactly the same smell in his perfume, despite the inconstancies of using

A display of historic perfume bottles in the Farina House Perfume Museum
(Duftmuseum im Farina-Haus)

non-synthetic ingredients. This he did by establishing a rigid set of reference samples that is still used today. It was the pinnacle of the perfumer's art and it is little wonder that Farina is known as the Father of Modern Perfume.

Farina's strategy of appealing to an audience outside Cologne was an enormous success, and his account book reads like a Who's Who of European nobility and royalty. Emperor Charles VI of Austria, for example, sent a bottle (or *flacon*) of *Original Eau de Cologne* to all those whose support he needed to legitimise his Pragmatic Sanction, by which his daughter Maria Theresia could succeed him as empress. Empress Maria Theresia herself became a valued customer, as did the likes of King Louis XV of France, King Frederick the Great of Prussia, Empress Elisabeth of Austria, and Queen Victoria of England (Marlene Dietrich, Indira Gandhi, and Diana, Princess of Wales would join the list). Farina's scrupulously maintained account books together with copies of the many letters he wrote to customers now form the most complete company archive in Europe. The desk where he generated much of this paperwork is preserved in the company's museum, alongside a collection of historic perfume bottles, and a selection of the many imitations that the perfume inevitably spawned. In 1874 a law was passed in the Reichstag protecting brand names and *Johann Maria Farina gegenüber dem Jülichsplatz* was the very first one to be registered.

Other places of interest nearby: 3, 4, 5, 6, 7, 10

3 The Fountains of Cologne

Innenstadt (Altstadt-Nord) (Borough 1), a tour of fountains
beginning with the Frauenbrunnen (Women's Fountain) in the
courtyard of Obenmarspforten 21
Stadtbahn 1, 7, 9 Heumarkt; Bus 132
(From 2015: Nord-Süd-Stadtbahn Rathaus)

Lovers of classical music will know the colourful tone poem *Fontane di Roma (Fountains of Rome)* by Italian composer Ottorino Respighi (1879–1936), brilliantly evoking the city where he settled in 1913. Like Rome, Cologne is embellished with a large number of fountains *(Brunnen)* – more than a hundred at the last count – but they have yet to inspire such wonderful music. This seems a pity since they make an aesthetic and therapeutic contribution to the urban scene. What follows is an anti-clockwise odyssey of some of those to be found in Altstadt-Nord.

The journey begins with the Frauenbrunnen (Women's Fountain) inside the courtyard of Obenmarspforten 21. The work of German ceramic artist Anneliese Langenbach (1926–2008) it depicts ten women, representing the different nationalities to have inhabited Cologne during its two thousand year history, from the time of the pre-Roman Ubii tribe and the Romans, through the Franks, Jews and Prussians, right up to the present day. Outside on tiny Gülichplatz is the Fastnachts-brunnen erected in 1913. This fountain consists of a bronze cauldron decorated with characters from Cologne's famous Carnival, for which *Fastnacht* is another name (see no. 71).

Heading north past the Town Hall (Rathaus) one passes the modern Theo-Burauen-Brunnen on Kleine Budengasse, erected in honour of Cologne's mayor from 1956 to 1973. On nearby Alter Markt is another Carnival-related fountain, the Jan von Werth-Brunnen, erected in 1884. It recalls the love story of Jan and Griet, which is enacted each year at Severinstor (Altstadt-Süd) during the opening of Cologne's Carnival season. Moving eastwards through Marsplatz, where an old hand-operated public water pump is still standing, charming Ostermann-platz is reached. Here is the Ostermann-Brunnen, which was erected in the late 1930s to commemorate the Cologne songwriter Willi Ostermann (1876–1936), whose songs are always a favourite during Carnival.

Further north is the Heinzelmännchen-Brunnen on Am Hof. Dating back to 1900 the fountain's sculptures depict the elf-like *Heinzelmännchen*, who according to legend came out at night to do the work of Cologne's manual workers. Also shown is the suspicious Cologne wife,

The Frauenbrunnen (Women's Fountain) stands in a courtyard at Obenmarspforten 21

who fearing that her husband would become lazy, sprinkled dried peas across his workshop floor causing the dwarves to fall over, as a result of which they never returned.

In the forecourt of Cologne Cathedral (Kölner Dom) is the Taubenbrunnen (Pigeons' Fountain) designed in 1953 by the German artist Ewald Mataré (1887–1965), whose work was denounced as degenerate by the Nazi regime. It is notable for being the first abstract fountain to be erected in Cologne after the Second World War.

A couple of streets westwards, in the courtyard of the Museum of Applied Arts (Museum für Angewandte Kunst) on An der Rechtschule, is another fountain by Mataré. The Stefan-Lochner-Brunnen takes the form of a slender pillar, topped with an angel holding an artist's palette, and marks the five hundredth anniversary of the death of Cologne's greatest Late Gothic painter, whose work can be found in the Wallraf-Richartz Museum on Obenmarspforten (Altstadt-Nord) (see no. 11).

Farther westwards is the Römerbrunnen (Roman Fountain) on Appellhofplatz, although it actually only dates from 1915. The fountain celebrates Cologne's Roman heritage and depicts the Capitoline She-Wolf suckling Romulus and Remus, an image taken from the legend of the founding of Rome. The westernmost point of this journey is marked by the Löwenbrunnen on Erich-Klibansky-Platz, which carries the names of more than a thousand Jewish children murdered by the Nazis.

Next is the DuMont-Brunnen on Breite Strasse, installed in 1986 in celebration of the Cologne publishing house nearby, and adorned with literary motifs. A few streets away in Offenbachplatz is an altogether different fountain installed in 1966 by the Cologne sculptor Jürgen Hans Grümmer (1935–2008). He used glass from Berlin's ruined Gedächtniskirche, as well as pieces from the luxury yacht of Aristotle Onassis. The tour finishes with the Bierbrunnen at the bottom end of Schilderstrasse, designed by students in the early 1970s, and sponsored by a Cologne brewery. The beer that once gushed forth from the fountain has today been replaced by water!

Other places of interest nearby: 2, 4, 5, 6, 7, 10

4 The Invention of the Stumbling Stone

Innenstadt (Altstadt-Nord) (Borough 1), the Stumbling Stone
(Stolperstein) on Rathausplatz
Stadtbahn 1, 7, 9 Heumarkt; Bus 132
(From 2015: Nord-Süd-Stadtbahn Rathaus)

Outside the entrance to Cologne's Town Hall (Rathaus) on Rathausplatz, where in 1933 Nazi troops ousted mayor Konrad Adenauer (1876–1967) in favour of Gauleiter Josef Grohé (1902–1987), there is a small brass plate embedded in the cobblestones. On its surface is inscribed a decree issued by Reichsführer-SS Heinrich Himmler (1900–1945) ordering the deportation of Cologne's "Zigeunerische Personen" (by which he meant Roma and Sinti) to the concentration camp at Auschwitz. The plaque is the work of Berlin-born artist Gunter Demnig (b. 1947), who in 1990 marked the route taken by the deportees – from an assembly point in Bickendorf to Deutz railway station – in chalk on the pavement. When one resident expressed surprise that gypsies had ever lived in her neighbourhood Demnig got the idea to render his chalk line in metal, so as to create a permanent reminder of those who had died.

The little brass plaque in Rathausplatz is an example of what Demnig calls a *Stolperstein*, or stumbling stone. Designed to surprise pedestrians on the street they are usually located in front of the last known residence of victims of the Nazi regime. Demnig laid his first stumbling stone illegally in Berlin in 1996, and after several years of negotiations was permitted to install more. Other countries have followed, including Austria, Poland, Hungary, the Czech Republic, and Italy, bringing the total number of stumbling stones across Europe to approximately twenty five thousand.

Demnig has stated that his aim is to bring back from obscurity the individual names of the millions of Jews, resistance fighters, homosexuals, and Roma and Sinti who perished at the hands of the Nazis between 1933 and 1945. The stones, which carry the name, date of birth, and date and place of death, are intended to reinstate some sort of identity to the victims, most of whom received neither a funeral nor a grave marker. Unlike conventional Holocaust memorials, which usually consist of individual wall plaques and standing monuments, stumbling stones derive their impact from being modest yet omnipresent. Dem-

A Stumbling Stone (Stolperstein) outside the Town Hall (Rathaus) on Rathausplatz

nig has referred to his ongoing project as a social sculpture, which when viewed as a whole is the biggest art monument in the world.

The author of the current work came across the background to one of Cologne's stumbling stones whilst conducting his research. Standing alongside him was an American, who explained that he was in Cologne to attend the installation of a *Stolperstein* for his grandfather, Michael Marx, who had lived at Eigelstor 110 (Altstadt-Nord). In late March 1939, with war looming and anti-Semitism rife, Marx dispatched his son to the safety of Rotterdam but elected to remain in Cologne to nurse his sick wife. By 1941 he had been placed in a forced labour camp on Neusser Strasse (Nippes), and on 20th July 1942 he and other Jewish residents of Cologne were deported by train, supposedly to be relocated in Poland. In reality they were transferred to cattle wagons and taken to the death camp of Maly Trostinets on the outskirts of Minsk, Belorussia. That none of them survived makes the stumbling stone outside Eigelstor 110 even more poignant.

Anyone can contact Gunter Demnig and sponsor a *Stolperstein* for around a hundred Euros, which pays for the materials and the artist's time. The historical research for each stone is done voluntarily, either by the surviving family or else by local citizens or students. In many cases the family attend the installation of the stone, bringing some sort of closure for those who have mourned for so long.

Similar to Gunter Demnig's stumbling stones are the so-called *Totensteine*, or death stones, clustered on the riverbank at the end of Markmannsgasse (Altstadt-Nord). The work of artist Tom Fecht (b. 1952) they are part of a Europe-wide initiative initiated in 1992 to memorialise the victims of AIDS, in locations where they once lived, worked, and socialised.

Other places of interest nearby: 2, 3, 5, 6, 7, 10

5 Excavating the Goldsmiths' Quarter

Innenstadt (Altstadt-Nord) (Borough 1), the Archaeological Zone/
Jewish Museum (Archäologische Zone/Jüdisches Museum)
on Rathausplatz
Stadtbahn 1, 7, 9 Heumarkt; Bus 132
(From 2015: Nord-Süd-Stadtbahn Rathaus)

Until recently Cologne's Rathausplatz was a barren area of civic paving, used as a thoroughfare between Hohe Strasse and Alter Markt, and as a meeting point for those attending weddings at the Town Hall. There is now another good reason to come here, since recent archaeological excavations have revealed the fascinating but fragile remains of one of the most important Jewish quarters in Europe. With the excavations complete the area has been opened to the public in conjunction with the adjacent Roman Governor's Palace *(Praetorium)* as the Archaeological Zone/Jewish Museum (Archäologische Zone/Jüdisches Museum) (see no. 1). Visitors now have the unique opportunity of witnessing two thousand years of urban development in Cologne, within an area of just seven thousand square metres.

There has been a Jewish community in Cologne since the first century AD. In 321 the Roman Emperor Constantine I (272–337) decreed that Jews participate in the town Senate *(Curia)*. As such this is the oldest written source for a Jewish community north of the Alps. Documentary evidence suggests the Jews were initially allowed to live peacefully in Cologne; archaeological evidence shows their ghetto to have been focussed on Rathausplatz, where the ruins of a synagogue, one of the largest in Germany, have now been revealed. The synagogue existed at least as early as the ninth century, and occupied the site of a fourth century structure of unknown purpose.

Although many of Cologne's Jews were killed during a pogrom dating from the start of the Crusades in 1096, the community quickly re-established itself and experienced something a golden age – quite literally! During this period many Jews rose to positions of wealth as gold merchants and pawn brokers, both professions proscribed by Christians. The recent excavations have uncovered the remains of a row of twelfth and thirteenth century houses along Portalsgasse, between the aptly named Judengasse and Unter Goldschmied, the latter recalling the presence of Jewish goldsmiths here.

Archaeologists uncovering the remains of Cologne's medieval synagogue on Rathausplatz

Of particular interest is Haus Bardowick, which may have been the first guild house of the goldsmiths, the foundations of which include the remains of a Roman under-floor heating system *(Hypocaust)*. Haus Nichols is named after the goldsmith Nichol, who lived here in the mid-thirteenth century, although the first documented owner was the goldsmith Theoderich von Metz. To the rear of the building was a Jewish bakery. Haus zum Golde, as its name suggests, was also connected with goldsmithing, its owner Maria Goltslegerrsa running a gold leaf business here. Haus Koppe is interesting in that it features a stone pillar that would have supported a vault, like the one still intact in the twelfth century Girkeller at Lintgasse 14 (the only fully extant Romanesque patrician house in Cologne is the Overstolzenhaus at Rheingasse 12 (Altstadt-Süd)).

Between the houses and the synagogue lay the so-called *Mikveh*, a ritual plunge bath constructed around 1170. The bath was used as a means of removing religious impurity, purifying ritual objects touched by gentiles, and for cleansing women before marriage and after menstruation. Since only living water can be used in such rituals the bath is located seventeen metres below street level – *Mikveh* means sunken in Hebrew – where groundwater rises and falls with the level of the Rhine.

Despite the Archbishop of Cologne issuing an edict protecting the Jews in 1266 the community suffered a second pogrom in 1349, principally as a response to the arrival of the Black Death in Cologne. The history of the medieval Jewish quarter ended in 1424, when continuing prejudice saw the remaining Jews expelled across the Rhine to Deutz and their synagogue converted into a chapel for the town council. Not until the arrival of the French in the 1790s would the Jews be allowed to return to the west bank (see no. 65).

Other places of interest nearby: 2, 3, 4, 6, 7, 8

6   Churches in Ruins

Innenstadt (Altstadt-Nord) (Borough 1), the Old Church of
St. Alban's (Alt-St.-Alban-Kirche) on Quatermarkt
Stadtbahn 1, 7, 9 Heumarkt; Bus 132
(From 2015: Nord-Süd-Stadtbahn Rathaus)

By the end of the Second World War, Allied air raids had reduced ninety percent of central Cologne to ruins, prompting the architect and urban planner Rudolf Schwarz (1897–1961) to dub the city the "world's greatest heap of debris" (see no. 28). Schwarz conceived the master plan for the reconstruction of Cologne in 1947, which involved the construction of several major new thoroughfares and the reconstruction of Cologne's twelve great Romanesque churches (see no. 31). The destruction of these churches had meant a huge cultural loss for Cologne, and their rebuilding, whilst questioned by some art historians, was generally approved.

Less well known are the dozen non-Romanesque city churches damaged in the war, for example the Herz-Jesu-Kirche and the Mauritiuskirche, which have been left partially ruined as monuments to the futility of war. Another is the eleventh century Church of St. Alban on Quatermarkt (Altstadt-Nord), which was one of the oldest parish churches in Cologne until its destruction in 1943. After the decision was taken not to rebuild, a new St. Alban's Church was built in Stadtgarten (Neustadt-Nord). Since 1959 the atmospheric ruins of Old St. Alban's (Alt-St.-Alban-Kirche), together with the thought-provoking statues *Trauernde Eltern (Grieving Parents)*, have stood as a memorial for the dead of both world wars. The statues are copies by the sculptor Ewald Mataré (1887–1965) of originals by Käthe Kollwitz (1867–1945), which can be found in a military cemetery in Flanders, where her own son was killed and buried. (The Käthe Kollwitz Museum is at Neumarkt 18–24 (Altstadt-Nord).)

A different approach was taken with the Church of St. Kolumba (St.-Kolumba-Kirche) at Kolumbastrasse 4 (Altstadt-Nord), first documented in 980 and also one of Cologne's most important parish churches. Severely damaged in 1943 only a few outside walls and a Gothic statue of the Virgin Mary survived unscathed. In 1947 the architect Gottfried Böhm (b. 1920) erected a chapel inside the ruins to shelter the statue, which was known thereafter as *Madonna in den Trümmern (Our Lady of the Ruins)*. Candles, stained glass, and a shell-like

Only bare brick walls remain of the Old Church of St. Alban's (Alt-St.-Alban-Kirche) on Quatermarkt

ceiling imbue the chapel with a special atmosphere. Over the entrance to the chapel Böhm placed a sculpture of a bear, recalling a local legend in which the virginal Saint Kolumba was saved by a bear from losing her chastity.

In 2007 the ruins were sensationally transformed into a new home for the Cologne Diocese Museum (Kunstmuseum des Erzbistums Köln), an important collection of Christian artwork founded in 1853. The Swiss architect Peter Zumthor (b. 1943) ingeniously combined both the medieval ruins and the chapel together with an entirely new outer structure to create a unique and contemplative space known as the Kolumba Museum. Walkways enable visitors to view the foundations of the old church, as well as even older archaeological remains from the Roman period. In terms of urban planning the resuscitated ruins have restored something of the lost heart of what was once one of Cologne's most beautiful areas.

Another city church partially destroyed during the Second World War is the Antonite Church (Antoniterkirche) at Schildergasse 57 (Altstadt-Nord), the oldest Protestant church in Cologne. An oasis amidst the bustle of Cologne's main shopping street, this simple Gothic structure was erected in the mid-fourteenth century. Suspended over the font is a copy of *Der Schwebende Engel (The Floating Angel)* by the sculptor Ernst Barlach (1870–1938), the original of which was cast in 1927 and hung in the cathedral of Güstrow in Mecklenburg-Western Pomerania, where Barlach lived and work. Considered degenerate by the Nazi regime it was removed from the church, only to be replaced by a further copy in 1953.

Other places of interest nearby: 2, 3, 4, 5, 7, 8

7 An Unusual Statue for a Prussian King

Innenstadt (Altstadt-Nord) (Borough 1), the statue of King
Frederick William III on Heumarkt
Stadtbahn 1, 7, 9 Heumarkt; Bus 132
(From 2015: Nord-Süd-Stadtbahn Heumarkt)

In 1815 following the military defeat of France, Cologne fell under Prussian rule. A useful reminder of the regnal years of the various Prussian kings during this period can be found at the Hohenzollern Bridge (Hohenzollernbrücke), which is adorned with four imposing equestrian statues: Frederick William IV (1840–1861) and Wilhelm I (1861–1888) at the eastern end; Frederick III (1888) and Wilhelm II (1888–1918) at the west. One king, however, is missing. The statue of Cologne's first Prussian king, Frederick William III (1797–1840) is tucked away on Heumarkt, the former site of the city's medieval hay market, and its controversial story makes for interesting reading.

Unlike the statues on the bridge, which represent an expression of Prussian military might, the equestrian statue of Frederick William III is a very different affair. This is perhaps to do with the fact that it was under Frederick's ineffectual rule that the Prussian army was soundly defeated by the French at the Battle of Jena and Auerstedt in 1806.

Although the inhabitants of Cologne disliked Prussian rule they benefitted economically and culturally. This prompted the city's mayor to commemorate the fiftieth anniversary of the start of Prussian rule with a statue of the missing king. The idea met with little enthusiasm, however, since Prussian rule was still unpopular, and there were few people willing to finance it. Interested artists were thin on the ground, too, but eventually local sculptor Gustav Blaeser (1813–1874) stepped forward and the result was astonishing.

Eventually unveiled in 1878 the statue depicts the king on horseback atop a pedestal, the base of which carries reliefs of the most important men of his day, including the composers Beethoven and Mendelssohn, the philosophers Lessing and Hegel, the explorer Humboldt, the architect Schinkel, and the military commanders Scharnhorst and Gneisenau. Thus, in contrast to the bellicose posturing of Cologne's other Prussian statues, Frederick William III is presented in a cultural and economic context, as well as a military one. Indeed, only six out of the total of sixteen other men depicted are from a military background.

The equestrian statue of King Frederick William III on Heumarkt

In this unusual and subtle way the artist honoured the late king whilst at the same time snubbing gently the harshness of Prussian rule. Needless to say the statue was not considered 'kingly' enough in Prussian court circles.

Liked or loathed the huge equestrian statue soon became a popular rendezvous, with people arranging to meet "ungerm Stätz" ("under the tail"). This they continued to do until the Second World War, when an aerial mine blew the statue to pieces. No-one really missed it until the 1980s, when some fragments were re-discovered, sparking a discussion about whether the statue should be reconstructed. The debate was fuelled when an artist placed a polystyrene foam replica of the statue on the surviving pedestal, which remained in

Sculptures adorn the pedestal of the statue of King Frederick William III

place until it was destroyed during a storm. In 1990 the statue was re-cast in iron by the sculptor Raimund Kittl and re-erected. It remained in place until November 2007, when it was again removed. This time the horse's legs had become dangerously brittle due to the iron alloy used in the re-casting containing too much lead. It was feared by the authorities that revellers climbing the statue during the city's impending Carnival season might endanger themselves.

Controversy continued to surround the statue when it was realised that it was too big to fit under the city's bridges or through its tunnels. Instead, the colossal horse and rider were transported by ship to a workshop in nearby Godorf, in the district of Rodenkirchen. Finally, in 2010 and at a cost of 20 000 Euros, a revitalised king and horse were unveiled in Heumarkt once again (the accompanying figures around the pedestal are the originals, and still bear the scars of the Second World War). After one hundred and thirty years it seems King Frederick William III has finally been forgiven his shortcomings.

Other places of interest nearby: 4, 5, 6, 8, 9, 10

8 The Most Popular Theatre in Germany

Innenstadt (Altstadt-Nord) (Borough 1), the Hänneschen Puppet
Theatre (Hänneschen Puppenspiele) at Eisenmarket 2–4
Stadtbahn 1, 7, 9 Heumarkt; Bus 132
(From 2015: Nord-Süd-Stadtbahn Rathaus)

The Hänneschen Puppet Theatre
(Hänneschen Puppenspiele)
on Eisenmarket

It is quite possible that the most popular theatre in Germany features puppets speaking in Cologne dialect! That is certainly the case according to theatregoers in Cologne, who note with understandable pride that all ten weekly performances at the Hänneschen Puppet Theatre (Hänneschen Puppenspiele) at Eisenmarket 2–4 (Altstadt-Nord) have been sold out since the late 1980s.

The Hänneschen Puppet Theatre – since 1926 owned by the City of Cologne, hence its full name of Hänneschen Puppenspiele der Stadt Köln – was founded in 1802 by Johann Christoph Winters. As a *Stockpuppen* theatre it features puppets held aloft on sticks, operated by humans hidden behind a stage, rather than marionettes suspended from above on strings. The theatre is named after the star of the show, Hans Knoll, known to all as Hännesche, who inhabits the fictional world of Knollendorf. He can sometimes be glimpsed in the puppet workshop around the corner at Marmannsgasse 3, alongside racks of tiny costumes and glass-fronted cabinets filled with rows of miniature heads.

The theatre has been located in Eisenmarkt since the 1930s and can hold a capacity audience of around three hundred. Afternoon performances are aimed primarily at children, and are generally light-hearted, slapstick affairs. The evenings are reserved for adult audiences, and tend to carry more socio-political clout. During these performances the plots regularly take up current events in the city, which is only loosely disguised as Knollendorf. The characters represented by the puppets are local and universal archetypes, which the audience are quick to warm to or else dislike. Hännesche is the main protagonist, a headstrong young hero with blond hair and a bright red waistcoat. The equally popular Bärbelche, with whom he often appears, serves to provide an affectionate, commonsense counterpoint to Hännesche's more impetuous actions. Another well-observed pairing is the brown-suited Besteva, a hen-pecked old gentleman, and his wife in green, the shrewd Maritzebell. The list of characters goes on.

Inside the puppet workshop on Marmannsgasse

Two of the most instantly recognisable inhabitants of Knollendorf are Tünnes and Schäl, and many Germans outside Cologne will have encountered them before. Indeed, so popular are they that they have their own bronze statues in a small square to the rear of Alter Markt 24. Tünnes, with his red hair and even redder nose, is a loyal, rustic type dressed in the traditional garb of a cabbage farmer. He may enjoy a drink or two and be somewhat naïve but he's not stupid. His name is the Rhenish form of Antonius. By comparison, Schäl is dressed in a gentleman's frock coat but has an untrustworthy air about him. A small-time crook he's always trying to outwit others but is rarely as clever as he thinks. His name is somewhat ambiguous meaning both cross-eyed in dialect as well as cunning. The two characters embody aspects of industrial and rural life in Cologne during the nineteenth century.

The character of Tünnes was created by the puppet theatre's founder, Johann Christoff Winters. Schäl, on the other hand, appeared later and was the brainchild of Franz Millowitsch, a rival puppet master, who had tried unsuccessfully to join the Hänneschen Puppet Theatre. Instead he operated a mobile puppet theatre without a licence on the old pontoon bridge across the Rhine to Deutz, using the character of Schäl as an attack on Winters. His son, Josef Caspar Millowitsch, established his own puppet theatre in Cologne during the mid-nineteenth century, which eventually substituted real actors for puppets and is today the Volkstheater Millowitsch at Aachener Strasse 5 (Altstadt-Süd). Little could Franz Millowitsch have known that his great grandson, Willy Millowitsch (1909–1999), would one day become one of Germany's favourite actors, and that a bronze sculpture of him would end up in front of the Hänneschen Puppet Theatre.

Other places of interest nearby: 4, 5, 6, 7, 9, 10

9 Private Passions Made Public

Innenstadt (Altstadt-Nord) (Borough 1), some small museums
including Papa Joe's Biersalon at Alter Markt 50–52
Stadtbahn 1, 7, 9 Heumarkt; Bus 132
(From 2015: Nord-Süd-Stadtbahn Rathaus)

As a major cultural centre of the Rhine region, Cologne is home to more than thirty mainstream museums and many more galleries. Exhibitions range from Roman archaeological remains to contemporary graphics and sculpture. As a result it is all too easy to overlook the city's smaller specialist museums, such as the Mustard Museum (Senfmuseum) and the Money History Collection of the Cologne Savings Bank (Geldgeschichtliche Sammlung der Kreissparkasse Köln), which are the result of private passions (see nos. 19 & 32). Here are a few more of them.

A unique (and noisy!) collection is to be found at "Papa" Joe Buschmann's Roaring Twenties-style beer saloon *(Klimperkasten)* at Alter Markt 50–52. Despite its obvious attractions to the tourist trade the collection of old-fashioned penny arcade machines, one-armed bandits and pianolas it contains is a serious business. It's certainly worth calling by on the hour to see and hear them, when they all swing into action. And you might like to wash the experience down with a Kölsch, too!

Another specialist collection is Joyce Merlet's Museum of Puppet History (Museum der Puppengeschichte) at Unter Goldschmied 3 (Altstadt-Nord). Founded in 1977 this combined museum and shop contains thousands of dolls both antique and new, made of porcelain, wax, plaster, and plastic; one of the most collectible is a wax doll from 1730. Also displayed are dolls' houses and furniture, stuffed animals and teddy bears, as well as tin toys, Christmas decorations, and old books and games. A workshop on the premises offers a professional restoration service for worn out and damaged dolls and bears.

Different again but still no less passionate is the journalist and broadcaster Heribert Wüstenberg, who in 1999 founded the RadioMuseum Köln at Waltherstrasse 49–51 (Mülheim). And what better location since Cologne is one of Germany's most important media centres, where numerous radio and television stations (including Westdeutscher Rundfunk (WDR), RTL and VOX) have their headquarters. The museum, which is open on the second Sunday of each month, contains many artefacts relating to the development of radio broadcasting in Germany from the late nineteenth century onwards, as well as a large display of radios, tape recorders, gramophones, televisions, and jukeboxes. The museum even has its own amateur radio station with the call signal DL0RMK.

Last but by no means least is Edwin Preibisch, who runs a tobacconist with a difference at Bergerstrasse 136 (Porz). Since 1999 his shop has also been home to the Cigarette Lighter Museum (Feuerzeugmuseum), which contains fifty thousand objects associated with tobacco and smoking, the most important of which is a Ronson 'Banjo' from just after the Second World War, the first gas lighter to offer ignition and extinguishment in a single action. Of particular his-

A one armed bandit at Papa Joe's Biersalon

toric interest are the five hundred cigarette lighters from the factory of Karl Wieden in Solingen, near Düsseldorf, once one of the most prolific and innovative cigarette lighter manufacturers in the world.

Other places of interest nearby: 4, 5, 6, 7, 8, 10

10 A Medieval Sense of Humour!

Innenstadt (Altstadt-Nord) (Borough 1), the Kallendresser
Sculpture (Kallendresser-Skulptur) at Alter Markt 24
Stadtbahn 1, 7, 9 Heumarkt; Bus 132
(From 2015: Nord-Süd-Stadtbahn Rathaus)

High above street level at Alter Markt 24 (Altstadt-Nord) there is a
very curious sculpture. Close scrutiny reveals a squatting man with his
trousers pulled down, his posterior revealed to all those walking below.
This somewhat surprising figure in copper is the work of the German
sculptor Ewald Mataré (1887–1965), an artist denounced as degenerate
by the Nazi regime (see nos. 3 & 11). Mataré, however, was only reinter-
preting an older medieval sculpture that had adorned a building at Alter Markt 40, which was destroyed during the Second World War. This
begs the question as to what was the function of the original sculpture?

According to the popular history of Cologne the answer lies in the
proximity of Alter Markt to the nearby Benedictine abbey of St. Martin
the Great (Gross-St.-Martin-Kirche). The old house at Alter Markt 40
was called the Haus zur Sonne, and lay at the edge of the abbey's neu-
tral territory. It is said that the monks handed over a criminal to the
authorities so that he could be brought to justice, even though he had
sought sanctuary with them. To express their displeasure at this action the inhabitants of Alter Markt erected the sculpture on the wall
at number 40 so that its exposed rear was visible to the monks as they
walked below. When this building was destroyed, the sculpture and the
tradition was kept alive at number 24 instead.

It has also been suggested, since Alter Markt lies directly opposite
Cologne's Town Hall (Rathaus), that the figure was used to express public discontentment with the city council; the council was administered
by Cologne's medieval guilds, who had erected the Town Hall tower
in 1407–1414 (in turn the tower represented the victory of the guilds
over the rule of the patricians, who themselves had reconstructed the
Town Hall in 1330 as a symbol of their own independence from the
archbishop).

As if in riposte three sculpted posteriors appear on the tower as well,
where they act as pedestals for three of the statues adorning the tower,
namely Katharina Henot (1576–1627), who was unfairly accused of being a witch and hung, Archbishop Konrad von Hochstaden (1205–1261),
responsible for laying the foundation stone of the cathedral, and Ulrich

Zell (d. 1507), Cologne's first book printer. The message from the guilds is made even more potent when every hour the so-called *Platzjabbeck*, a grotesque clock jack, sticks his tongue out towards Alter Markt.

High on a wall on Alter Markt the cheeky Kallendresser Sculpture (Kallendresser-Skulptur) bears his all

The local name for a sculptured figure revealing its posterior is *Kallendresser* and it too has an interesting origin. During the Middle Ages, when household sanitation was less developed – and humour perhaps more so – it was common practice for people to relieve themselves into the roof gutters. In Cologne such miscreants were referred to as *Kallendresser*, a name derived in part from the word *Kalle*, being dialect for gutter.

A slightly less playful example of medieval humour in stone are the monstrous heads that can be found embedded in certain walls of the Martinsviertel, the quarter of narrow cobbled streets around the Church of St. Martin the Great (Gross-St.-Martin-Kirche). Known as *Grinköpfe* (in dialect *Grinköppe*) the heads are set above the keystone of doorways, the mouth wide open to reveal a set of dangerous-looking iron incisors. Not surprisingly passers-by have assumed that such ghoulish carvings must surely be an instrument of torture! The truth, as is so often the case, is far more prosaic. The heads acted as a support for a pulley mechanism by which the occupants of the building could lower and raise heavy goods between street level and their cellars. The iron teeth dissuaded the curious from tampering with the mechanism or attempting to break into the building. Examples of *Grinköpfe* can be found at the sixteenth century Gasthaus zum Peter at Heumarkt 77, at the Brauhaus Sünner im Walfisch at Salzgasse 13, and also at Buttermarkt 35, Markmannsgasse 13, and at the corner of Auf dem Rothenburg and Lintgasse 22–26.

Other places of interest nearby: 4, 5, 6, 7, 8, 9

11 Cathedral Curiosities

Innenstadt (Altstadt-Nord) (Borough 1), a tour of curiosities in
Cologne Cathedral (Kölner Dom) at Domkloster 4
Stadtbahn 5, 16, 18 Dom/Hauptbahnhof; Bus 132

There is no shortage of superlatives when it comes to describing the most famous landmark in Cologne. Cologne Cathedral (Kölner Dom), or more correctly the Cathedral Church of St. Peter and St. Mary (Hohe Domkirche St. Peter und St. Marien), the seat of the Catholic Archbishop of Cologne, was constructed between 1248 and 1880. Not only is it the largest church in Germany but it also boasts the world's second tallest spire. It is also the largest Gothic church in Northern Europe, its choir has the largest height to width ratio of any medieval church, and it presents the largest façade of any church anywhere. Little wonder that it attracts thirty thousand visitors a day, and that hidden in its historic fabric are more than a few oddities and curiosities.

This tour begins outside the cathedral's main west façade, where a series of sturdy bronze doors installed in 1887 are the work of the little-known church architect and painter Hugo Schneider (1841–1925). It's a shame how few people pause to marvel at his wonderfully intricate designs. The left-hand corner of the façade deserves special attention as it was here that a Second World War bomb once threatened to bring down the northwest spire. The insertion of an emergency brick buttress was required, which remained in place until 2005, when it was replaced with the newly carved blocks of sandstone seen today. Within the thickness of the stonework there is a spiral staircase, something considered too audacious by the architects of the older, south-western corner of the façade. They instead placed their staircase inside an offset pier, which resulted in the curious half-windows in that part of the building.

Moving around to the south, past the doors of the southern transept, with their unusual motifs by the German sculptor Ewald Mataré (1887–1965), the cathedral workshop (Dombauhütte) is reached, where a team of expert stonemasons create new architectural elements to replace those eroded by the elements. When the flying buttresses high above were restored during the 1930s they were inscribed with the date and a Nazi swastika, although this is not visible from the ground. During restoration work in the 1950s and 60s the heads of politicians, such as Kennedy, Kruschev, MacMillan and De Gaul, were incorporated into the stonework. There are tiny carved footballers up there, too, recalling the World Cup in 1966, and a figure of the craftsman Alois Olmscheidt, who devoted forty eight years of his life to restoring the cathedral.

Passing around the eastern apse there is a small garden containing a battered colonnade. This once connected a Romanesque collegiate church with the cathedral's eighth century predecessor – the so-called Old Cathedral (Alter Dom) – which itself occupied the site of the early fourth century basilica of Maternus, Cologne's first known bishop. A little further on one reaches the Cathedral Treasury (Domschatzkammer), where part of the even older Roman city wall can be seen (see no. 12). The tour now returns to the main façade and enters the cathedral.

First stop is the northern transept, where there is a late seventeenth century Baroque Madonna, her white silk gown covered with the *ex-votos* of those who have been

The mighty twin towers of Cologne Cathedral (Kölner Dom)

cured by praying to her. To the left are some hanging metal rods, which indicate the number of years of the current archbishop's tenure. Moving towards the apse, the Chapel of the Holy Cross is passed in the northern part of the choir, where an inscribed stone records privileges given to the Jews by the archbishop in 1266. Despite this there is a carving on one of the early fourteenth century wooden stalls in the centre of the choir (the largest Gothic choir stall in Germany) that depicts a man being suckled by a pig, an example of medieval anti-Semitism. Immediately beyond the inscription is the Chapel of the Cross containing a miracle-working Crucifix donated by Archbishop Gero in 976. It is the oldest surviving monumental crucifix in the West. Another chapel, in the apse itself, is dedicated to Saint John and contains the world's largest technical drawing of a cathedral. Created around 1283 it is hidden behind a green velvet curtain to protect it from the sun.

In the centre of the apse, and directly behind the High Altar, lies an

Detail of a cathedral window sponsored by the owner of the Saturn electronics company

ornate golden reliquary said to contain the bones of the Three Kings, brought to the city from Milan in 1164 as war booty by Archbishop Rainald of Dassel (c. 1120–1167) (see no. 23). It is the largest reliquary to survive from the medieval period. Behind the reliquary, in the axial window of the apse, is one of the cathedral's very finest medieval windows; dating from c. 1260 it depicts the so-called Jesse Tree, which represents the lineage of the Messiah from Jesse of Bethlehem, through his son David. In the southern part of the choir is the Chapel of the Virgin, which contains the magnificent fifteenth century Altar of the Three Kings by the Late Gothic painter Stephan Lochner (c. 1400–1451).

The last two cathedral oddities are both windows. The first is a new window in the southern transept by Gerhard Richter (b. 1932). Unveiled in 2007 it consists of 11 500 panes of identical-sized glass, arranged randomly in seventy two colours. Critics of such modern, non-figurative windows would undoubtedly prefer the traditional window in the southwest corner of the cathedral, sponsored by the wealthy businessman Friedrich Wilhelm Waffenschmidt, on the occasion of his fifty fifth wedding anniversary in 2005. His name and that of his wife can be seen at the bottom of the window, and at the lower right is the image of a tiny planet – Saturn to be precise – after which Waffenschmidt's highly successful chain of electronics stores is named.

Other places of interest nearby: 2, 3, 4, 12, 13, 14

12 Walking the Roman Walls

Innenstadt (Altstadt-Nord) (Borough 1), a circular tour of the
Roman walls beginning in the Treasury of Cologne Cathedral
(Domschatzkammer)
Stadtbahn 5, 16, 18 Dom/Hauptbahnhof; Bus 132

Much of what remains today of Roman Cologne lies underground (see
nos. 1, 31, 60 & 72). What remains above ground is largely limited to
fragments of the four kilometre-long city wall, constructed at the time
of the city's foundation in the mid-first century AD. Unlike most modern cities it is still possible to follow the line of the wall, enabling one
to appreciate how the modern city has been constructed over an incom-
plete destruction of the ancient one.

This tour begins in the subterranean Treasury of the cathedral
(Domschatzkammer), into which a massive piece of the north wall pro-
trudes, seven metres high and twenty metres long. The treasury began
life as the Chapel of the Holy Sacrament on the north side of the cathedral, consecrated in 1277 by Albert the Great, where a vaulted cellar was
necessary to fill the earlier Roman ditch. The Roman wall comprised an
outer and inner face of small ashlars rising to eight metres, with a rubble and tile fill giving a width of two and a half metres. The wall disap-
pears under the cathedral's north transept only to reappear among the
parked cars of an underground car park in Trankgasse, directly beneath
the cathedral forecourt (the so-called Domplatte).

The wall was originally pierced by nine gates: three to the west,
three overlooking the Rhine, two in the south, and one in the north.
An arch from the north gate, which was dismantled in 1106, sits in front
of the cathedral, to where it was removed in 1971. In the Romano-Ger-
manic Museum (Römisch-Germanisches Museum) at Roncalliplatz 4
(Altstadt-Nord) there is a stone from the arch inscribed with the letters
'CCAA', a reminder of the city's original name – Colonia Claudia Ara
Agrippinensium.

Westwards on Komödienstrasse (where a map of the roman walls
is conveniently embedded in the pavement) there is a small piece of
wall outside a shop, beyond which, at the junction with the busy Nord-
Süd-Fahrt, stands the stubby remains of the Lysolphturm, one of only
five of the wall's original twenty one towers still visible. Beyond is a fine
stretch of Roman walling at the end of which is a well-preserved tower
at Am Römerturm 13, marking the original north-west corner of the

This chunk of Roman wall can be found in an underground car park on Trankgasse

wall. Used later as a communal lavatory by the Franciscan nuns of the Convent of St. Clara it is today a private residence.

The first fragment to be encountered of the west wall is the Saint Helenturm on St.-Apern-Strasse, although it is easy to miss beneath its mantle of ivy. The former site of one of the city's western gates, the Ehrentor, is recalled in murals and road fragments in the foyer of a savings bank beyond the junction with Ehrenstrasse.

Continuing south, where Im Laach makes a junction with Lungengasse, the street name Marsilstein marks where a Roman aqueduct entered the city with water from the Eifel region ninety kilometres away. Until the late eighteenth century a fragment of the aqueduct was still visible here, identified erroneously during the Middle Ages as the sarcophagus of a fictional local hero, Marsilius, who had saved the city during a siege (a relocated piece of the aqueduct can be scrutinised outside Cologne's Museum of Applied Arts (Museum für Angewandte Kunst) on Drususgasse).

Further south are several fragments of the west wall, including a piece jutting into a hairdressing salon on Bobstrasse. The longest continuous stretch of walling lies between two apartment buildings on nearby Mauritiussteinweg.

From here onwards the wall becomes more elusive. At the point where it turns eastwards there once stood a gate used by citizens on their way to the hippodrome. Along Alte Mauer am Bach a modern brick wall takes up the story, punctuated at both ends by two more ruined towers. Looking out from the top of the wall affords an impression of how a Roman soldier might have felt two thousand years ago.

The line of the wall now proceeds north-eastwards, past the former site of the city's main south gate, which lay at one end of the main street *(Cardo Maximus)*. Where the wall turns northwards there are the remains of an unusual structure at An der Malzmühle 1, which can be glimpsed in the courtyard of Mühlenbach 57 (the monument itself is only open by appointment). Discovered in 1965 it is known as the Ubiermonument and pre-dates the walls. It may have served either as a fortification of the *Oppidum Ubiorum*, the settlement that preceded the Roman city, or else as some sort of mausoleum.

Passing the Romanesque Church of Saint Maria im Kapitol at Kasinostrasse 6 (Altstadt-Süd), beneath which lie the remains of the *Capitolium* (the Roman Temple of the Capitoline Gods), the east wall heads northwards to the cathedral past Marspforte, where a temple to Mars once stood. A gateway called the Drachenpforte in the northern section of the east wall once gave access to the Roman harbour, which lay between the city wall and a river island on which warehouses were constructed (a part of the old harbour road has been reconstructed on the south side of the Romano-Germanic Museum (Römisch-Germanisches Museum) at Roncalliplatz 4 (Altstadt-Nord)). The harbour was eventually infilled during the third century to make way for what became the Alter Markt and Martinsviertel.

Other places of interest nearby: 2, 3, 4, 11, 13, 14

13   A Descent into Cologne's Crypts

Innenstadt (Altstadt-Nord) (Borough 1), a tour of crypts
beginning with the Church of St. Andrew (St.-Andreas-Kirche)
at Komödienstrasse 6–8
Stadtbahn 5, 16, 18 Dom/Hauptbahnhof; Bus 132

The tomb of Albertus Magnus in the crypt beneath the Church
of St. Andrew (St.-Andreas-Kirche) on Komödienstrasse

Concealed beneath several of Cologne's famous Romanesque churches can be found vaulted burial chambers known as crypts (from the Greek word *kryptós* meaning 'hidden') (see no. 31). Constructed originally as a place to store and display revered saintly relics, they are perhaps the city centre's most atmospheric locations.

A curious example lies beneath the Collegiate Church of St. Andrew (St.-Andreas-Kirche) at Komödienstrasse 6–8 (Altstadt-Nord), founded in the late tenth century by Archbishop Bruno, the brother of Holy Roman Emperor Otto I (962–973). Around the year 1200 work on the present building began in the Late Romanesque style, taking the standard form of a three-aisled nave, choir and apse, with a crypt below. In the fifteenth century the east choir was demolished to make room for a replacement in the Late Gothic style, the combination of sturdy Romanesque and more graceful Gothic elements being a striking feature of this church. During the rebuilding the crypt was lost and it was not until 1953 that it was rediscovered and restored, albeit in a modern style. The visitor can gain a sense of how the original must have appeared around the candlelit tomb of St. Albertus Magnus (c. 1200–1280), itself a reused Roman sarcophagus from the third century. Albertus was a Dominican friar, ecclesiastical scholar and bishop, who studied at an important Dominican priory nearby. His remains were stored there until the French occupation, when the priory was dissolved, and the relics moved to the church. Albertus is remembered for his advocacy of a peaceful coexistence between science and religion, and some have called him the greatest German philosopher and theologian of the Middle Ages.

An intact Romanesque crypt can be experienced several streets away to the west, beneath the Church of St. Gereon (St.-Gereons-Kirche) on Gereonskloster (Altstadt-Nord). Here there is a unique thirteenth century decagonal nave soaring thirty four metres above the ground to form a cupola, the third largest in Western Christendom after the Duomo in Florence and the Hagia Sofia in Constantinople. The nave is built directly on the remains of an early Christian *martyrium* from the fourth century, which contained the bodies of the three hundred and eighteen martyrs of the Theban legion who perished here, together with their captain Saint Gereon, during the persecution of the Christians under Diocletian. Below ground, and outside the parameters of the nave, lies the Romanesque crypt – just visible at the bottom of the stairs beneath the altar. Surprisingly intimate when compared with the lofty nave above, it follows the standard pattern for Romanesque crypts, namely three aisles separated by sturdy Romanesque columns, supporting a vaulted ceiling. Carolingian-inspired mosaics, Gothic wall paintings, and stained glass windows installed in the 1960s imbue a unique atmosphere. The Crucifixion altar at one end was created in 1540 and signals the start of the Renaissance in Cologne.

In Altstadt-Süd there are three further churches with crypts. Cologne's largest Romanesque church is that of St. Maria im Capitol (St.-Maria-im-Capitol-Kirche) at Kasinostrasse 6, which was consecrated in 1049 by Pope Leo IX (1002–1054). The church boasts Germany's first instance of the trefoil or clover-leaf apse. The building occupies the former site of the *Capitolium* (the Roman Temple of the Capitoline Gods), the nave retaining the temple's predefined proportions (see no. 1). The spaciousness of both the church and the larger-than-usual crypt beneath it reflects the importance of the building's benefactor, a Benedictine abbess called Ida, whose grandfather was Holy Roman Emperor Otto II (967–983).

The Church of St. Cecilia (St.-Cäcilien-Kirche) at Cäcilienstrasse 29 (Altstadt-Süd) is a former twelfth century convent church, which since 1956 has been home to the Schnütgen Museum (Museum Schnütgen) of Medieval Art. The crypt is entered from beneath the Nun's Gallery and contains a collection of funerary-related exhibits.

This crypt lies beneath the Church of St. Maria im Capitol (St.-Maria-im-Capitol-Kirche) on Kasinostrasse

Finally, the Church of St. Severin (St.-Severins-Kirche) on Severinskirchplatz is the most southerly of Cologne's great Romanesque churches, and was completed in the Gothic style. Below the floor of the church are two distinct subterranean structures demonstrating two thousand years of funerary history. The first is an archaeological showroom in which the remains of a well-to-do Roman cemetery have been revealed, as well as a funerary chapel from the fourth century, out of which the present church grew. Immediately adjacent is the Romanesque crypt, again in the usual triple-aisled form with columns, which is notable for some fine wall murals and a display of ancient fabrics found inside the reliquary of Saint Severin (the crypt can only be visited on Fridays at 4 pm).

Other places of interest nearby: 1, 3, 11, 12, 14, 15

14 The Birthplace of Electronic Music

Innenstadt (Altstadt-Nord) (Borough 1), the former WDR Studio
for Electronic Music in the Funkhaus on Wallrafplatz
Stadtbahn 5, 16, 18 Dom/Hauptbahnhof; Bus 132

Electronic music can be broadly defined as music that employs electronic musical instruments and electronic music technology in its production. An intrinsic element of many of today's modern musical genres (for example electronic dance music) its origins stretch back to the invention in 1908 of the triode, an electronic amplifying vacuum tube, which led to the generation and amplification of electrical signals. From this date onwards composers endeavoured to use emerging technologies in their works, assisted enormously by the invention during the 1940s of professional tape recorders and high fidelity magnetic audio tape. Two distinct electronic musical movements soon emerged: Musique concrète in France, which used natural and industrial acoustical sounds as its source, and Elektronische Musik in Germany, in which purely experimental music was synthesized entirely from electronically produced signals.

The principles of Elektronische Musik were laid down by the German experimental acoustician, phoneticist and information theorist Werner Meyer-Eppler (1913–1960). In 1951 he joined forces with sound engineer Robert Beyer and composer Herbert Eimert to create a studio for electronic music. It was located in the modern headquarters of Northwest German Broadcasting (Nordwestdeutscher Rundfunk, NWDR) on Wallrafplatz (Altstadt-Nord), which had been constructed after the war for the transmission of live broadcasts. Opened in 1953 the Studio for Electronic Music became the most important studio of its kind in the world, and has since been hailed as the birthplace of electronic music.

One of the studio assistants during the mid-1950s was Karlheinz Stockhausen (1928–2007), who more than anyone else promoted and developed the ideas of Meyer-Eppler, with works such as *Elektronische Studie II* (1954), the first electronic piece to be published as a score. Generally acknowledged as one of the great visionaries of twentieth and early twenty-first century music, Stockhausen led the studio from 1963 until 1980. Other electronic music luminaries who visited the studio

The composer Karlheinz Stockhausen at work in Cologne's Studio for Electronic Music on Annostrasse

during this period included Karel Goeyvaerts (1923–1993), Henri Pousseur (1929–2009), and Gottfried Michael Koenig (b. 1926).

Guided tours are today available of the NWDR studios – since 1956 Westdeutscher Rundfunk (WDR) – although little reference will be made to the Studio for Electronic Music (visit www1.wdr.de). This omission is because the studio was dismantled during renovation work in 1986, and relocated to premises at Annostrasse 86 (Altstadt-Süd), which were formerly used by the WDR to film ballets. Stockhausen continued to work here periodically alongside other musical pioneers such as John Cage (1912–1992) and Mesias Maiguashca (b. 1938), and together they managed to continue and build upon the sense of charismatic avant-gardism that had defined the original studio.

A far greater change occurred in 2001, when the management at WDR decided to no longer support the creation of new electronic music. The sadness felt by studio employees was made more poignant by the fact that 2001 marked the fiftieth anniversary of the decision to first establish the studio. All was not lost, however, since the WDR were interested in digitising their huge archives of recorded transmissions, and agreed to secure new premises so that the studio could expedite the work for them. So it was that the studio relocated once again, this time to a cellar in Ossendorf (the premises on Annostrasse are now occupied by a post-production film company). The multi-track studio set-up of the 1970s has been re-installed here, and the digitisation work has been in progress ever since. Although no further original electronic music has been created, long-serving sound engineer Volker Müeller has been able to preserve much of the old equipment from Annostrasse. He remains confident that with the right funding a dedicated museum of electronic music will be established in Cologne's Media-Park (Neustadt-Nord). Only such a museum would remind people of the important part played by Cologne in the birth of electronic music.

Other places of interest nearby: 1, 3, 11, 12, 13, 15

15 A Shrine to Cutlery

Innenstadt (Altstadt-Nord) (Borough 1), the Glaub Besteckhaus
at Komödienstrasse 101–113
Stadtbahn 3, 4, 5, 16, 18 Appellhofplatz

Cutlery (*Besteck* in German) is the term used to refer to any hand implement used for the preparation, serving, and eating of food in the Western World. The most important items of cutlery are the knife, fork and spoon, and their origins date back to the dawn of civilisation. The world's first knives were sharpened stone blades manufactured during the Palaeolithic period, with clay and bone spoons appearing around 5000 BC; the fork is thought to have developed out of the knife and appeared during the ninth century BC. Although knives and forks were not used together on dinner tables until the late sixteenth century, all three implements had since Roman times been used individually for a great variety of separate tasks.

Those interested in the development and aesthetics of modern cutlery over the last few centuries must visit the Glaub Besteckhaus at Komödienstrasse 101–113 (Altstadt-Nord), since it is probably the most extensively-stocked cutlery store in Europe. A combination of shop and museum it was founded by Bodo Glaub in 1950. As a young man Glaub was enamoured by graphic representations of dining scenes and began to collect them: old prints, wood carvings, caricatures, and so on. After purchasing his first silver spoon from a Hamburg antiques dealer his collecting developed into a commercial concern, and the Glaub Besteckhaus opened for business. Managed today by Glaub's more than capable wife, Anita, the shop remains in its original location and still boasts its original retro-looking wooden display cabinets and neon signs installed in 1958.

A visit to the Glaub Besteckhaus is a unique experience for both cutlery expert and novice alike. The large window displays at the front of the shop, open each evening long after the shop doors have been shut, are crammed from top to bottom with cutlery, from easily affordable everyday knives and forks, to classic Art Nouveau and Bauhaus styles, contemporary Scandinavian examples, and antique nineteenth century Russian pieces. Together with the instore displays more than five hundred styles are represented in stainless steel, silver plate, sterling silver, solid silver, and gold, and there are handles to suit every pocket, too, from silver, mother of pearl and horn to wood and plastic.

Famous names include the German manufacturers Carl Mertens, Gebrüder Reiner, Pott, and Mono, as well as non-German producers such as Jean Puiforcat of France.

Probably of most interest to the non-specialist will be the displays of specialised cutlery, reflecting more recent eating habits. These include a snail fork *(Schneckengabel)*, salmon knife *(Lachsmesser)*, lobster pliers *(Hummerzange)*, crab cutlery *(Krebsbesteck)*, oyster openers *(Austernbrecher)*, and caviar cutlery *(Kaviarbesteck)*. Inside the shop can be found everything else associated with cutlery, including cutlery canteens, napkin rings, Irish horn egg spoons, children's inscribed birthday cutlery, presentation sugar tongs, and tiny boxed sets of miniature German cutlery no more than a centimetre long (the perfect gift for the person who has everything!). There are also amusing novelty items, such as the Sheffield-made George Butler's Slimming Spoon *(Schlankheitslöffel)*, which has a large hole in it!

The Glaub Besteckhaus also has an in-house workshop, where antique or much-loved cutlery can be restored.

Other places of interest nearby: 1, 3, 14, 16, 17, 18

16 Where Voices of Dissent are Still Loud

Innenstadt (Altstadt-Nord) (Borough 1), the Nazism Documentation Centre of Cologne (NS-Dokumentationszentrum der Stadt Köln) in the EL-DE-Haus at Appellhofplatz 23–25
Stadtbahn 3, 4, 5, 16, 18 Appellhofplatz

Cologne is a city renowned today for its tolerance and liberal-mindedness, although this hasn't always been the case. There are two addresses where the voices of those who felt compelled to speak out against the authoritarian regimes of their day can still be heard. Today's visitor to Cologne would do well to visit these addresses, if only to be reminded of the value of being able to speak one's mind without persecution.

The first address is Heumarkt 65 (Altstadt-Nord), where a wall plaque informs the passer-by that here between August 1848 and May 1849 stood the editorial offices of the Socialist newspaper *Neue Rheinische Zeitung*, the chief editor of which was Karl Marx (1818–1883). Marx was born in Trier in what at the time was the Prussian Province of the Lower Rhine. As a young man he was influenced greatly by the works of Kant and Voltaire, creating within him a distinctive blend of German profundity and French subversion. In May 1842 he had an article published in the *Rheinische Zeitung*, a paper that had been founded in Cologne in January the same year as a means by which intellectuals could voice their opposition to Prussian authoritarianism. Marx's article railing against the government's use of censorship was lauded widely in the progressive community.

In October 1842 Marx was named editor of the paper, and a month later he was visited by Friedrich Engels (1820–1895), who was on his way to study the condition of the working class in England. With Marx at the helm, and now under the influence of Engels, the paper took on a more radical stance, openly opposing Prussian governmental policy with increasing stridency. By early 1843 Marx's radical Socialist and Communist statements were effectively calling for revolution. Not surprisingly this was too much for the government, and the resulting censorship of the paper prompted Marx to resign on March 17th, after which the paper closed.

After several years in Paris and Brussels Marx returned to Cologne, where he published the *Neue Rheinische Zeitung* from his office on Heumarkt. Revolution was brewing across Europe and once again the paper became the target of governmental suppression. On 9th May 1849 Marx was ordered to leave the country, and the final issue of his paper was printed entirely in red ink! For now it seemed the sword had proved mightier than the pen.

Fast forward to the first half of the twentieth century and the *Rheinische Zeitung* had re-emerged as the mouthpiece of the German Social Democratic Party (Sozialdemokratische Partei Deutschlands), with editorial offices at Deutzer-Kalker-Strasse 46 (Deutz). In 1933 Hitler's stormtroopers occupied the building and installed the offices of their own *Westdeutscher Beobachter* there instead. Shortly afterwards a new upper storey was added to the building, the top of which featured a running motif of swastikas, which can still be made out today.

This brings us to the second address. Between December 1935 and March 1945 the seat of the Cologne branch of the Nazi Party's Secret State Police, or Gestapo (Geheime Staatspolizei), was the EL-DE-Haus at Appellhofplatz 23–25. The building was the centre of National Socialism terror in the Rhineland and now houses the Nazism Documentation Centre of Cologne (NS-Dokumentationszentrum der Stadt Köln). The Gestapo acquired the lease of the building whilst it was still under construction by its then owner, the businessman Leopold Dahmen,

Karl Marx edited a Socialist newspaper here in the early 1840s

Appellhofplatz was once a base for the Gestapo

whose initials it bears. In the basement the Gestapo built a series of cramped prison cells, where they could detain, interrogate and torture people, often for weeks at a time (four hundred people were executed in the courtyard to the rear of the building). A visit to the cells today, which appear much as they did in 1943 after refurbishment following an air raid, is a chilling experience.

Most affecting are the inscriptions scrawled by prisoners on their cell walls, which provide a poignant and unique document of their experiences. There are approximately eighteen hundred of them, including many in Russian, French, Polish and Dutch. Most were made during the last stages of the war, when a large number of forced labourers and prisoners of war were present in Cologne. The inscriptions take the form of signatures, dates, calendars, and parting words. Many of them retain their defiance: "I wish for no-one to be here only those who are my mortal enemies".

Other places of interest nearby: 1, 3, 15, 17, 18, 19

17 Street Names and House Numbers

Innenstadt (Altstadt-Nord) (Borough 1), French artefacts at
the Cologne City Museum (Kölnisches Stadtmuseum) at
Zeughausstrasse 1–3
Stadtbahn 3, 4, 5, 16, 18 Appellhofplatz

In 1475, in return for providing support at the Battle of Neuss against
the Duke of Burgundy, the Habsburg Emperor Frederick III (1452–1493)
conferred the status of Free Imperial City upon Cologne. This meant
three things: the city was freed from the burden of external taxation,
it was beholden to no-one except the Holy Roman Emperor, and its
City Council, in whom all local power resided, was answerable to none.
Such power inevitably brought the council and its citizens into conflict,
and several people were executed for attempting to expose corruption
within its ranks. The most famous was Nikolaus Gülich (1644–1686), a
man whose brave sacrifice subsequently warranted his own statue on
the walls of the Town Hall (Rathaus).

Gülich was also seen as a hero by supporters of the French Revolutionary Wars, waged against several European states between 1792
and 1802. Cologne's council had survived both the Reformation and the
Counter Reformation but by the time Napoleon's troops occupied the
city on 6th April 1794 its golden age as a centre for trade and industry
was over. Under the occupation of the French, and subsequently the
Prussians, the city's economic fortunes would now be revived. Funda-
mental changes in the way the city was governed would also bring about
rapid reform, including the dissolution of church property, the aboli-
tion of the trade guilds (which themselves had been established in 1396
to end the rule of the nobles over the citizens), the recognition of both
religious and commercial freedoms, the legal equality of all citizens, and
eventually the creation of a uniform German domestic market.

Cologne's twelve thousand inhabitants put up no resistance to the
French occupation and submitted peaceably to the numerous changes
imposed by their new rulers. It could be said they had little choice, since
the French introduced martial law, and erected a guillotine on Roncalliplatz (until that point executions were carried out at a site on Aachener
Strasse beyond the city walls, which Napoleon replaced with his new
Melaten Cemetery (Melaten Friedhof); see no. 77). But the French
also brought with them human rights, and much of their legislation

remained effective in the Rhineland long after their departure in 1814. Most significantly, Protestants and Jews were at last able to live and work in the city with equal rights, and everyone was free to engage in trade and manufacturing, regardless of their origin or religion.

A Napoleonic street sign on the wall at Zeughausstrasse 1–3

One of the most tangible changes wrought by the French on Cologne was the introduction of bilingual street names, an adjunct of the obligatory use of the French language. Occasionally when walking around Cologne today it is still possible to see these names on inscribed stones at street corners, for example at Apostelnkloster/Mittel Strasse, and An der Linde/Machabäerstrasse (Altstadt-Nord). A pair of such signs (removed from their original locations) can be viewed up close in the Cologne City Museum (Kölnisches Stadtmuseum) at Zeughausstrasse 1–3 (Altstadt-Nord). They are displayed on the ground floor of the museum as part of a small collection of Napoleonic-era artefacts, which includes a chart of German and French street names, weights and measures, banknotes, weapons, and a ceramic model of Napoleon, looking his usual imperious self! The building in which the museum has been housed since 1958 is a former armoury, and it too preserves its bilingual street sign at its north-eastern corner: it reads *R(UE): DE L'ARSENAL-ZEUGHAUS GAS(SE)*.

The French also introduced consecutive house numbers to Cologne, with Cologne Cathedral (Kölner Dom) receiving the number 1. The most famous number is 4711, which was given to the property on Glockengasse of the perfume manufacturer Wilhelm Muelhens. An impressive tapestry hanging on the wall of the building today illustrates a French soldier applying the number to the building. It is interesting to note that in the absence of trademark law Muelhens sold his perfume under the name *Farina*, which was the name of the inventor of *Original Eau de Cologne* a century earlier (see no. 2). This confusion continued until the late nineteenth century, when Muelhens' grandson was obliged by law to cease trading under the Farina name, and to use a name of his own invention, as a result of which he chose the number 4711. When city-wide house numbering was abandoned in 1811, in favour of numbering by street, the home of the newly-branded *4711* became Glockengasse 12.

Other places of interest nearby: 13, 14, 15, 16, 21, 22

18 The Horse Heads of Richmodstrasse

Innenstadt (Altstadt-Nord) (Borough 1), the Richmodis Tower
(Richmodis-Turm) at Richmodstrasse 6
Stadtbahn 1, 3, 4, 7, 9, 16, 18 Neumarkt; Bus 136, 146

Cologne's city centre has been subject to a steady process of urban renewal since Roman times. To gain an impression of how the streets
of Cologne have changed over the years one should visit www.bilder-
buch-koeln.de, a website containing thousands of images of Cologne
past and present. Comparing the old with the new can be a fascinating
experience, as is the case when scrutinising the view looking northwards from Neumarkt along Richmodstrasse (Altstadt-Nord). On the
left-hand side can be seen a typical late nineteenth century apartment
house, bristling with Historicist architectural detail. By contrast, the
right hand corner is occupied by the Richmodis-Haus, a fine building
from 1830 constructed in an unfussy neo-Classical style. Standing behind this building is a lofty octagonal tower known as the Richmodis
Tower (Richmodis-Turm), which was the only element in the ensemble
to survive the Second World War.

But let's return to those early photos of the Richmodis-Haus. If
one looks very carefully at the windows of the upper storey, the second
one in from the left contains something most unusual: a pair of white
wooden horses' heads! Their purpose was to remind passers-by of the
curious legend of Richmodis von Aducht, who died in 1349 as the Black
Death swept through Cologne. Her husband, the wealthy merchant
Mengis of Aducht, had the infected corpse buried quickly, stopping
only to adorn it with a gold chain and ring. This did not go unnoticed
by a pair of grave diggers, who returned later the same day and dug up
the coffin in order to remove its valuable contents. Upon removing the
coffin lid the men were horrified to see Richmodis open her eyes! As
the men fled Richmodis arose and returned to her husband's house and
knocked on the door. Mengis was dumbfounded and refused to admit
the stranger, saying that he would believe it more likely that his horses
could climb the stairs of his house and look out of an upstairs window
than for his wife to rise from the dead. As the words left his mouth so
his horses did just that, prompting him to open the door and be reu-
nited with his wife. According to the legend they lived happily ever af-

The white horses of Richmodstrasse

ter and installed a pair of artificial horses' heads in an upstairs window in memory of the incredible events.

Whatever one thinks of the story, there is some evidence to suggest that sculpted horses have been connected with Richmodstrasse ever since. In the Cologne City Museum (Kölnisches Stadtmuseum) at Zeughausstrasse 1–3 (Altstadt-Nord), for example, there is an intriguing life-sized wooden horse dating from the early sixteenth century. It comes from the Hackeneysche Hof, a hotel that once stood where the Richmodis-Haus was constructed (the word 'Hackeneysche' is derived from the Old French *Haquenée*, meaning a comfortable riding horse). Quite how the horse is connected with the Richmodis legend is unclear but it is known that the building was once occupied by two brothers, and that such wooden horses might have been used as a support for equestrian tournament armour. The brothers were granted the use of a pair of white horses on their coats of arms when they became knights in 1498.

Archive photographs of the department store that replaced the Richmodis-Haus in the 1920s depict clearly a pair of stone horses' heads high up on the building's façade. This building was destroyed during the war and replaced by a row of shops into which the Richmodis Tower was incorporated. In 1958 the horses' heads were re-carved and placed inside a window at the top of the tower, where they remain to this day.

Opinion seems divided on exactly where Mengis and Richmodis lived, although it was probably somewhere to the rear of where the old Richmodis-Haus stood. The tower, which may or may not have been a part of their property, is an example of a *Geschlechterturm* erected by wealthy medieval patrician families as a status symbol, although it is not thought that horses' heads (*Päädsköpp* in Cologne dialect) were ever originally displayed there.

At the base of the Richmodisturm there is a wall plaque recording that the German Romantic composer, conductor, and music teacher Max Bruch (1838–1920) was born here. Bruch's Opus 47 for cello and orchestra was based on Hebrew melodies, principally the melody of the *Kol Nidre* incantation from the Jewish Yom Kippur service. The initial success of this work led many to believe that Bruch himself was of Jewish ancestry, although in reality he was raised a Protestant. Rumour alone was enough to get his work banned by the National Socialists, as a result of which he is now all but forgotten in the German speaking world.

Other places of interest nearby: 1, 15, 16, 19, 30

19 The Fascinating History of Money

Innenstadt (Altstadt-Nord) (Borough 1), the Money History
Collection of the Cologne Savings Bank (Geldgeschichtliche
Sammlung der Kreissparkasse Köln) at Neumarkt 18–24
Stadtbahn 1, 3, 4, 7, 9, 16, 18 Neumarkt; Bus 136, 140

The long history of Cologne is well represented in the coinage produced by the city over the last two thousand years. The first mint was established by the Romans in 257 AD, and later re-established by Emperor Otto I (962–973) for the production of Pfennigs, which still carried the traditional *Colonia* monogram used by the Romans. Cologne would become one of the most important mints in the Holy Roman Empire. To find out more there is no better place than the Money History Collection (Geldgeschichtliche Sammlung), located suitably in the light and airy banking hall of Germany's largest savings bank, the Kreissparkasse Köln at Neumarkt 18–24 (Altstadt-Nord).

Of far greater interest than it might sound the Money History Collection was instigated by the bank in 1954, and today boasts some forty thousand exhibits. The permanent display (a mere two thousand objects spread across forty showcases lining the walls) details not only the development of money in Cologne and Germany but also around the world from China to ancient Greece.

Anything and everything to do with money is on display, including coins and banknotes, coin scales *(Münzwaagen)*, and money boxes *(Sparbüchsen)*. Long before the invention of money in the seventh century BC, scales were used to weigh precious metals as a means of payment. They continued to be used across Europe to verify the authenticity of gold coins well into the nineteenth century, when paper money became dominant. Cologne was also an exporter of beautifully-made coin balances, supplied in small wooden carrying cases.

The origin of the money box also stretches back to before the invention of money, since man has long saved objects of value as a precautionary measure. The first coins were probably saved in pots or bags, out of which the more secure purse, money box and safe developed. The museum contains several Roman examples, some of which were found when the savings bank itself was constructed, as well as others from as far away as Java and South America. Popular around the world is the piggy bank, the pig being a longstanding symbol of luck and fer-

A Javanese piggy bank

tility. Late nineteenth century examples designed to encourage children to save include an American cast-iron frog, and a Hans and Gretel chocolate dispenser manufactured by the Cologne chocolate manufacturer Stollwerck (see no. 32).

Perhaps the most interesting display in the museum concerns the means of payment used by non-European cultures, notably in Africa and Oceania. This is a subject close to the heart of museum curator Thomas Lautz, who has made numerous journeys to record the use of this so-called traditional money *(traditionelle Zahlungsmittel)*, notably the remote Islands of Papua New Guinea and the Solomons. On the Micronesian island of Yap he discovered that ring-shaped stones are used as currency, with high denominations being as large as a cartwheel! Traditional money developed quite independently of European money, and served different functions, including ritual payments, dowries, and the demonstration of personal power. Much of it, such as shells, amber and skins, comprised natural materials in an unrefined state, whereas others, such as axes, arm bands, and beads, had both value and functionality.

Those not interested in money *per se* might find the museum's thematic displays more stimulating, covering topics such as jewellery made from coins, curious-shaped coins, oversized and undersized coins, and the history of forgeries *(Münzfälschungen)*: the inclusion of different metals in the modern Euro is a good example of the ongoing fight against the forger. The museum also hosts regular temporary exhibitions (called 'Das Fenster', or The Window), which are drawn from both private collections, as well as Cologne's other museums.

Coin collectors might like to attend one of Cologne's regular coin auctions, which have been hosted since 1968 by Tyll Kroha's Kölner Münzkabinett at Neven-DuMont-Strasse 15 (Altstadt-Nord) (www.tyllkroha.com). Kroha assisted the bank in establishing its money museum in the 1950s.

Other places of interest nearby: 1, 15, 16, 18, 19, 30

20 Panama Hats and a Good Cup of Tea

Innenstadt (Altstadt-Nord) (Borough 1), a tour of unusual
shops beginning with Jürgen Eifler at Friesenwall 102a
Stadtbahn 3, 4, 5, 12, 15 Friesenplatz

The high streets of Europe look increasingly similar these days. Fortunately for Cologne it has managed to retain a healthy number of independent specialist retailers. These idiosyncratic bastions of local colour are manned by knowledgeable staff, each with a passion for their products. This tour takes in some of those to be found in Altstadt-Nord.

The journey begins at Friesenwall 102a, where for more than twenty five years Jürgen Eifler has been making hats and caps by hand. His wonderful shop, which contains a cap studio to the rear and a workshop next door, is fitted out with furniture used by another Cologne hatter a century ago. One wall is lined with bolts of cloth stacked to the ceiling, including Scottish Hebridean Harris Tweed, Irish tweed from Donegal, and finest Italian kashmir. Others are fitted with shelves on which are displayed Panama hats made from Ecuadorean straw, silk-finished top hats, trilbies, rabbit felt fedoras, and Harris Tweed caps. Any spaces remaining are occupied by historical artefacts associated with the hatter's trade, such as hat boxes, wooden forms for hat stretching, rolls of eighty-year-old hat bands, sewing machines, and posters.

A couple of roads away at Apostelnstrasse 44 is the poultry and game shop Gustav Brock, identified by the stag's head on the outside wall. Inside, the produce is displayed on old-fashioned white marble counters, and the walls are adorned with stuffed pheasants, ceramic ducks, and a large wild boar's head. Across the road at number 21 is Filz Gnoss, a shop specialising in products made from felt (woollen cloth milled with soap and warm water). This versatile raw material has many uses, including slippers, hats, drinks coasters, table mats, and even cathedral keyrings!

Around the corner at Hahnenstrasse 2–4 is Peter Heinrichs pipe and cigar emporium. Founded in 1908 and today spread across three separate shops it is advertised as "Das Haus der 10 000 Pfeifen" (The House of Ten Thousand Pipes) and boasts a cigar warehouse and a smoking lounge.

A brisk walk along Hahnenstrasse/Cäcilienstrasse leads to An St. Agatha, where at number 37 is Honig Müngersdorff. This family firm was established one hundred and fifty years ago and sells not only honey but also every possible honey-related product, including beeswax candles, shampoo, sun lotion, soap, mead, beer, sweets, and cosmetics. A couple of doors down at Antoniterstrasse 41 is Cologne's English Shop. Appealing to Anglophiles and homesick expatriates it sells Heinz baked beans, Marmite, Strongbow cider, Cadbury's chocolate, Tetley's tea bags, and salt and vinegar crisps.

North of busy Schilderstrasse is Sterck Joh. Jos & Zoon at Neue Langgasse 4. Established in the 1950s as an independent enterprise (but now part of a larger Bremen-based concern) this reliably traditional store features an elegant S-shaped wooden counter topped with old fashioned weighing scales. More than sixty types of tea are available, including Gu Zhang Mao Jian Chinese green tea, fine Oolong 'White Glory', 'Butterfly' Jasmine flower tea, and 'Temple of Heaven' Gunpowder tea. Their own roasted coffees include mild, big-beaned Meragogype from Mexico, aromatic coffee from Java, and spicy Costa Rican.

At the end of the street runs bustling Breite Strasse. Half a dozen individual shops can be found hereabouts, beginning at the eastern end with Musikhaus Tonger at Brückengasse 6. This treasure house for music lovers has several floors of instruments, sheet music, CDs, and books. At Breite Strasse 25–27 is Hoss an der Oper, a traditional delicatessen that has been owned by the same family for more than a century, selling all manner of fine foods, including sausages, preserves, oil, vinegar, paté, and wine.

Schirm Bursch at Breite Strasse 104 stocks hundreds of umbrellas, parasols and walking sticks, available in every size, style and colour, many of them made in the in-house workshop. One final shop on Breite

Handmade hats at Jürgen Eifler on Friesenwall

Strasse is Monika Nachbar Beauty Hair Accessories at number 161, which specialises in male grooming. This is the place for badger fur shaving brushes, horn-handled cut-throat razors, and tortoise-shell combs, and to the rear is one of Cologne's few wet shave salons.

Running north from Breite Strasse is Auf dem Berlich, where at number 26 is Antiquariat Stefan Kruger, a paradise for second-hand book buyers. A highlight is the cellar which is filled with ten thousand paperbacks on sale for no more than a couple of Euros each. Close by at number 30 is the CCAA-Glasgalerie Köln, which specialises in hand-blown reproductions of Roman glassware.

Other places of interest nearby:
16, 17, 18, 19, 21, 29

Tea and coffee at Sterck Joh. Jos & Zoon on Neue Langgasse

21 How Cologne Might Have Looked

Innenstadt (Altstadt-Nord) (Borough 1), the Gerling-Hochhaus
at Gereonshof 10–26
Stadtbahn 12, 15 Christophstrasse

During the years of the Weimar Republic, votes cast in Cologne in favour of the Nazi Party in Reichstag elections were always below the
national average. This is perhaps unsurprising when one considers
that Cologne had defied its ruling archbishops in 1288 and its ruling
patrician families in 1396. Free-thinking, liberal-minded Cologne met
its match, however, during the 1930s, when Adolf Hitler as German
Chancellor decreed that the capital of the Nazi administrative district
of Cologne-Aachen become a "Gateway to the West". Had his megalo-
maniac plans for the rebuilding of the city come to fruition, Cologne
would look very different today.

To get an impression of what Hitler had in mind for Cologne one
should visit the Nazism Documentation Centre of Cologne (NS-Doc-
umentationszentrum der Stadt Köln) at Appellhofplatz 23–25 (Altstadt-Nord) (see no. 16). Architectural plans and photographs show
that Hitler's plan called for the wholesale demolition of much of the
city centre. In its place would be built a series of monumental party
and public buildings of the type planned for Nazi Germany's other
major cities such as Berlin, Munich, and Hamburg. Only the cathedral
would be left standing, together with a few Romanesque churches and
some of the old medieval streets south of the cathedral, as a reminder
of past glories.

Each city was allocated its own architect, approved by Hitler personally, who would be responsible for expediting the ambitious rebuilding plans. In Cologne that architect was Clemens Klotz (1886–1969),
whose professional career had begun in the city in 1911 with the design
of Modernist residential and office buildings. For Hitler Klotz planned
a series of new buildings immediately north of the cathedral. In Deutz
on the east bank of the Rhine he proposed an extension of the existing trade fair site, a new railway station, and a huge Nazi Party centre
(Gauforum), including a Hall of German Work and extensive parade
grounds. Meanwhile, the green space to the west of the city at the start
of Aachenerstrasse, freed up by the earlier demolition of the old city
walls, would also be transformed into a parade ground, surrounded by

A model of how Cologne might have looked under Adolf Hitler

a cultural and business centre, including new museums and an opera house.

Although planning for the new Cologne continued until 1944, as with Nazi Germany's other cities very little ever left the drawing board, as the country's resources were increasingly diverted towards the war effort. Certainly plenty of demolition occurred, but much of it was courtesy of Allied air raids (see no. 28). Indeed, all that exists today of Klotz's grand plan is the Aachener Weiher, an ornamental lake on Aachener Strasse, and a representative ensemble of reconstructed medieval houses on Ostermannplatz (Altstadt-Nord).

For an idea of how Cologne might have looked one must turn to some post-war buildings. One is an office and residential building at Neumarkt 1b (Altstadt-Nord), erected in 1952 to a design by Klotz, who continued working in Cologne after the war. Its unfussy façade with identical rows of windows, balconies with neo-Classical pendants, and a pillared top-storey loggia are reminiscent of official buildings constructed in Berlin and Munich during the thirties. Having said that, such features are also descended directly from 1920s Modernism, a style banned for residential use by the Nazi regime in favour of more traditional forms (see no. 73).

Similar design elements can be found on a monumental scale in a group of buildings constructed for the Gerling Insurance Company

(Gerling-Versicherungsgruppe) on Gereonshof (Altstadt-Nord) between 1953 and 1958. The main architect here was Helmut Hentrich (1905–2001), who whilst studying in Berlin in the 1920s had been greatly influenced by the Modernist architecture of Ludwig Mies van der Rohe (1886–1969) and Hans Poelzig (1869–1936). During the same period he also came into contact with the Third Reich architects Albert Speer, Friedrich Tamms, and Rudolf Wolters. Both influences are strong in the Gerling complex, which consists of several low ranges grouped around an open square, over which looms the fifty six metre high Gerling-Hochhaus. When walking through the somewhat oppressive square it is difficult not to feel as if one were in some type of martial forum, like the one constructed for Hitler in front of

The Gerling-Hochhaus on Gereonshof

the Führerbau, his official residence in Munich (even the balustraded porches of the two buildings are similar). This effect is reinforced by the presence of tall ceremonial flagpoles, lamp standards reminiscent of those designed by Speer in Berlin, and bronze reliefs by Arno Breker (1900–1991), once Hitler's official state sculptor, whose oversized neo-Classical sculptures were once seen as representing the momentum and will power of the Nazi Party. For many commentators the echoes of the Third Reich are too strong to ignore, although this is not to suggest that the architect was making any political statement, indeed his later works carry no such overtones.

Other places of interest nearby: 16, 17, 20

22 The Horrors of Klingelpütz

Innenstadt (Altstadt-Nord) (Borough 1), the site of the former
Klingelpütz Prison between Klingelpütz, Vogteistrasse,
Gereonswall and Kyotostrasse
Stadtbahn 12, 15 Hansaring; S-Bahn 6, 12, 13 Hansaring

In the northwest corner of Altstadt-Nord, in the lee of a stretch of preserved medieval city wall, there is a small park. Bounded by Vogteistrasse, Gereonswall, Klingelpütz, and Kyotostrasse the park appears
to be very normal, nondescript even, where children come to play, the
elderly pause on benches, and workers enjoy their lunch hour. But all
is not as it seems. In the centre of the park there is a small hill, formed
from the heaped-up rubble of a building that once stood here. A modest
memorial nearby informs the curious observer that the building was
the notorious Klingelpütz Prison.

The street name Klingelpütz has its origins in a family called Cling-
elmann, who during the thirteenth century owned several wells hereabouts (well being *Pütz* in Kölsch dialect, from the Latin *puteus* and the
French *puits*). The prison inevitably took the same name when it was
built here between 1836 and 1838, as the main Prussian prison for the
Rhineland. It continued in service until 1969, when it was replaced by
a new prison in the district of Ossendorf, and the old prison was demolished. Of the many prisoners who passed through its doors, two of
them warrant particular attention.

The first is the German serial killer Peter Kürten (1883–1931), Germany's answer to Jack the Ripper, who was executed here by guillotine
on 2nd July 1931. Convicted of a series of violent sex crimes, assaults and
murders against adults and children he confessed to seventy nine of-
fences, and claimed to have committed his first murder aged just five.
Born into a large, poverty-stricken family Kürten witnessed his alco-
holic father frequently abuse his mother and sisters, and he followed
suit. The location of many of his crimes led to the media dubbing him
the 'Vampire of Düsseldorf'. After the execution Kürten's brain was dis-
sected by scientists in an effort to explain his behaviour, the remains
finding their way eventually to Ripley's Believe it or Not! Museum in
the American state of Wisconsin.

The second noteworthy inmate is German Communist and
anti-Nazi resistance fighter Bernard Bästlein (1894–1944), who was
imprisoned here for a year in April 1939. He was born the son of an

The star-shaped Klingelpütz Prison before its demolition

enthusiastic member of the German Social Democratic Party (Sozial-demokratische Partei Deutschlands), Germany's oldest parliamentary political party, and it is therefore unsurprising that he also joined the SPD. After working in an armaments factory he went to fight on the Western Front where, inspired by revolutionary movements in Russia at the time, he began extolling the virtues of peace through revolution. On his return home he realigned himself politically with the Communist Party of Germany (Kommunistische Partei Deutschlands). When the party began to incite industrial unrest in Hamburg Bästlein was at the forefront and was arrested for "conspiracy to commit high treason". Despite an amnesty that restored his freedom he continued as an activist, becoming KPD district leader in Cologne in 1930, and a member of the Prussian Federal State Parliament in 1932. On 5th March 1933 he was finally elected to the Reichstag, although his tenure was short-lived. In May he was arrested by the Nazis, again on a charge of treason, and imprisoned. He spent much of the period between 1935 and 1944 in prison, where his experiences only strengthened his belief that the Hitler regime as well as capitalism were the two greatest threats to German society. He was eventually executed on 18th September 1944 in Brandenburg-Görden Prison after a court deemed him "unteachable and unreformable".

During the years of the Third Reich Klingelpütz Prison became the central place of execution for those found guilty by the Nazi Special Court (Sondergericht) at Appellhofplatz 1, where a series of show trials were staged as a deterrent to anti-Nazi resistance. Gross overcrowding was commonplace in the prison, with up to ten thousand people being held in just one of the wings in 1944, despite the fact that the entire building was only designed for eight hundred. The memorial to be found at the site today was placed there on 1st September 1979, exactly forty years after the start of the Second World War. The work of Rhenish metalworker Hans-Karl Burgeff (1928–2005) it takes the form of a low brick pedestal on top of which is a copper plaque turned green by the weather. Half of the plaque depicts a window grille of the

Only a plaque and a grass-covered hill recall Klingelpütz Prison

type that would have been commonplace in Klingelpütz. The other half carries an inscription recalling the one thousand innocent people sent to the guillotine here between 1933 and 1945.

Other places of interest nearby: 17, 23, 24, 27

23 In the Footsteps of Pilgrims

Innenstadt (Altstadt-Nord) (Borough 1), holy relics in the
Church of St. Ursula (St.-Ursula-Kirche) at Ursulaplatz 24
Stadtbahn 12, 15 Hansaring; S-Bahn 6, 12, 13 Hansaring

The Middle Ages in Europe was a time during which the remains of
saints, as well as things purported to have been touched by saints, were
believed to be imbued with supernatural healing powers. Churches
containing relics became centres for pilgrimage and inevitably generated income for the surrounding area. Splinters of bone from the bodies of saints, fragments of the True Cross, stone from the Holy Sepul-
chre, and even water from the River Jordan all found their way from the
Holy Land back to Europe. The procurement of holy relics for churches
in Europe became an industry in its own right.

Sancta Colonia – Holy Cologne – was no exception, indeed it became
the archetypal European pilgrimage centre after relics claimed to be
those of the Three Kings were brought to the city from Milan as war
booty in 1164 by the Archbishop of Cologne Rainald of Dassel (c. 1120–
1167). The relics were installed in a highly ornate golden reliquary, the
largest of its type to survive from the medieval period, which can be
seen today behind the High Altar of Cologne Cathedral (Kölner Dom)
(see no. 11). Moreover, the construction of the cathedral itself was a
response to the huge influx of pilgrims that resulted from the presence
of the relics in the city.

Inspired by the cathedral many parish and monastic churches in
Cologne secured their own relics, some of which were displayed in
reliquary boxes similar to that of the Three Kings. A good example is
Saint Heribert's reliquary (Heribertschrein) of 1170 in the Church of
St. Heribert (St.-Heribert-Kirche) at Tempelstrasse 2 (Deutz), known
also as Deutz Cathedral (Düxer Dom). Another example in the Church
of St. Andrew (St.-Andreas-Kirche) at Komödienstrasse 6–8 (Altstadt-
Nord) dates from the the sixteenth century and contains the skulls of
the seven Jewish Maccabean brothers, their mother and their teacher,
who were martyred in the second century BC. Yet another, containing the authenticated fourth century remains of Saint Severin, can be
found in the chancel of the Church of St. Severin (St.-Severins-Kirche)
on Severinskirchplatz (Altstadt-Süd).

So important have the relics of the Three Kings been to the liveli-
hood of Cologne that three crowns appear on the city's coat of arms.

The eleven black flickering flames that appear beneath them recall an earlier set of relics, namely those of Saint Ursula and her ten virginal companions. Ursula was a Romano-British princess martyred with her companions in Cologne in 383 by the invading Huns, whose capture of the city was subsequently prevented by divine intervention. The Church of St. Ursula (St.-Ursula-Kirche) in which the relics are stored stands at

The Golden Chamber (Goldene Kammer) in the Church of St. Ursula (St.-Ursula-Kirche) on Ursulaplatz

Ursulaplatz 24 (Altstadt-Nord). A parish church since 1804 it was first constructed in 1135 on the site of a Late Roman cemetery, in which according to local legend the remains of the martyrs had been discovered in 1106, and venerated thereafter. In the seventeenth century the interior of the church was subject to a Baroque refurbishment during which the extraordinary Golden Chamber (Goldene Kammer) seen today was installed. A place to store the church's rich collection of relics this lavishly decorated room contains a series of shelves on which reliquaries in the form of gilded busts are placed. The upper surface of the walls, as well as the ceiling, are entirely covered with a mosaic made from the bones of those exhumed from the old cemetery.

Incidentally, so as to satisfy demand for relics of Ursula and her companions from churches elsewhere their number was later inflated by relic traders from eleven to eleven thousand!

For an idea of pilgrims praying for help today visit the Church of St. Maria in der Kupfergasse (Kirche St. Maria in der Kupfergasse) at Schwalbengasse 1 (Altstadt-Nord), where a steady stream of believers come to pray before a seventeenth century Black Madonna (Schwarze Muttergottes).

Other places of interest nearby: 13, 22, 24, 27

24 The Sinking of the *Cöln*

Innenstadt (Altstadt-Nord) (Borough 1), the lifeboat wreck
inside the Eigelsteintorburg
Stadtbahn 12, 15, 16, 18 Ebertplatz; Bus 127, 140

The Eigelsteinturburg just south of Ebertplatz (Altstadt-Nord) is one of the few gateways still remaining from Cologne's medieval city wall (see no. 35). Constructed during the first half of the thirteenth century it was used by the French Emperor Napoleon and his wife Joséphine during their triumphant entrance into the city on the evening of 13th September 1804. Although the city wall is long gone people still visit the old gateway. They are drawn not only by its history and the pleasant cafés clustered around it but also by something quite unique: hanging inside an alcove on the gate's eastern side is a wrecked lifeboat.

The story of how a lifeboat came to be hanging in a Cologne gateway is a fascinating but little-known one. In May 1908 at the Germaniawerft in Kiel a start was made on the construction of the Kolberg Class light cruiser *S.M.S. Cöln*. This class of German cruiser was the first to be driven entirely by steam turbines. The *Cöln* entered service with the German Imperial Navy (Kaiserliche Marine) in 1911. She had an overall length of 130.5 metres, with propeller shafts capable of generating nineteen thousand horsepower (giving a top speed of 26.8 knots), and a dozen 10.5 centimetre rapid fire guns. Her crew in peacetime numbered three hundred and eighty, which was increased to four hundred and eighty five during combat. The *Cöln*, however, was not to see much active service.

Shortly after the start of the First World War the *Cöln* became the flagship of Rear Admiral Leberecht Maas, assigned to the defence of Heligoland, off the north-west coast of Germany. It was 28th August 1914 and a British flotilla of cruisers and destroyers – the Harwich Force under Commander Reginald Tyrwhitt – made a raid on German shipping near the naval base at Heligoland. Providing cover was the First Battle Cruiser Squadron under Vice Admiral Beatty. Around 7 am the Harwich Force sank a German torpedo-boat, prompting the Germans to deploy two light cruisers to the scene, which were soon joined by several more from Wilhelmshaven, including the *Cöln* under the command of Captain Meidinger (battle cruisers, however, were unable to provide support due to low water in the harbour).

The *Cöln* quickly encountered the British light cruiser *H.M.S. Arethusa* and eight destroyers, which had engaged the German light cruiser *Mainz*. Outgunned and with the *Arethusa* badly damaged, Tyrwhitt requested urgent support. Beatty's squadron hove into view at 12.40 pm, taking the Germans by surprise. The superior speed and

A wrecked lifeboat hangs inside the Eigelsteintorburg

firepower of the British battle cruisers proved decisive, and the Germans lost not only the *Mainz* but also the *Ariadne* and the *Cöln*, the latter sunk as she tried to escape from Beatty's flagship battle cruiser *H.M.S. Lion*. Seven hundred and twelve German sailors were killed in the fighting and four hundred and nineteen were taken prisoner.

The *Cöln* went down at approximately 2.30 pm taking many of her crew with her. Two hundred men survived the sinking but of those all but one drowned. The sole survivor, a Cologne stoker by the name of Adolf Neumann, managed to cling to the battle-damaged remains of a lifeboat for seventy six hours before being picked up. The lifeboat itself was washed ashore three days later on the East Frisian island of Norderney; it was donated to the City of Cologne the following year. At first the lifeboat was hung in the Town Hall (Rathaus) but since 1926 it has been displayed in its current position, where every year on the anniversary of the sinking a wreath is placed in memory of those who perished.

Since 1909 five ships have carried the name *Cöln* (or *Köln*), and the anchor from one of them, the German Navy frigate *Köln IV*, can be seen displayed beneath the lifeboat. An iron nameplate hanging alongside it bearing the distinctive arms of Cologne was taken from the ship when it was decommissioned in 1982. A renovation of the wrecked lifeboat, as well as the installation of the anchor and various inscriptions, was undertaken in 2008 by the Freundskreis Fregatte Köln e.V.

Other places of interest nearby: 22, 23, 25, 27

25 The Underground Chandelier

Innenstadt (Neustadt-Nord) (Borough 1), the Chandelier Hall
(Kronleuchtersaal) on the corner of Theodor-Heuss-Ring and
Clever Strasse
Stadtbahn 12, 15, 16, 18 Ebertplatz; Bus 127, 140

In 1828 the English poet Samuel Taylor Coleridge (1772–1834) made reference to the lack of sewers in Cologne by noting that the city had "two and seventy stenches, All well defined, and several stinks!" It is difficult to imagine what it must have been like to live in such a city between the medieval period and the first half of the nineteenth century. Like other cities across Europe Cologne's population was burgeoning – and so too was its volume of wastewater. With no means to process it, raw sewage was channelled into the river along open ditches, filling the narrow streets of the Altstadt with noxious odours and facilitating the spread of disease.

The first modern sewage systems in Europe were built in London and Paris during the 1850s, and consisted of a radial network of brick-built tunnels conveying effluent discreetly away from built-up areas. Unfortunately for Cologne, a safe and reliable public water supply was not made available until 1863, despite repeated (and apparently unaffordable) offers from both German and English hydraulic engineers (see no. 39). The first modern sewer system took even longer and was not inaugurated until 1890, some eighteen hundred years after the Romans had first attempted such a thing (see no. 1).

Cologne's nineteenth century sewer system can be visited every last Sunday in the month between March and September on a fascinating tour offered by the city's drainage and flood service department (Stadtentwässerungsbetriebe Köln) (Tel. 0049-(0)221-22126845, www. koelntourismus.de). This rarely-seen world is entered by means of a sturdy steel trap door at the corner of Clever Strasse and Theodor-Heuss-Ring (Neustadt-Nord). A steep staircase leads downwards to where a service tunnel connects to a subterranean chamber known as the Regenentlastungsbauwerk. With a width of 3.8 metres and a height of 4.6 metres this surprisingly elegant space gives access to an important junction of the city's network of storm and wastewater drains (it is interesting to note that this particular location was selected because previously it had been a harbour, created immediately north of the medieval city wall during the French occupation).

The Chandelier Hall (Kronleuchtersaal) in the sewers on Theodor-Heuss-Ring

Under normal conditions only the main canal is filled with wastewater, a slow-moving, murky mass of dark grey water with a distinctive aroma! It runs northwards to Cologne's first mechanised wastewater treatment plant in Niehl, which opened in 1905. However, in times of exceptionally heavy rain the water in the canal is supplemented by water running off the streets above, and all too soon the level rises, slopping over the side, and running into the storm drain alongside it. This carries the excess water directly into the Rhine. When it's not raining visitors are able to take a short stroll along the storm drain to peer into its numerous side tunnels.

A unique and surprising feature is the twelve-armed chandelier

A sudden cloud burst floods the Chandelier Hall (Kronleuchtersaal)

suspended from the ceiling of the chamber, giving rise to the name Kronleuchtersaal, or Chandelier Hall. The chandelier's presence dates back to the opening of the sewer system in 1890, which was to have been attended by the Prussian Emperor Wilhelm II (1888–1918). As if the state-of-the-art sewers were not enough to impress him, a pair of candlelit chandeliers were also installed. In the event the emperor never arrived but the chandeliers remained in place. Having succumbed to rust over the years they were replaced by a single, electric-powered chandelier in 1990. An inscribed stone tablet on the wall nearby records the names of the mayor at the time, as well as the two architects responsible for the construction (Johann Stübben and Carl Steuernagel).

During the tour it is explained how the centre of Cologne, as well as the boroughs of Deutz, Nippes and Ehrenfeld, were all connected to the wastewater system by 1900. Today, Cologne's two thousand or more kilometres of wastewater tunnels drain effluent and excess rainwater from across the entire city to five modern water purification plants (Rodenkirchen, Wahn, Stammheim, Langel, and Weiden), where filtration tanks are used to clean the water before it is fed into the Rhine.

Cologne's original sewer system is still fully functional today, despite the population having increased four-fold since 1890. In addition to tours, the sewers also play host to occasional jazz and classical music concerts, attended by up to fifty people, who come here not only to enjoy the unusual surroundings but also the special acoustics provided by the Chandelier Hall.

Other places of interest nearby: 24, 26

26 A Pioneer of Post-War Modernism

Innenstadt (Altstadt-Nord) (Borough 1), a tour of works
by Wilhelm Riphahn commencing with the Restaurant Bastei
at Konrad-Adenauer-Ufer 80
Stadtbahn 12, 15, 16, 18; Bus SB40

The name of Modernist architect Wilhelm Riphahn (1889–1963) may not be well known outside architectural circles but in his home town of Cologne he has left a distinctive and long-lasting impression. That he became an architect seems inevitable considering the fact that his father and his mother's father were both building contractors. As a young man Riphahn studied architecture in Munich, Dresden, and Berlin, where he served several apprenticeships, and in 1913 he established himself as a self-employed architect in Cologne.

Riphahn's first major commissions date from the early 1920s, when he came to the attention of fellow Modernist and director of town planning, Adolf Abel (1882–1968). Riphahn was asked to supply designs for new housing estates being constructed in the green belt surrounding Cologne (see no. 73). Expedited in the pared down Modernist idiom of the so-called *Neue Sachlichkeit* (New Objectivity) these estates were a response to Germany's housing shortage after the First World War, and a fulfillment of the promise of Article 155 of the 1919 Weimar Constitution to provide "a healthy dwelling" for all Germans ("Lich, Luff und Bäumcher" – light, air and trees – according to a motto in Cologne dialect at the time). They included the GAG-Wohnsiedlung in Bickendorf (Ehrenfeld) and the Weisse Stadt and Blauer Hof in Buchforst (Mülheim).

One of Riphahn's most memorable designs, and the first stop on this tour, is the Restaurant Bastei at Konrad-Adenauer-Ufer 80 (Altstadt-Nord), which takes its name from the base of the Prussian defensive bastion on which it was ingeniously constructed in 1924; dating from 1891 the bastion had been partially demolished in 1911 and supported a searchlight station during the First World War. A sturdy column rises above the brick-built remains on top of which Riphahn placed a disk-shaped, glazed balcony offering panoramic views across the Rhine. The balcony is supported on a radiating framework of light steel struts, each reaching eight metres outwards, originally over the river itself. Damaged during the Second World War the structure was

Wilhelm Riphahn's Restaurant Bastei on Konrad-Adenauer-Ufer

rebuilt in 1958 with Riphahn overseeing the work.

Before the Nazi regime put an end to Modernist construction in favour of more conservative building styles, Riphahn designed two large commercial buildings in the style in central Cologne. The oddly-named Indanthren-Haus on Breite Strasse was a high street clothing and textiles store for the German chemical company BASF, pioneers of a light- and water-fast dye called Indanthren. The other, which is the second stop on this tour, was a cinema, the UFA-Palast at Hohenzollernring 22–24 (Neustadt-Nord). Constructed in 1931 in only five months this building was one of the most spectacular in Cologne at the time, its concrete portico stretching far across the pavement to protect waiting cinemagoers. With seats for three thousand people it was for a time the largest cinema in Germany. Unfortunately, despite such statistics the cinema closed its doors in March 2010, and they have yet to reopen.

With the collapse of the Nazi regime Riphahn was once again able to practice in Cologne. The third and final stop on this tour is Hahnenstrasse (Altstadt-Süd), where between 1947 and 1950 Riphahn participated in the post-war urban renewal of the city's important east-west axis between Heumarkt and Rudolfplatz. Riphahn designed several flat-roofed, two-storey, pre-cast concrete pavilions for use as apartments, shops, and offices. One of these buildings, at Hahnenstrasse 6, became the premises of the British Council, which like the Amerika Haus around the corner at Apostelnkloster 13–15, was a focus for the

Inside Riphahn's Die Brücke (The Bridge) on Hahnenstrasse

post-war re-education of the German populace after years of indoctrination by Nazi propaganda. Known as *Die Brücke (The Bridge)* the upper storey of the building hangs over the pavement on a series of columns, creating an arcade through which pedestrians can pass. *Die Brücke* was vacated in the late 1990s and has subsequently been occupied as an exhibition space by the Cologne Art Association (Kölnischer Kunstverein), one of the oldest art associations in Germany.

Riphahn remained busy throughout the 1950s and into the early 1960s, designing several of Cologne's best known public buildings. They included the new Cologne Opera House (Oper Köln) and Schauspielhaus Köln, both of which stand on Offenbachplatz (Altstadt-Nord), as well as the Institut Français (Französisches Kulturinstitut) at Sachsenring 77 (Neustadt-Süd), one of the first and now one of the last foreign cultural institutes established in West Germany.

Other places of interest nearby: 24, 25

27 Cologne's Original Skyscraper

Innenstadt (Neustadt-Nord) (Borough 1), the Hansahochhaus
at Hansaring 97
Stadtbahn 12, 15 Hansaring; S-Bahn 6, 12, 13 Hansaring

For a brief period during the early 1880s the 157 metre-high twin spires of Cologne Cathedral (Kölner Dom) made it the tallest building in the world. Even today the cathedral boasts the second highest spires after the single spire of Ulm Cathedral, and visitors can clamber their way up 576 steps to a viewing platform inside one of them, located some ninety eight metres above the ground. It was not until 1925, however, that Cologne received its first skyscraper *(Wolkenkratzer)*, the so-called Hansa Hochhaus at Hansaring 97 (Neustadt-Nord). Despite being only sixty five metres high it was the tallest tower block in Europe at the time, and a visit there today brings back memories of the Golden Age of the skyscraper.

The Hansahochhaus was constructed between 1924 and 1925 – six years before the completion of the Empire State Building – to a design by the Aachen-born architect Jakob Koerfer (1875–1930). Constructed around a skeleton of steel the red-brick tower comprises seventeen storeys. Sturdy corner buttresses and pointed windows around the top of the tower hark back to medieval military and church architecture, an impression counterbalanced by the pared-down Modernist façade, with its curious stylised ceramic animal heads at pavement level, simple rectangular windows, and the presence of a futuristic non-stop *Paternoster* that transports office workers as far as the fifteenth floor. The term Brick Expressionism *(Backsteinexpressionismus)* is used to describe such buildings, being a specific variant of Expressionist architecture popular in the larger cities of Northern Germany and the Ruhr in the 1920s.

The Hansahochhaus originally included not only offices but also shops, a showroom for the Adler motor car company, and a cinema. For a good impression of how the building appeared when it was first built visit the foyer of the hotel at Hansaring 97, where there is a magnificent black-and-white photograph. Around the top of the tower in the photograph can be seen the trade name of the Munich-based film company EMELKA (Münchner Lichtspiel-Kunst), whose films were once shown in the tower's cinema.

During the Second World War the Hansahochhaus served as a con-

The Hansahochhaus on Hansaring was Cologne's first skyscraper

venient lookout post for the spotting of enemy aircraft, and on the third and fourth floors a camp was established for the containment of eight hundred forced labourers. In the 1970s the Cologne-based home electronics giant Saturn moved into the tower, and it is their name that adorns the structure today.

Many more skyscrapers have appeared on the skyline of Cologne since the construction of the Hansahochhaus. In 1928, for example, the 80 metre-high Messeturm was constructed at Kennedy Ufer 27 (Deutz), as a beacon for Cologne's extensive trade fair grounds (Kölnmesse). The carved heads at the top of the tower represent Hermes, the great messenger of the Greek gods, as well as the god of commerce.

A sculptural detail on the Hansahochhaus

During the 1930s Hitler planned to raze much of central Cologne and erect a series of grandiose Nazi party and public buildings. Of these projects nothing ever left the drawing board, and it wasn't until after the war that the next skyscraper appeared. The 56 metre-high Gerling-Hochhaus was built at Gereonshof (Altstadt-Nord) in 1953, as headquarters for the Gerling insurance company, and the building gives an impression of how Cologne might have looked had Hitler's plans succeeded (see no. 21).

From the late 1960s comes the Herkules-Hochhaus, an apartment block at Graeffstrasse 1 (Ehrenfeld). At 102 metres in height it is considerably taller than the Hansahochhaus built more than forty years earlier but it lacks that building's elegance, its uniform glass and steel appearance broken only by the use of blocks of different colours. And yet to contemporary eyes its very simplicity has helped it to date rather better than the 147 metre-high Colonia-Haus at An der Schanz 2 (Nippes), which was Germany's highest apartment block when completed in 1973. The tallest building erected in Cologne during the 1980s is the 138 metre-high Funkhaus Am Raderberggürtel (Rodenkirchen), the former broadcasting house of the radio station Deutsche Welle.

Currently the highest tower block in Cologne is Jean Nouvel's 165 metre-high KölnTurm in the MediaPark (Neustadt-Nord), completed in 2001. This is dwarfed, however, by the tallest structure in Cologne, the 266 metre-high Colonius Telecommunications Tower (Colonius-Fernmeldeturm), erected in 1981 on Innere Kanalstrasse (Neustadt-Nord); since its viewing platform is closed, a visit to the rooftop of the 103 metre-high KölnTriangle office block at Ottoplatz 1 (Deutz) is recommended instead.

Other places of interest nearby: 22, 23, 24

28 The World's Greatest Heap of Debris

Innenstadt (Neustadt-Nord) (Borough 1), the Herkulesberg rubble mountain on Herkulesstrasse between Mediapark and Innere Kanalstrasse
Stadtbahn 12, 15 Christophstrasse/Mediapark, then walk along Gladbacher Strasse/Subbelrather Strasse

In 1945 the architect and urban planner Rudolf Schwarz (1897–1961) dubbed Cologne "the world's greatest heap of debris". Schwarz, who devised the master plan for the post-war reconstruction of Cologne, including the construction of the new North-South Drive (Nord-Süd-Fahrt), was not exaggerating. Cologne endured no less than two hundred and sixty two Allied air raids in the Second

The Herkulesberg is a pile of Second World War rubble

World War, during which the city centre was largely obliterated. On the night of 30th May 1942 alone the first thousand bomber raid conducted by the Royal Air Force known as Operation Millennium made some fifty nine thousand people homeless. Almost one and a half thousand tons of explosives were dropped, laying waste to nearly two hundred and fifty hectares of built-up area in the process. By the end of the Second World War, one and a half million Allied bombs had reduced ninety five percent of Cologne to ruins, filling the shattered streets with an estimated fifty three million cubic metres of rubble and other debris. Fewer than four hundred houses survived the ferocious aerial onslaught intact.

Before work could begin on rebuilding, the streets of Cologne had to be cleared of rubble. This was done using specially-constructed wagons *(Schuttkipper)* hauled by narrow-gauge locomotives, an example of which can be seen in the Rhineland Industrial Railway Museum (Rheinisches Industriebahn-Museum) at Longericher Strasse 249 (Nippes) (see no. 59). The wagons were manufactured in the Westwaggon carriage factory in Deutz in 1948, and feature a pivoting mechanism for easy loading and unloading. Other examples are displayed in the Cologne City Museum (Kölnisches Stadtmuseum) at Zeughausstrasse 1–3

A Schuttkipper used to
clear wartime rubble
from Cologne

(Altstadt-Nord) and in the KVB Tramway Museum Thielenbruch
(KVB-Strassenbahn-Museum Thielenbruch) at Gemarkenstrasse 139
(Mülheim) (see no. 53).

The rubble was removed to green spaces beyond the old inner ring
of Prussian-built fortresses (Innere Festungsgürtel), resulting in the
appearance of eleven artificial hills known as *Trümmerberge* (rubble
mountains). One can be found in the park between Vingster Ring and
Ostheimer Strasse (Kalk), and another is in the Hiroshima-Nagasaki-
Park (Neustadt-Süd). The largest of them, the aptly-named Herkulesberg, lies to the north of Herkulesstrasse (Neustadt-Nord), between
Innere Kanalstrasse and MediaPark. It covers an area of around 130 000
square metres and contains much of the rubble removed from the
centre of Cologne. Despite the proclamation by Rudolf Schwarz that
Cologne was the greatest heap of debris in the world, the Herkulesberg
is actually one of the smaller debris mountains in Germany. With a
height of twenty five metres it would be dwarfed if placed alongside
Berlin's Teufelsberg or Munich's Olympiaberg, both of which reach
fifty metres or more.

So important and so pervasive was the removal of rubble from the
bombed out cities that the first definable genre of post-war filmmaking in Germany was called *Trümmerfilm* (literally 'rubble film'), since
it depicted people clearing the streets for rebuilding. Although only
a short-lived genre, the actual process of rebuilding lasted until well
into the 1990s, when the reconstruction of the Romanesque Church of
St. Kunibert (St.-Kuniberts-Kirche) at Kunibertskloster 6 (Altstadt-
Nord) was finished.

29 A Car in Concrete

Innenstadt (Neustadt-Nord) (Borough 1), Wolf Vostell's
Ruhender Verkehr at the junction of Hohenzollernring and
Flandrische Strasse
Stadtbahn 1, 7, 12, 15 Rudolfplatz; Bus 136, 146

Berlin and Cologne are cities that have inspired a lot of post-war street art, and the German artist Wolf Vostell (1932–1998) has been active in both. His controversial work reflects the fact that such places have fallen victim to one particularly unpleasant aspect of modern urban living: motor cars and the traffic jams they cause!

At the junction of Flandrische Strasse and Hohenzollernring there is a large block of concrete seemingly abandoned in the middle of the dual carriageway. This is Vostell's artwork *Ruhender Verkehr (Static Traffic)*. A closer look at the block reveals that it is in the shape of a car – an Opel 'Kapitän' with the number plate K-RM 175 to be precise – over which Vostell poured concrete in 1969, whilst the engine was still running. Like similar 'cars in concrete' elsewhere *Ruhender Verkehr* represents Vostell's protest against what he saw as the glorification of the car as a status symbol.

The motor age transformed European cities beyond recognition, and Cologne was no exception. In the early 1880s the medieval city wall encircling the city's Altstadt was demolished and replaced by the Kölner Ring, a six kilometre-long boulevard of which the Hohenzollernring was just one element. As motor vehicles became ever more prevalent on the city's streets so further outer 'rings' were constructed, namely the Gürtel, the Militärring, and the Kölner Autobahnring. The landscape of Cologne was changed forever.

Although Vostell knew the clock could never be turned back he felt obliged to engage the public in an ongoing dialogue on man's potentially doomed love affair with the motor car. In Berlin Vostell sensationally installed a pair of up-ended Cadillacs entombed in concrete on Rathenauplatz. Inaugurated in 1987 to mark the 750th anniversary of the founding of Berlin the artwork caused a stir from the moment it was unveiled. The title of the work, *Zwei Beton-Cadillacs in Form der nackten Maja (Two Concrete Cadillacs in the Shape of the Naked Maja)*, with its seemingly obscure reference to the famous painting by the Spanish artist Francisco Goya (1746–1828), suggests a measure of self-parody and mockery: undoubtedly for some the thought of a big American car is as

Wolf Vostell's sculpture Ruhender Verkehr on Hohenzollernring

enticing as a reclining female nude! Perhaps more importantly, like the concrete-covered Opel in Cologne, the work also passes comment on the stultifying and quite literally solidifying effects of gridlocked cars on the urban landscape. It is no coincidence that in both cities Vostell selected locations where cars regularly form traffic jams, forcing drivers to confront the artworks and ponder their meaning. Despite the best efforts of Vostell's vociferous critics to get the sculptures removed they are still in place – and still making people think: surely the best response a modern artist can hope for.

No stranger to extending the borders of art it is perhaps worth noting that in 1959 Vostell became the first ever artist to incorporate a television set into one of his works *(Deutscher Ausblick)*. Vostell was also a co-founder during the 1960s of the Fluxus Movement, an international network of intermedia artists, composers, and designers, and a pioneer of video art and so-called 'Art Happenings'. Recognition from his peers came in 1992 when Cologne honoured Vostell with a major retrospective of his work.

No less controversial than Wolf Vostell is the Taschen book company, whose European headquarters can be found at Hohenzollernring 53. Founded in Cologne in 1980 by Benedict Taschen the company has published innovative and beautifully-designed books about everything from art, architecture and film to oriental carpets, tattoos and luxury hotels. It is, however, with what Taschen call their "sexy books" that the company has gained real notoriety, publishing bestselling volumes on breasts, derrières, and porn stars. The books can be found at a branch of Taschen located farther along Hohenzollernring at number 28.

Other places of interest nearby: 19, 20, 36, 37

30 The World in a Museum

Innenstadt (Altstadt-Süd) (Borough 1), the Rautenstrauch-
Joest Museum – Cultures of the World at Cäcilienstrasse 29–33
Stadtbahn 1, 3, 4, 7, 9, 16, 18 Neumarkt; Bus 136, 146

On the afternoon of Sunday 13th January 2008 the doors of Cologne's venerable Rautenstrauch-Joest Museum at Ubierring 45 closed for good. For just over a century they had given access to one of Germany's leading ethnological collections, but increasingly cramped conditions and repeated floodings now demanded a change of address. So it was that in October 2010 the museum reopened in a striking new building at Cäcilienstrasse 29–33 (Altstadt-Süd).

The core of the Rautenstrauch-Joest Museum was assembled by the Cologne-born ethnologist Wilhelm Joest (1852–1897), whose extensive globetrotting was financed by his parents. They in turn had benefitted from the commercial success of Joest's grandfather, Carl, who made a fortune from Cologne's largest sugar refinery. After studying linguistics and natural sciences Wilhelm Joest set off around the world, acquiring artefacts reflecting the daily life and rituals of the peoples he encountered. In his early twenties he visited the Orient and North Africa, following this up with a journey the length of Canada and the Americas. In 1879 he made a breathless tour of Asia, taking in Sri Lanka, India, Afghanistan, Thailand, Cambodia, Mongolia and Japan, before returning to Germany via Manchuria and Siberia. In 1883 Joest circumnavigated the entire continent of Africa, and then set out for the South Seas, where aged just forty five he succumbed to Black Fever on the remote island of Ureparapara. Fortunately, Joest's collection of more than three thousand five hundred objects was in safe hands, since his sister Adele and her husband Eugen Rautenstreich donated it to the City of Cologne. After Eugen's death Adele financed the construction of the original museum building, which opened as the Rautenstrauch-Joest Museum in 1906.

The museum's original aim of engendering respect for non-European cultural legacy still holds true today, although the way in which it is achieved is now very different. Exhibits from the museum's holdings of sixty thousand objects are no longer presented geographically but rather comparatively, emphasising what unites human cultures, rather than what separates them. Humans around the globe face the same challenges: their solutions are defined only by their natural and social settings: a Eu-

Figures from papua New Guinea in the Rautenstrauch-Joest Museum on Cäcilienstrasse

ropean solution represents but one of many possible solutions.

The innovative concept behind the new Rautenstrauch-Joest Museum is that of a walk-through gallery following the broad storyline "People In Their Worlds". The gallery traverses three floors punctuated by thematic sections and attendant focus points *(Blickpunkte)*.

The visitor's journey begins in the foyer, where the museum's largest exhibit, an ornately carved rice barn of the Toraja people of Sulawesi in Indonesia provides a prologue. Combining both social and religious aspects of its owners the structure sets the scene for the entire museum, as does the *Gamelan* orchestra from Central Java, providing a ceremonial welcoming gesture.

Entering the walk-through gallery the visitor encounters two broad theme complexes, the first of which is "Comprehending the World". Sub-themes observed from a European perspective include crossing borders (illustrated by the story of Wilhelm Joest himself), prejudices (using the European perception of Africa), museums (featuring an open archive of three hundred objects from Papua New Guinea), and art (illustrated by a rotating display of sculpture).

The second theme complex is "Shaping the World" in which sub-themes observed this time from a global perspective include living spaces (represented by a North American Plains Indian *tipi*), clothing and adornment (the focal point is a Hawaiian nobleman's feather cloak of 1820), death and the afterlife (exhibits here include wooden figurines from the Bismarck Archipelago representing deceased ancestors, a richly-carved Maori royal funerary boat, and a wooden coffin in the form of a bull in which Balinese Hindu high priests are cremated), religions (represented by Buddhist cult figures from South East Asia), and rituals (illustrated by African masks).

A series of short videos of farewell rituals provide an epilogue for visitors as they return to their own worlds. After spending a few hours in this fascinating museum the visitor will probably feel almost as well travelled as Wilhelm Joest did himself!

A bull-shaped coffin used to cremate Balinese Hindu priests

The subject of ethnology is presented in a different way in Cologne's fascinating Museum of East Asian Art (Museum für Ostasiatische Kunst) at Universitätsstrasse 100 (Altstadt-Süd) (see no. 30). Dotted amongst the silk wall hangings and carved Buddhas are everyday items such as a fresh water vessel used in tea ceremonies (Mizusashi), a portable backgammon set (Sugoroku), and a travelling smoking set with pipe (Dôchû tabakobon).

Other places of interest nearby: 1, 2, 3, 6, 18, 19

31 A Dozen Romanesque Churches

Innenstadt (Altstadt-Süd) (Borough 1), a tour of Romanesque
churches beginning with the Church of St. Maria in Lyskirchen
(Kirche St. Maria in Lyskirchen) at An Lyskirchen 8
Stadtbahn 1, 7, 9 Heumarkt; Bus 106, 978
(From 2015: Nord-Süd-Stadtbahn Heumarkt)

Romanesque architecture, as its name suggests, was inspired by the
sturdy vaulted architecture of the Romans. The style dates back to the
eleventh century, when it was carried from France across Europe by
clerics on pilgrimage, followed by journeymen masons seeking work.
The most striking legacy of the period are its churches – and Cologne
can boast a dozen superb examples within its Altstadt alone: six in Altstadt-Süd and six in Altstadt-Nord.

A Romanesque church represents heavenly Jerusalem as a sacred
castle. Strong walls forming a cross-shaped plan signify the temporal
power of the Church in protecting its congregation, with towers and
spires providing a manifestation of God's power on earth. The western façade has a fortress-like character, because the side of the setting
sun was regarded as a gateway of darkness and evil. To the east, where
the sun rises, is placed the altar, representing Christ as the light of the
world. Romanesque churches differ from early Christian basilicas in
their use of subdivided space, creating transepts, a chancel, and a nave.

The smallest of Cologne's Romanesque churches is the Church
of St. Maria in Lyskirchen (Kirche St. Maria in Lyskirchen) at An
Lyskirchen 8 (Altstadt-Süd). Located on a quiet backstreet and constructed between 1210 and 1220 it is also the only one to have survived
intact in its original condition. The simple pink façade is of particular
interest because its door lintel features a marker recording Cologne's
worst ever flood on 28th February 1784; it is difficult to imagine the
Rhine having ever risen so high. The interior of the church, meanwhile,
is an urban oasis, the earthy colours of the walls, the lack of seating,
and the thirteenth century frescoes imparting more the feeling of an
abandoned country chapel than a city church.

The veneration of saints during the medieval period necessitated
that some Romanesque churches were given subterranean crypts, providing clergy and worshippers' with direct access to holy graves (see nos.
1 & 13). Atmospheric examples, some of which contain earlier Roman
remains, can be found in the Church of St. Andrew (St.-Andreas-Kirche),

the Church of St. Martin the Great (Gross-St.-Martin-Kirche), and the Church of St. Gereon (St.-Gereons-Kirche) in Altstadt-Nord, and in the Church of St. Cecilia (St.-Cäcilien-Kirche), the Church of St. Maria im Capitol (St.-Maria-im-Capitol-Kirche), and the Church of St. Severin (St.-Severins-Kirche) in Altstadt-Süd. That saintly relics were all the rage is witnessed by the bone-filled Golden Chamber in the Romanesque Church of St. Ursula (St.-Ursula-Kirche) (Altstadt-Nord) (see no. 23).

Cologne's four other Romanesque churches also contain extraordinary features. The Church of St. Kunibert (St.-Kuniberts-Kirche) at Kunibertskloster 6 (Altstadt-Nord) is the youngest,

The entrance to the Church of St. Maria in Lyskirchen (Kirche St. Maria in Lyskirchen)

founded in the seventh century by Bishop Kunibert (c. 600–663). It features a stunning cycle of early thirteenth century stained glass windows in its apse. By contrast, the Church of St. Aposteln (St.-Aposteln-Kirche) at Apostelnkloster 10 (Altstadt-Nord) features modern Expressionistic wall paintings by Gottfried Herrmann (1907–2002), added to the choir between 1988 and 1994. The Church of St. George (St.-Georgs-Kirche) on Waidmarkt (Altstadt-Süd) is unique in being the only remaining Romanesque columned basilica in the Rhineland; completely open, its reused Roman columns would originally have supported a flat roof. To one side is a tiny courtyard containing graves of the victims of the last Allied air raid on Cologne on 2nd March 1945. Finally, there is the Church of St. Pantaleon (St.-Pantaleons-Kirche) at Am Pantaleonsberg 8 (Altstadt-Süd), the city's earliest instance of Romanesque architecture, and notable for its Baroque organ and pulpit. (Incidentally, the Church of St. Mariä-Himmelfahrt (St.-Mariä-Himmelfahrts-Kirche) at Marzellenstrasse 26 is Cologne's only true Baroque church.)

Other places of interest nearby: 6, 7, 8, 31, 33

32 Don't Forget the Mustard

Innenstadt (Altstadt-Süd) (Borough 1), the Mustard Museum
(Senfmuseum) at Holzmarkt 79–83
Stadtbahn 3, 4 Severinstrasse; Bus 106

Each year over half a million visitors pass through the doors of Cologne's Imhoff Chocolate Museum (Imhoff-Schokoladenmuseum) at Am Schokoladenmuseum 1a (Altstadt-Süd). Combining striking modern architecture with several thousand mouth-watering exhibits, this state-of-the-art museum is located on the tip of a peninsula jutting out into the Rhine. It was founded in 1993 and pays homage not only to the three thousand year long history of chocolate but also to the Cologne-based Stollwerck chocolate company, which was revitalised after the Second World War by Hans Imhoff (1922–2007). Highlights of the museum include a tropical greenhouse in which cacao trees are grown (from which the cocoa bean is harvested), glass-sided chocolate making machines into which visitors can peer, and a hot milk chocolate fountain three metres high.

Those with more of a savoury tooth, however, should visit the less well known but no less interesting Mustard Museum (Senfmuseum), which is located directly opposite the Chocolate Museum at Holzmarkt 79–83. It could be said that a tasting here may well leave an even more indelible memory!

The Mustard Museum is operated by mustard miller Wolfgang Steffens, whose pride and joy is an historic mustard mill dating back to 1810. It is one of only two traditional mustard mills in operation in Germany and is one of the oldest in Europe. In actual fact Steffens' mill is one of a pair located originally in Belgium, which were acquired by him in 1997. In poor condition he lovingly restored them, removing one to the Rhenish town of Cochem in 2001 and the other to Cologne in 2009, where both now function as working mustard museums.

Six times daily Steffens gives a working demonstration of his mill. In a large vat he places the mustard seed – imported from Eastern Europe and Canada since it is no longer farmed in Germany – which is mashed with vinegar and water. The mash is then fed between two sturdy millstones, each weighing 525 kilogrammes. This releases the potent essential oils that give traditional mustard its unmistakeable taste and smell. In industrial mustard production a lot of heat is generated, which tends to vaporise the essential oils, and so horseradish

A restored mustard mill is the highlight of the Mustard Museum (Senfmuseum) on Holzmarkt

is added to retain the sharp taste. The grinding stones of a traditional mustard mill generate little heat thus leaving the potency of the oils intact – and one can really taste the difference! This will be discovered after the milling demonstration, when visitors are given the chance to taste some of Steffens' award-winning mustards, 360 kilogrammes of which he produces daily.

The museum shop contains everything for the real mustard devotee, including a large array of gourmet cold-milled mustards using traditional and secret recipes dating back to 1820. These include garlic mustard (Knoblauch-Senf), which goes well with roast meat and in salad dressings, sweet honey mustard (Waben-Senf), which is recommended as an accompaniment to smoked salmon, cayenne pepper mustard (Cayenne-Senf) for grilled meats, and curry mustard (Indisch-Curry-Senf) for use with poultry and in dips. Unique varieties include a Riesling mustard (Riesling-Senf), which makes a good sauce for perch, and a sweet mustard made with wine (Mühlen-Senf), which is based on a monastic recipe from the fifteenth century and recommended for use with game. The Beer mustard (Bier-Senf), made with locally-brewed Gaffel-brand *Kölsch*, is almost good enough on its own!

And it should be remembered that mustard is much more than just

A sack of mustard seed waiting to be milled

a tasty condiment. Its powerful antibacterial properties, propensity to stimulate the gastric juices, and beneficial influence on the liver and gall bladder have long been appreciated. Indeed, as long ago as 1597 the English herbalist John Gerard wrote in his *Great Herball, or Generall Historie of Plantes* that Sinapis Alba (i.e. the white mustard plant) "doth helpe digestion, warmeth the stomacke, and provideth appetite". Potential purchasers will also be pleased to learn that the essential oils in mustard contain natural preservatives, giving the product a long and natural shelf life. Incidentally, the best containers for the storage of mustard are salt-glazed stoneware vessels, which can also be purchased in the museum shop, together with a range of other mustard-infused products including sauces, preserves, spreads, and chutneys.

A steam engine once used in the Stollwerck chocolate factory is displayed in a park opposite Annostrasse 27 (Altstadt-Süd). Around the corner at Dreikönigenstrasse 23 is the Bürgerhaus Stollwerck, built originally in 1906 as a Prussian military provisions store, which was later used as a store by the Stollwerck company. It today serves as a cultural centre and café.

Other places of interest nearby: 7, 31, 33

33 Casanova and the Chapel of Misery

Innenstadt (Altstadt-Süd) (Borough 1), the Elendskirche
St. Gregor at An St. Katharinen 5
Stadtbahn 3, 4 Severinstrasse; Bus 132, 133
(From 2015: Nord-Süd-Stadtbahn Severinstrasse)

People are spoilt for choice when it comes to visiting churches in Cologne. In addition to Cologne Cathedral (Kölner Dom), Altstadt boasts a dozen magnificent Romanesque churches, and a further thirteen are to be found out in the suburbs. These aside, however, there are many other churches and chapels worth visiting, one of which, the Elendskirche St. Gregor (or St. Gregorius im Elend) at An St. Katharinen 5, is especially intriguing.

The name of this little chapel has a poignant origin since it recalls a pair of former medieval cemeteries where homeless people, non-Catholics, suicide victims, and those who had been executed were buried with little ceremony. The use of the German word *Elend*, meaning misery, recalls their sorry fate.

During the sixteenth century the old cemetery gave way to property development, which included the construction of a private chapel for the Catholic de Groote family. Constructed in the red-brick Baroque style it was used by them until 1764, after which they formed a family trust and had the chapel extended into a church, and opened thereafter for public services (the family still administers the church and has sole access to it one day each year). The initial design of the building was by the little-known architect and sculptor Balthasar Spaeth; it was at this time that the building received its distinctive rounded corners and took the name Elendskirche St. Gregor. The numerous carved skulls were also added to the façade, being a Catholic Baroque device symbolising death and the transience of life.

The de Groote family first arrived in Cologne along with an influx of Catholic immigrants from the Netherlands during the sixteenth century. Unlike the Protestants, who did not get their own church in the city until 1802, the Catholics received considerable privileges, and Franz Jakob Gabriel de Groote even rose to the rank of mayor.

An extraordinary story surrounds Franz Jakob and his wife Maria Ursula Columba Pütz, whom he married when she was just fifteen. During the carnival season in 1760 the then twenty five year old Ma-

Skulls adorn the Elendskirche St. Gregor on An St. Katharinen

ria encountered none other than Giacomo Casanova in a local theatre. She must have left an impression on him since according to Casanova's memoirs he hid in the confessional of the family's chapel until after it had been locked, in an attempt to see her again. Several hours later, through a door connecting the chapel with an adjoining building, the mayor's wife eventually appeared. During the conversation that followed she revealed to Casanova her great love for her husband and how this had been demonstrated by her bearing him six children. Unfortunately for "Mimi", as Casanova refers to Maria in his memoirs, she was destined to die from tuberculosis aged just thirty three.

Despite suffering serious damage during the Second World War the church was extensively restored and reopened in 1967. The building seen today differs little from the original eighteenth century structure. Although the exterior can be viewed at all times, the interior is only visible during mass on Fridays at 7pm (tours by appointment only, tel. 0049-(0)221-31-42-75). A visit is certainly worthwhile if only to see the Baroque organ and pulpit, as well as the de Groote and Pütz family arms on the ceiling above the High Altar (they appear also in the gable at the top of the main façade).

The site of the de Groote family home on the north side of the church is now partially occupied by the Schönstattkapelle, a small chapel that is part of the Schönstätter Marienschwestern organisation. Founded in 1926 it is the longest established secular institute of the Roman Catholic Church, and is administered by women who are free to come and go as they please.

Other places of interest nearby: 32, 34, 35

34 Silver Screen Cologne

Innenstadt (Altstadt-Süd) (Borough 1), the Odeon Cinema
(Odeon Lichtspieltheater) at Severinstrasse 81
Stadtbahn 3, 4 Severinstrasse; Bus 132, 133
(From 2015: Nord-Süd-Stadtbahn Severinstrasse)

The history of cinema in Germany can be traced back to November 1895, when Max and Emil Skladanowsky demonstrated their newly-invented *Bioskop* film projector at the Wintergarten music hall in Berlin, pre-dating by almost two months the first public display of the Lumière brothers' *Cinematographe* in Paris the same year. By the time of the Weimar Republic (1918–1933) the German film industry was booming, turning out more than six hundred feature films a year, with the legendary UFA film studio in Berlin rivalling Hollywood itself. Since those heady days the industry has waxed and waned with the country's turbulent history, from the strictly controlled propaganda films of the Nazi era and the *Trümmerfilm* ('rubble film') genre of the immediate post-war period (reflecting everyday life in a devastated Germany), to the morally simplistic and hugely popular *Heimat* films of the 1950s, which accompanied West Germany's economic recovery *(Wirtschaftswunder)*.

Unlike Berlin, Cologne during these years was not a centre for film production, but like all German cities it had its fair share of cinemas. One of these, the Odeon Cinema (Odeon Lichtspieltheater) at Severinstrasse 81 (Altstadt-Süd), illustrates well the vicissitudes of the German film industry from the 1950s until the present day. The 374-seat cinema was opened as the Rhenania in 1956, when West German cinema attendance was at its post-war peak. It was built on the site of the former Vrings Opera House (Vrings-Oper), which had been destroyed during the war (the name comes from Vringsveertel, being Cologne dialect for Severinsviertel, the quarter named after Saint Severin).

The first films to be screened at the Rhenania undoubtedly included *Heimat* films, together with comedies, musicals, adaptations of operettas, and hospital melodramas, all of which were popular genres at the time. German rearmament and the founding of the Federal Defence Force (Bundeswehr) a year earlier also gave rise to popular apolitical films depicting the ordinary German soldier during the Second World War.

In the late 1950s, cinema attendance stagnated and then declined

Take to the red carpet at the Odeon Cinema (Odeon Lichtspieltheater) on Severinstrasse

throughout the 1960s. By 1969 West German cinema attendance had fallen to less than a quarter of what it was when the Rhenania opened, and numerous German film companies went out of business. The number of films made in West Germany (now mainly westerns and crime films) was halved, as was the number of screens, which reached an all-time low in 1976. Average incomes in West Germany had risen and the number of television sets rose dramatically, taking people away from the cinemas. Cologne was no exception and the Rhenania was converted into the Theater im Vringsveedel (known also as the Trude Herr-Theater after its proprietor).

In 1994 the Theater im Vringsveedel was acquired by a subsidiary of the German media group Kinowelt-Medien AG for conversion back to a cinema. By this time the fortunes of German filmmaking had been revived somewhat through the efforts of the so-called New German Cinema (Neuer Deutscher Film), a group of directors who rejected co-operation with the existing film industry, seeking support instead from television companies. Despite the turn of the millennium witnessing a resurgence in returns at the German box office, trouble at Kinowelt-Medien AG saw the Odeon close its doors once again. Fortunately this only lasted for three months, and with financial assistance

The Metropolis on Ebertplatz still retains some glamour

from the North Rhine Westphalia Film Foundation (Filmstiftung NRW), Germany's largest regional film grant programme, the cinema reopened as the Odeon in 2002.

The Odeon today is one of the few cinemas in Cologne that still offers a taste of the golden age of cinema (others include the Metropolis at Ebertplatz 19 and the tiny, seventy-seat Filmpalette at Lübeckerstrasse 15 (Neustadt-Nord)). With a programme of two films a day, including international films on Sunday and children's films in the afternoons, the Odeon is a truly traditional cinema. The mood is enhanced by an elegant red-carpeted staircase leading up to the main auditorium, as well as an intimate house bar.

To experience film- and television-making up close it is possible to take a studio tour of the Magic Media Company (MMC) at Am Coloneum 1 (Ehrenfeld) (www.mmc.de). Established in 1991, Cologne's largest multimedia facility has been used for numerous successful international co-productions, including the romantic comedy *Amélie* (2001). With a combination of attractive foreign-friendly regional subsidies and state-of-the-art facilities, Cologne and North Rhine Westphalia looks set emulate some of the cinematographic successes achieved in Berlin almost a century ago.

Other places of interest nearby: 33, 35

35 Portals to the Past

Innenstadt (Altstadt-Süd) (Borough 1), the Ulrepforte
at Sachsenring 42
Stadtbahn 15, 16 Ulrepforte

In 785 Cologne became the seat of an archbishopric providing the foundation for the commercial success of Europe's largest medieval town. A prerequisite for any strategically located medieval city was an effective wall, and in 950 and again in 1106 Cologne's existing Roman circuit wall was extended on all sides (see no. 12). The city soon outgrew this extension and between 1180 and 1259 an entirely new wall was erected. More than five kilometres in length it would be the greatest city wall in the Western world and would protect Cologne for the next seven centuries.

Cologne's medieval city wall was demolished from 1881 onwards, to create much-needed space for housing, by which time it had long been replaced by a new series of Prussian-built fortifications farther out of the city (see no. 82). Despite this, the line of the medieval wall can still be traced today, since a semicircular ring road – the Kölner Ring – was built in its place. Before setting out to explore it, however, one should visit the Cologne City Museum (Kölnisches Stadtmuseum) at Zeughausstrasse 1–3 (Altstadt-Nord), where there is a highly informative model of the medieval city, made in 1914 at a scale of 1:750. Not only are the stout walls depicted clearly but also the fifty two watch towers and the twelve gateways that punctuated them (with a further twelve facing the Rhine).

When exploring what's left of the medieval wall most visitors gravitate to one of the three surviving main gateways: the Severinstor on Chlodwigplatz in the south, the Hahnentor on Rudolfplatz to the west, and the Eigelsteintor on Ebertplatz in the north (see no. 24). Much restored these thirteenth century structures illustrate well the construction process of using massive blocks of black basalt in the lower courses and calcareous tufa higher up.

Perhaps more enlightening and certainly less frequented is the Ulrepforte on Sachsenring, west of the Severinstor, which was one of the first medieval gateways to be constructed in around 1220. Having lost its original purpose it was reused in 1446 as the base for a windmill. In 1861 it doubled as the workshop of a rope maker, and was eventually restored as the fairytale tower seen today. Westwards along Kartäuser

Wall runs a restored stretch of crenellated medieval wall, with a watchtower at either end (the Sachsenturm at the east and the Prinzen-Garden-Turm at the west).

To the east of the Severinstor another windmill was constructed on the medieval wall. Known as the Bottmühle it was first built in wood in the 1580s and then rebuilt in stone in the seventeenth century. Further east again, where the city wall reaches the Rhine, stands the Bayenturm (Bavaria Tower), the strongest of all the towers in the medieval wall. The tower is today known also as the FrauenMediaTurm and contains an information centre for the history of the women's emancipation movement.

Another restored stretch of walling stands on Gereonswall, in the north-west of the city, and incorporates a semicircular projecting bastion, a deep ditch, and a watch tower (again reused as the base for a windmill).

The fairytale Ulrepforte on Sachsenring

One final wall fragment is the curious Kunibertstürmchen, a tower now incorporated into a modern housing block on Konrad-Adenauer-Ufer. Like the Bayenturm it marked the place where the city wall reached the Rhine, this time to the north.

A medieval gate with a difference is the Dreikönigenpförtchen on Lichhof (Altstadt-Süd). It is Cologne's only remaining sanctuary gate, the land beyond it being subject to canon rather than secular law. Unproven is the belief that Archbishop Rainald of Dassel (c. 1120–1167) brought the relics of the Three Kings into Cologne through this gate in 1164.

Other places of interest nearby: 33, 34

36 Hotel Secrets, Secret Hotels

Innenstadt (Neustadt-Süd) (Borough 1), a tour of idiosyncratic
hotels beginning with the Hopper Hotel et cetera at Brüsseler
Strasse 26
Stadtbahn 1, 7 Moltkestrasse; Bus 136, 146

Some of Cologne's famous hotels contain secrets, whilst other less well
known ones are secrets in themselves. Here are a handful of them.

The Hopper Hotel et cetera is located in the fashionable Belgian
Quarter (Belgisches Viertel) at Brüsseler Strasse 26 (Neustadt-Süd).
Hidden behind the sturdy walls of a former monastery the hotel's forty
nine rooms occupy the monks' former cells and are each decorated individually with modern art. The monastery opened in 1894 as a cloister
and chapel for the Merciful Montabaur Brothers, where twenty brothers fed the poor and infirm regardless of denomination, their work
funded by charitable donations (in 1934 alone they served 2920 lunches
and distributed 4000 portions of bread). In 1974 the remaining seven
brothers relocated to an old people's home in Deutz, after which the
cloister was sold off to the aid organisation Malteser Hilfdienst. Today,
the building is once again providing food and shelter, albeit this time
for a price, and the former chapel, which was almost totally destroyed
during the Second World War, is recalled by an atmospheric mural on
the back wall of the hotel bar.

The combination of historic fabric and modern interior design is
continued in two other Hopper hotels in Cologne. The Hopper Hotel
St. Josef at Dreikönigenstrasse 1–3 (Altstadt-Süd) was built originally
in 1891 as a Kindergarten, to help care for the children of workers occupied in the new factories of Cologne's Südstadt, which proliferated
during the second half of the nineteenth century. The school was run
by the Sisters of Christian Love (Schwestern der Christlichen Liebe)
from Paderborn, who took in paying lodgers to help cover their running costs. During the 1920s the sisters also established a *Volksküche*,
providing up to five hundred meals a day to those suffering during Germany's era of hyperinflation.

The Hopper Hotel St. Antonius at Dagobertstrasse 32 (Altstadt-
Nord) opened originally in 1904 as a hostel for itinerant journeyman
at the instigation of Cologne's *Gesellenverein* (Journeymen's Association), which had been instigated by cathedral vicar Adolph Kolping
(1813–1865) in 1849. The building's sympathetic restoration as a hotel

The restaurant of the Hopper Hotel et cetera on Brüsseler Strasse is a former chapel

has ensured the survival of the original lattice windows and vaulted dining hall.

Another historic building that has been successfully converted into a hotel is the Hotel im Wasserturm at Kaygasse 2 (Altstadt-Süd). Situated inside a listed 130-year-old water tower the hotel boasts a luxurious interior courtesy of celebrated French architect Andrée Putman. The actor Brad Pitt was moved to say that he could well imagine Rapunzel letting her golden locks down the hotel's castle-like walls!

Two of Cologne's most storied hotels are to be found adjacent to the cathedral in Altstadt-Nord. Le Méridien Dom Hotel at Domkloster 2a is a five-storey (and five star) hotel, with just as many secrets. Opened as the Hotel du Dome in 1857 it was here in room 206 that the legendary double agent Mata Hari (1876–1917) stayed in 1916. Adolf Hitler proudly signed the guest book in March 1936, after the Wehrmacht marched into the demilitarised Rhineland. In 1944, the hotel's then director, a vigorous opponent of the Nazi regime, hung himself in the attic after being denounced by his employees. The hotel bar, incidentally, is named after the actor Peter Ustinov (1921–2004), who for thirty years was a regular visitor.

Equally historic is the Hotel Excelsior at Trankgasse 1, which

The name of the Hotel im Wasserturm on Kaygasse betrays its origins

opened as the Grand Hotel in 1863. From one of its windows the Prussian Emperor Wilhelm I (1861–1888) witnessed the completion of the cathedral in 1880. After the First World War the hotel served as the seat of the General Headquarters of the British Forces of the Rhine. Some 280 000 soldiers were commanded from the hotel and in 1919 Winston Churchill organised a military parade here. The British occupation of Cologne lasted from December 1918 until 1929, with Mayor Konrad Adenauer (1876–1967) cooperating amicably with British military governor Sir Charles Ferguson.

We finish with what is perhaps Cologne's cosiest hotel, Das kleine Stapelhäuschen at Fischmarkt 1–3. It opened in 1950 in a former Late Gothic storage building *(Stapelhaus)* located on one side of Cologne's old fish market. At the apex of the building is a bedroom containing the medieval crane once used to raise goods up from the pavement below, the only remaining example of its type in Cologne.

Other places of interest nearby: 29, 37, 38

37 Europe's First Art Hotel

Innenstadt (Neustadt-Süd) (Borough 1), the Hotel Chelsea at
Jülicher Strasse 1
Stadtbahn 1, 7 Moltkestrasse; Bus 136, 146

The concept of the 'Art Hotel',
in which original works of
art adorn both public areas
and private rooms, is now a
Europe-wide phenomenon,
fuelled in part by the growing
popularity of weekend city
breaks. A list of them might
include London's Caesar Hotel (original Roman mosa-
ics from Syria), Berlin's Arte
Luise Kunsthotel (philosoph-
ical statements painted in the
stairwell), Madrid's Hotel Urban (totem poles in the foyer),
and Stockholm's Nordic Light
Hotel (where patrons can ma-
nipulate light installations in
their bedrooms to suit their
individual mood). The Jones
in London's Bayswater even
boasts its own curator, whose
job it is to regularly change
the display of paintings on
the walls!

Catering not only to the
art lover but also to the independent thinking traveller,
Art Hotels offer personalised
accommodation in a char-

The distinctive Kippenberger Suite at the Hotel Chelsea
on Jülicher Strasse

acterful environment. As such, they are far removed from the identical rooms of traditional hotels, in which art is commonly used only to
break up the wall space. With an increasing number of Art Hotels to
choose from, however, it shouldn't be forgotten where, when, and how

The artist Martin Kippenberger often stayed for months at a time in the Hotel Chelsea

the first one was founded, especially since the answer can be found at Cologne's Hotel Chelsea at Jülicher Strasse 1 (Neustadt-Süd).

The story begins in 1985, when the fast-living, hard-drinking German artist Martin Kippenberger (1953–1997) became a regular customer at the Café Central, adjacent to the Hotel Chelsea. In the summer of 1986 Kippenberger ('Kippi' to his friends) came into contact with the hotel's proprietor, Dr. Werner Peters, whom he persuaded into having a bet over a Football World Cup game. Confident following an earlier successful bet, Kippenberger offered one of his drawings against a double room for a week including breakfast in bed. Kippenberger won the bet and took up residence at the Chelsea!

When the week was over Kippenberger told Peters that he liked the idea of living in a hotel rather than his own house, and suggested that the exchange of art against lodging might be extended. With the prospect of more pictures with which to adorn his rooms Peters agreed enthusiastically, and the hotel became Kippenberger's preferred residence whenever he stayed in Cologne, often for several months at a time. This unique symbiosis between artist and hotelier thus gave rise to Europe's first Art Hotel.

The rooms of the Hotel Chelsea still contain many pieces of contemporary art, some of which are by artists such as Walter Dahn (b. 1954), A. R. Penck (b. 1939), Jiří Georg Dokoupil (b. 1954), and Albert (b. 1954) and Markus Oehlen (b. 1956), who together with Kippenberger were members of the Neue Wilde group of experimental artists in the early 1980s. Art lovers will always find something of interest here, as do artists and gallery owners, for whom the Hotel Chelsea and the Café Central have become something of a home-from-home. Indeed, that's exactly how the American conceptual artist Joseph Kosuth, whose neon installation is in the hotel foyer, described it when he stayed.

The Hotel Chelsea continues to be enhanced artistically, most dramatically in 2001 when a spectacular new roof was added. Designed in the Deconstructive style it has the appearance of a random pile of geometric shapes, contrasting sharply with the plain 1960s style of the rest of the building. The roof contains seven new hotel bedrooms, one of which is named in honour of Martin Kippenberger, who died in Vienna aged just forty four from liver cancer.

As well as sculpting a crucified toad, creating his own museum in a former slaughterhouse on a deserted Greek island, and opening a petrol station in Brazil called Gas Station Martin Borman, Martin Kippenberger also ran a Dadaesque night club in Berlin during the late 1970s. Cologne was once the creative centre of the Dadaists, focussed around the painter and sculptor Max Ernst (1891–1976), whose home and studio at Kaiser-Wilhelm-Ring 14 (Altstadt-Nord) was destroyed during the Second World War.

Other places of interest nearby: 29, 36, 38, 78

38 The Sound of Chinese Bells

Innenstadt (Neustadt-Süd) (Borough 1), the Museum of
East Asian Art (Museum für Ostasiatische Kunst) at
Universitätsstrasse 100
Stadtbahn 1, 7 Universitätsstrasse

Those seeking calm and tranquillity in Cologne might head to one of
the city's churches or parks for quiet contemplation (see nos. 31 & 58).
There is one uniquely peaceful location, however, that is neither of
these and yet combines elements of both. The Museum of East Asian
Art (Museum für Ostasiatische Kunst) at Universitätsstrasse 100 (Neustadt-Süd) is located in the Hiroshima-Nagasaki-Park and contains
some of the finest Asian religious art in Europe.

Established in 1913 the museum was the first of its kind in Germany. At its heart is the Japanese collection of its founders, Adolf Fis-
cher (1856–1914) and his wife Frieda, consisting of Buddhist paintings
and wooden sculptures, Japanese painted screens, coloured woodcuts,
and lacquer work. Several private collections have subsequently been
absorbed into the museum, including Chinese furniture and ceremonial bronzes, Chinese and Japanese calligraphy, and Chinese, Japanese
and Korean ceramics.

The original museum building on Hansaring, a traditional stone
structure with a pitched roof, was destroyed during the Second World
War. The current building, which opened in 1977 could not be more
different, being a series of interconnected Modernist cubes in concrete
and glass. It was designed by the Japanese architect Kunio Maekawa
(1905–1986), a former pupil of Le Corbusier, and is centred on a meditative Japanese water garden created by the Japanese sculptor Mas-
ayuki Nagare (b. 1923). This symbiosis of Japanese architecture and
garden design imbues the museum with a distinct, almost spiritual
identity.

Visitors enter through a foyer that feels as if it is floating on an
adjacent ornamental lake, the Aachener Weiher. In one corner are set
a row of fourteenth century Luohan figures, the appointed disciples of
the Buddha. From their expressions it is easy to see why they are an
inspiration to young Buddhist monks. In keeping with the concept of
the founders, all the exhibits are presented as autonomous works of art,
used to illustrate specific styles of an individual artist or period. This
case of "less is more" encourages the visitor to concentrate longer on

A rare set of Chinese bells in the Museum of East Asian Art (Museum für Ostasiatische Kunst) on Universitätsstrasse

fewer objects, an experience enhanced by the use of low-level lighting.

In the first gallery are examples of East Asian Buddhist art: delicate Japanese silk wall hangings, a magnificent Chinese silk triptych depicting the Buddha, and the seated sixteenth century wooden figure of the thirteenth century Japanese priest Eison, whose crimson eyes seem to follow the viewer around the room. The next gallery is devoted to Japanese calligraphy inspired by Zen Buddhist teachings, which since the fourteenth century has been referred to as *Bokuseki* ('ink traces'). Influenced by art imported from China they are mostly on paper wrapped around a wooden pole to facilitate easy storage and transportation. A wonderful eighteenth century example depicts a hundred old blind men, representing man's endless quest for enlightenment.

Perhaps the most intriguing item in the museum comes next: a set of nine *Yongszhong*-type bronze bells from the Zhou dynasty (850–650 BC), once used to propitiate the spirits of dead ancestors. The bells are all synchronised in pitch, although the large so-called *Bo* bell may not originally have been part of the set. The haunting sound of the bells, which are the only such set outside China, can be heard on a recording alongside the exhibit. It is interesting to note that the world's first bells were manufactured by the Chinese around 2000 BC (Germany's oldest bell, the so-called *Saufang* dating from the early seventh century, hangs in Cologne's Schnütgen Museum of Medieval Art at Cäcilienstrasse 29 (Altstadt-Süd)).

This Japanese water garden lies at the heart of the Museum of East Asian Art (Museum für Ostasiatische Kunst)

In the same room is the sculpture of a horse and groom, an outstanding example of Chinese bronze work from the Eastern Han Dynasty (2nd–3rd centuries AD). The museum concludes with a series of beautiful objects dating back to prehistoric times, including Chinese jade from 3000 BC and ornate bronze mirrors of the Tang Dynasty (7th–9th centuries AD).

Immediately west of the Museum of East Asian Art, beyond the busy Universitätsstrasse, is the Clarenbach Canal, a chestnut-lined waterway that also offers a measure of tranquillity in the city. It was created in the early 1920s by the city planner Fritz Schumacher (1869–1947) and the garden architect Fritz Encke (1861–1931), as part of an unfinished project to channel fresh air into the city centre.

Other places of interest nearby: 36, 77, 78

39 Homage to a Water Reservoir

Innenstadt (Neustadt-Süd) (Borough 1), the Water Storage Tank
Severin at Zugweg 29–31
Stadtbahn 15, 16 Chlodwigplatz; Bus 132, 133
(From 2015: Nord-Süd-Stadtbahn Bonner Wall)

Saint Severin was the third known bishop of Cologne and lived during the fourth century. Little is known of him other than that in 376 he founded a monastery in Roman Cologne, on what is today Severinskirchplatz, in honour of the martyrs Cornelius and Cyprian. Out of this establishment grew the Church of St. Severin (St.-Severins-Kirche), the southernmost of Cologne's twelve Romanesque churches (see no. 31). Although Severin died around AD 400 – the church contains his bones in a gold reliquary – he remains ubiquitous in this part of the city, where he has two streets (Severinsstrasse and Severinswall) and a medieval gate (Severinstor) named after him. Undoubtedly the most unusual location to carry the saint's name, however, is the colossal Water Storage Tank Severin at Zugweg 29–31.

Since the late nineteenth century the triangle of land formed by Zugweg, Bonner Wall, and Ohmstrasse has been given over to the RheinEnergie company, where it has been responsible for the city's water and power supply. Between 1883 and 1905 a complex of red-brick buildings, including pump rooms, machine halls and chimneys, were erected here, the façades and interiors of which are today classed as historically important examples of industrial architecture (the main entrance is marked by an imposing, ivy-clad, neo-Gothic turret). Chief among the buildings is the Water Storage Tank Severin (Wasserspeicher Severin), an underground reservoir with a storage capacity of approximately twenty million cubic litres of drinking water. The vault of the tank, which lies just beneath ground level, is 4.5 metres high and supported by one hundred and ninety four columns, giving it the feel of a subterranean church.

The reservoir is known for its remarkable but unintentional acoustics, enabling sounds to resonate for up to forty five seconds, making it the longest echo ever recorded. This was best demonstrated in December 1984 when the reservoir lay empty for maintenance work. The experimental artist Hinnerick Bröskamp assembled a group of musicians from around the world, together with members of Cologne's Tanzforum der Oper, to perform a unique music and dance project. Called

Ornate brickwork marks Cologne's nineteenth century waterworks on Zugweg

Vor der Flut – Hommage an einem Wasserspeicher (Before the Flood – Homage to a Water Reservoir) the performance was experimental, thought provoking, and meditative and can be viewed online at the video sharing website YouTube. Although the tank was subsequently re-filled it was emptied again in 2010, having been superceded by a new reservoir elsewhere. The old reservoir is thus now available permanently for concerts, events, and visitor tours, and its incredible echo can be appreciated by everyone.

An unforgettable tour of this man-made wonder, which illustrates the collection, purification, and storage of drinking water in Cologne, is possible by appointment with RheinEnergie AG (tel. 0049-(0)221-178-4660, www.rheinenergie.de). Another tour offered by the same company takes place at the Weiler Waterworks (Wasserwerk Weiler) on Blockstrasse (Chorweiler), where there is also an open-air display of old pumping engines and filtration tanks.

Cologne did not gain access to a centralised water supply until 1863, despite repeated (apparently unaffordable) offers from both German and English hydraulic engineers. The city's first waterworks opened in 1872 on the Alteburg, supplying the city centre with clean drinking water (the city's first public gas works were inaugurated a year later). Demand increased rapidly with industrialisation and the Severin I waterworks were established on Zugweg in 1885. This was replaced by the facility seen today (Severin II) during the early 1890s, and the storage tank was constructed in 1899–1900.

Cologne's first power station was built alongside the Severin works around the same time, guaranteeing Cologne a reliable supply of water and power from the same location (see no. 42). Supply continued until

The empty Water Storage Tank Severin is now used for concerts

the Zugweg facility was put out of action by an air raid in March 1945, although both supplies were restored by 1948. Cologne's water, gas, electricity and transport utilities were turned into corporations in 1960 under the umbrella of Stadtwerke Köln GmbH (SWK). In the early 1990s it was decided to once again align Cologne's water, electricity and gas companies to best suit the trading conditions in the new Europe, and on 2nd July 2002 the company that is today RheinEnergie AG was created to serve the entire Rhine region.

Dotted around Cologne are numerous wall markers recording the level reached by the city's worst floods. One is painted over the door of the Church of St. Maria in Lyskirchen (Kirche St. Maria in Lyskirchen) at An Lyskirchen 8 (see no. 31). Another is at the nearby corner of Am Leystapel and Filzengraben: the level reached in 1882 can be seen at the top of the ground floor window, whereas that reached in 1784 is at the top of the first floor window. Other markers are on the so-called Schmitz-Säule at An Gross St. Martin (Altstadt-Nord), and in the choir of the Elendskirche St. Gregor at An St. Katharinen 5 (Altstadt-Süd) (see no. 33). The level of the Rhine itself has been given since 1810 by the Pegelhaus on Frankenwerft (Altstadt-Nord).

Other places of interest nearby: 79

40   The Last of the Swing Bridges

Innenstadt (Deutz) (Borough 1), the swing bridge
on Alfred-Schütte-Allee
Stadtbahn 7 Drehbrücke

Swing bridges have long been used as a means of traversing waterways without impeding the passage of shipping. Their primary structural support is a vertical pin, usually at the bridge's centre of gravity, about which the bridge pivots horizontally. Small swing bridges need only be pivoted at one end, opening as would a gate, although in such cases a substantial subterranean foundation is needed to support the pivot. When a ship needs to pass, road traffic is stopped, and then manpower or motors are used to rotate the bridge approximately ninety degrees about its pivot point.

During the late nineteenth century the Rhine port of Cologne was given two new harbours in which ships could easily and safely dock, unload, reload, and depart. One of them, the Rheinauhafen was constructed on the west bank, whilst the other, the Deutzer Hafen, was constructed on the east. Similar in construction they consist of a promontory facing downstream thereby creating a haven for ships on the side facing the riverbank. The two harbours were also equipped with small swing bridges, located close to the end of each promontory.

Of the two, the Rheinauhafen swing bridge is best known, since it now provides direct access to the Imhoff Chocolate Museum (Imhoff-Schokoladenmuseum), which is one element of the highly successful transformation of the old docks on this side of the river into a high profile residential, business and leisure quarter. The bridge was constructed in 1888 – a decade before the harbour itself was inaugurated – and was operated by water pressure generated by an electrically-operated pump located in the nearby Malakoff Tower (Malakoffturm).

Although a few cranes have been preserved along the quayside of the Rheinauhafen, together with the renovated former customs' hall, *Siebengebirge* warehouses, and several other structures, the area today lacks the colour and commotion of an old harbour. The Deutzer Hafen, by comparison, still serves something of its original purpose, and therefore remains the more authentic of the two.

A harbour in Deutz was first planned in 1888, when the area was incorporated into Cologne (prior to this a harbour was forbidden for fear of creating competition with Cologne). Construction work com-

The old swing bridge on Alfred-Schütte-Allee in Deutz

menced in 1895, creating a harbour one thousand and ninety eight metres long by eighty eight metres at its widest point. Between 1906 and 1908 the electrically-operated swing bridge seen today was installed on Alfred-Schütte-Allee, and during the 1920s three steam- and four electric-powered cranes were installed. Up until the Second World War the harbour's largest operators were the millers Leysieffer & Lietmann, and Heinrich Auer.

After the war the largest company at the harbour was Kampffmeyer, who built the Ellmühle for the grinding of wheat and rye, with a storage capacity of sixty thousand tons. Other post-war operatives included the Theo Steil scrapyard, the Carl J. Weiler steel company, an asphalt manufacturer, and a fuel depot. All were serviced by a harbour railway operated by Häfen und Güterverkehr Köln (HGK), whose marshalling yard still lies at the southern end of the harbour in the district of Poll. It is the swing bridge, however, that remains the focus of this fascinating industrial ensemble, with its elegant grey green-painted *Jugendstil* ironwork, ornate operator's cabin, and lantern-topped obelisks. All around are half-concealed railway tracks, cranes, old warehouses, cobbled streets, and sturdy iron mooring rings. The scene is completed by the presence of Cologne's fire boat, which relocated here from the Rheinauhafen in 1994.

Love locks attached to the Hohenzollern Bridge
(Hohenzollernbrücke)

A sign of recent times has been the disappearance of the harbour's timber companies, and the gradual appearance of non-traditional enterprises reusing former industrial premises, such as the Essig-fabrik events venue at Sieg-burgerstrasse 110. However, with a projected increase in the volume of container traf-fic on the Rhine it looks like the Deutzer Hafen will con-tinue to serve as a harbour and industrial hinterland for at least a few more years to come.

Cologne's most celebrated bridge is the four hundred and nine metre-long Hohen-zollernbrücke completed in 1859. An unusual feature is the recent appearance of thou-sands of engraved padlocks, placed there by sweethearts to symbolise their love. These love locks *(lucchetti d'amore)* first appeared on the Ponte Milvio in Rome, and have sub-sequently been spotted on bridges as far away as China. After being attached to the bridge the keys are tossed into the river below.

Other places of interest nearby: 41

41   Is That Really a Church?

Innenstadt (Deutz) (Borough 1), the Church Bunker at Helenen-wallstrasse 21–29
Stadtbahn 1, 7, 9 Deutzer Freizeit

In August 1939 Reichsmarschall Hermann Göring (1893–1946) proclaimed that no Allied bomber would ever reach the River Ruhr. When the first Allied aircraft successfully dropped bombs on Berlin in June 1940 a frustrated Hitler responded by initiating a crash programme of air raid shelter building across Germany, primarily to protect himself, his staff, and those workers considered crucial to the war effort (Göring's own personal shelter in Berlin had been constructed as early as 1936). In Cologne, as in other important German cities, these shelters came in a variety of shapes and sizes, including underground complexes *(Tiefbunker)* and colossal overground towers *(Hochbunker)* (see no. 60).

The civilian population was also catered for but they remained vulnerable throughout the war since there was only ever the time and resources to construct shelters for around ten percent of them. This accounts for the high civilian mortality rate from 1942 onwards, when Allied Bomber Command began the deliberate area bombing of residential districts in an attempt to weaken German morale.

Many Second World War shelters remain in Germany today and it is interesting to note when visiting those above ground that some incorporate surprising decorative details. Neo-Classical cornices, neo-Renaissance conical red-tiled roofs, and Tuscan-style staircase balustrades all appear incongruous against the stark, steel-reinforced concrete construction of most of the shelters. The most striking of them has to be the existence of what appears to be a church belfry on the roof of a *Hochbunker* at Helenenwallstrasse 21–29 (Deutz).

One popular explanation for the presence of such details is that they helped disguise the real purpose of the shelters from bombers overhead. However, even with the benefit of the technical wizardry of Google Earth, this author found it difficult to distinguish any of these structures from their neighbours, and that was in clear daytime weather. So why, therefore, would a wartime shelter be deliberately disguised as a village church or a Renaissance tower, when it would probably never be seen at close quarters by the enemy? The answer probably lies with the department of Joseph Goebbels (1897–1945), Hitler's

Reichsminister of Propaganda, which undoubtedly convinced people that such a structure would be avoided by the bombers. Anything that made an air raid shelter look less like an air raid shelter was useful to the war effort, since it bolstered morale amongst the workers and civilians using it, and delayed the realisation that German victory in the war was fading fast. As with most of Goebbels' activities the effect was short-term. Few citizens in Cologne, a city located in the far west of

Germany, on a major river that provided useful navigation to the enemy, would have believed for long that their city was impervious to attack.

The shelter with the mock belfry on Helenenstrasse in Deutz, today nicknamed the Church Bunker, was probably constructed by forced labourers in 1943. The colourful paintwork that now enlivens it was added in 1989. It is not unique though, since another church bunker stands at Marktstrasse 6c (Rodenkirchen), and has again been painted in the post-war period. Constructed in 1942 it consists of two floors above ground and one below, and is used today as a shooting range.

A third church bunker can be found at Berliner Strasse 20 (Mülheim). Also constructed in 1943 by forced labourers, this one looks most like a church from the ground since it also has a pitched roof. Used subsequently as a storage hall, and even as a hotel and restaurant, it today

Another church-shaped air raid shelter is in Rodenkirchen

contains the Kulturbunker Mülheim, a multi-purpose cultural venue used for concerts, exhibitions and films. That the capacity audience is four hundred and fifty persons gives an idea of the former capacity of the shelter – but there the similarity ends: today the former shelter is a place to relax and enjoy life, and it even offers its own beer garden. How times have changed!

Other places of interest nearby: 40

42 A Road under the Rhine

Innenstadt (Deutz) (Borough 1), the District Heating Tunnel
(Fernwärmetunnel) at the corner of Messeplatz and
Kennedyufer
Stadtbahn 1, 7, 9 Deutzer Freiheit

An inconspicuous concrete cylinder in Deutz, at the corner of Messe-platz and Kennedyufer, provides an entrance to one of Cologne's technological wonders. Beyond a flood-proof door is a spiral staircase, leading downwards for twenty five metres. At the bottom is a tunnel conveying pipes for the city's District Heating Network *(Fernwärme-netz)* from one side of the Rhine to the other. The tunnel is walkable and can be visited on an exciting tour by appointment with Cologne's power provider, RheinEnergie AG (tel. 0049-(0)221-178-4660, www. rheinenergie.de).

Cologne's District Heating Tunnel *(Fernwärmetunnel)*, which is four hundred and sixty one metres in length, connects the heating network of the Innenstadt with Deutz on the east bank. Water heated in the city's three power stations (Niehl, Merkenich, and Innenstadt Süd) is pumped through a network of underground feed and return pipes, of which those in the tunnel are part, to around six thousand homes and businesses on both sides of the river, providing them simultane-ously with heating and hot water. The pipes are so well insulated that the water cools by only five degrees between power station and end user.

The concept of District Heating *(Fernwärme)* was first introduced into Cologne in the early 1960s. Over time the city's traditional, coal-fired power stations have been supplemented by four combined heat and power ('cogeneration') plants *(Kraft-Wärme-Kopplung)*, namely the three already mentioned, and another in Merheim. Running costs are cheaper in cogeneration plants because steam is used both to propel the turbines that generate power *and* to heat the water in the District Heating Network (heat that was traditionally lost to the atmosphere). The facility in Niehl, for example, converts 86 % of its fuel input into power and heat, as opposed to less than 50 % in a coal-fired power sta-tion that generates electricity alone. Atmospheric pollution is also significantly reduced. At the time of writing, more than 80 % of heat in Germany's district heating networks is provided by cogeneration plants, of which over 40 % are powered by natural gas. To see a co-

Cologne's District Heating Tunnel (Fernwärmetunnel) beneath the Rhine

generation plant in action visit the Heizkraftwerk Merkenich at Merkenicher Hauptstrasse 2, where tours are again available courtesy of RheinEnergie AG.

The tunnel beneath the Rhine was excavated between 1983 and 1985, at a depth of six metres beneath the surface of the riverbed. Its successful construction through loose river gravel was considered a bold engineering effort at the time, necessitating the boring of the tunnel and then the insertion of a series of concrete rings thirty centimetres thick, each inserted from the Deutz side using hydraulic rams. During the operation some interesting artefacts were unearthed, including fragments of Second World War bombs and pieces of steel from the original Hohenzollern Bridge (Hohenzollernbrücke), blown up deliberately by German engineers in March 1945. Those walking through the tunnel, which is only three metres in diameter and therefore somewhat claustrophobic, will emerge eventually on the west bank of the Rhine at Breslauer Platz.

The history of Cologne's public power and heating supply is inextricably tied up with that of its public water supply. The city's first waterworks were established in 1872, followed a year later by the city's purchase of the Imperial Continental Gas Association, a private English company responsible for gas supply and street lighting in Cologne since 1841. The first public electricity supply was inaugurated in 1891 on Zugweg (Altstadt-Süd), and was the first power station in Germany to generate an alternating current. The waterworks were relocated to the same site around the same time (see no. 39). Supply continued una-

Pipes emerging from the District Heating Tunnel (Fernwärmetunnel) beneath Messeplatz

bated until the facility was put out of action during an air raid in March 1945. The city's water supply was restored quickly but power relied on coal, which was in short supply, and so it was not restored until 1948. Cologne's gas supply, which since the 1870s had been sourced locally in Ehrenfeld and since 1933 from the Ruhr, was not restored until 1951. All three utilities, water, gas and power, were made into corporations in 1960 only to be brought under the umbrella of the company Rhein-Energie AG in 2002.

Other places of interest nearby: 43

43 The World's First Engine Factory

Innenstadt (Deutz) (Borough 1), the Motor Monument
(Motorendenkmal) on Ottoplatz
Stadtbahn 1, 9 Bahnhof Deutz/Messe; Bus 150, 250, 260

In 1894 the German engine designer Karl Friedrich Benz (1844–1929) unveiled his four-wheeled *Velo* automobile with mass production in mind. Twelve hundred of them were manufactured between 1894 and 1901, making it the first production automobile in history. Today, approximately fifty million motor vehicles are manufactured each year.

The success of all modern vehicle production rests on the internal combustion engine, the invention of which dates back at least as far as the early 1800s, with the scientific principles behind it dating back much farther. Of the many inventors and engineers responsible for subsequently developing the engine one of the most important was Cologne-based Nikolaus August Otto (1832–1891), who was the first to build and sell it commercially.

The son of a farmer, Otto arrived in Cologne with the dream of manufacturing and selling small stationary engines. Between 1861 and 1863 he pioneered the first internal combustion engine to efficiently burn fuel inside a single piston cylinder. Although other internal combustion engines had been invented (notably by the Belgian engineer Étienne Lenoir) these were not based on four separate strokes (intake-compression-power-exhaust). Otto's single cylinder, four-stroke gas engine (Einzylinder-Viertakt-Gasmotor) would pave the way for the motorisation of the world.

In 1864 Otto set up the world's first engine factory in Cologne (under the name N. A. Otto & Cie), at the junction of Servasgasse and Am Alten Ufer (Altstadt-Nord), just behind the cathedral. His work soon caught the attention of fellow engineer Eugen Langen (1833–1895), and together they began to develop stationary engines fuelled by the gas used in street lighting. However, despite winning a prize at the Paris Grand Exhibition in 1867 the company became insolvent.

Otto and Langen opened a new and larger factory in 1872 on Deutz-Mülheimer-Strasse (Deutz). As the Gasmotoren-Fabrik Deutz AG the company this time expanded rapidly, and in 1876 the renowned engineers Gottlieb Daimler (1834–1900) and Wilhelm Maybach (1846–

One of Nikolaus Otto's four-stroke gas engines adorns Ottoplatz

1929) joined its ranks. Although Otto patented his engine the German courts did not consider it as covering all in-cylinder compression engines, or even the four-stroke cycle, as a result of which in-cylinder compression became universal. Consequently, the door was open for engineers such as Karl Benz (as well as Daimler and Maybach, who founded their own company in 1880) to build their own four-stroke engines, and eventually to pioneer the use of liquid fuels.

Otto's enormous contribution to the development of engine technology, as well as the economic success of Cologne, was celebrated in 1931, when the Siemens Ring Foundation (Stiftung Siemens-Ring) placed an Otto engine on a podium in front of Deutz Railway Station (Deutzer Bahnhof). This was followed in 1939 by the railway station forecourt itself being re-named Ottoplatz. Langen's name is rightly inscribed on the podium, too, since he created and applied new production methods in the factory on Deutz-Mülheimer-Strasse, the red-brick machine halls of which can still be seen at the junction with Auenweg (the name Klöckner-Humboldt-Deutz AG on one of the building's recalls the company's name in 1938); Langen was also co-owner of the nearby Van der Zypen & Charlier carriage works (see no. 50).

The company founded by Otto and Langen now goes by the simple name of DEUTZ AG, with headquarters at Ottostrasse 1 (Porz). It is one of the largest producers of diesel motors worldwide, and is still in possession of Otto's original four-stroke test engine (*Versuchsmotor*) of 1876. It is only rarely shown to the public, and so to view an Otto engine up close visit instead the Cologne City Museum (Kölnisches Stadtmuseum) at Zeughausstrasse 1–3 (Altstadt-Nord), where one is displayed on the first floor.

Other places of interest nearby: 42

44 An Award Winning Petrol Station

Innenstadt (Deutz) (Borough 1), the Arena Petrol Station
(Arena-Tankstelle) at Deutz-Kalker-Strasse 103
Stadtbahn 1, 9 Deutz-Fachhochschule

Few city guides feature petrol stations for obvious reasons, since these days they are rarely considered attractive and almost never garner awards for their design. There is a petrol station in the borough of Deutz, however, that succeeds on both these counts, making it worthy of a visit – even if only to fill up your tank!

The Arena Petrol Station (Arena-Tankstelle) at Deutz-Kalker-Strasse 103 (Deutz) was built in 1959 for the Shell petroleum company, to a design by the Cologne architect Herbert Baumann. It's named after the nearby Köln Arena, today the LANXESS Arena. The highly distinctive structure consists of a single-storey, L-shaped main building, jutting into the forecourt like the prow of a ship, which originally contained a customers' waiting room and two washrooms. At either end of the main building are slightly higher terminal units in which repair shops and a car showroom were located.

The most astonishing element of the design is the roof, consisting of a diamond-shaped slab of steel-reinforced concrete, which projects twelve metres out from the main building, and would have protected the petrol pumps from the elements. Supported on a concrete column inside the waiting room the roof appears to be floating, much like a silk handkerchief on the wind (although in reality it represents a stylised shell inspired by the original proprietor's name). This dynamic design element raises the building above the mundane functionality of most petrol stations, indeed it could just as easily be the terminal of an airport, the entrance to a cinema, or the head office of a successful company.

Taken in the context of the late fifties, the roof is not so surprising when one considers that European petrol station design at the time was following American precedents, which themselves were mirroring the excesses of American car design, notably the overly emphasised tail fins of the Cadillac. As cars became more daring in design, so did petrol stations, especially their roofs, which were their one really distinctive feature. Like cinema buildings, petrol stations were designed to lure paying customers off the road.

Times changed quickly though, and the rising costs of both petrol

The Arena Petrol Station (Arena-Tankstelle) on Deutz-Kalker-Strasse

and staff saw the number of petrol stations in West Germany dwindle by half between 1965 and 1980. Cologne's Arena Petrol Station was one of the victims, and it closed for business in 1973. Seemingly destined for demolition it was saved in 1982 by a preservation order, after which numerous new uses were suggested, including a hotel, kindergarten, and art gallery. Eventually, in 1997 the site was sold to a pair of Turkish businessmen, Selehatin Topracki and Hidir Mak, who were determined that the site should reopen as a petrol station. In 2000, their financial commitment to the project of 3.5 million Euros, despite warnings of failure, paid off, and the run-down ruin was transformed into a viable business venture, this time under the Esso brand.

The architect responsible for the renovation, Werner Krause, received the Renault Traffic Design Award for his efforts. The jury, under presidency of German architect and city planner Thomas Sieverts (b. 1934), were impressed by the attractive integration of the renovated building into the modern urban scene, the skilful way in which two new steel and glass forecourt pavilions paid homage to the original structure of 1959, the enlargement of the existing facility without aesthetic detriment to the original structure, and the overall high quality of the renovation work within the strict guidelines of Germany's monument protection law. Undoubtedly in an age of generic, architecturally sterile petrol station-cum-supermarkets, the Arena Petrol Station now appears both striking and glamorous. What driver could resist calling in?

Almost contemporary with the petrol station is another relic of the automotive age in Cologne. The Auto-Kino at Rudolf-Diesel-Strasse 36 (a street named after the inventor of the diesel engine) opened in 1962 and was the third American-style drive-in cinema in Germany after Berlin and Frankfurt. With parking spaces for 1218 cars it was the biggest of its type in Europe at the time.

45 On the River at Zündorf

Porz (Borough 7), a visit to the villages of Zündorf and Weiss
Stadtbahn 7 Zündorf

Despite there being no less than eight road, rail, and pedestrian bridges connecting Cologne with the east bank of the Rhine, there is still demand for good, old-fashioned ferry services. One of them, for example, departs from Konrad-Adenauer-Ufer and makes regular crossings over to the trade fair halls (Kölnmesse) in Deutz. Rather more off the beaten track, and certainly more characterful, is the ferry connecting the village of Zündorf (Porz) with the district of Weiss (Rodenkirchen). The former is known for its history and architecture, the latter for its nature conservancy, making the journey quite an adventure.

The village of Zündorf is located conveniently at the terminal of Stadtbahn Line 7, from where it is a short walk down to the riverbank and the ferry terminal. On the way one can reflect on the history of Porz (Zündorf included), which only became a borough of Cologne in 1975. Long before that it had been a part of the Kingdom of Prussia, and prior to 1815 it was briefly part of a Grand Duchy under Napoleon. Most significantly, though, during the Middle Ages Porz became an important part of the German Duchy of Jülich-Cleves-Berg, which eventually controlled much of present-day North Rhine-Westphalia, with the exception of the city of Cologne, which although also a part of the Holy Roman Empire, was an independent clerical state under the Archbishop of Cologne.

During this period the village of Zündorf became an important place for one very specific reason. Since 1259 Cologne had been in possession of the so-called *Stapelrecht*, that is the legal right of storage. This meant that goods transported through the city by road or river had to be stored in a city *Stapelhaus* (storage hall) and offered for sale in the local markets there for at least three days. This generated considerable income for Cologne, and a tower from Cologne's main *Stapelhaus* on Frankenwerft is still standing today. Merchant vessels, however, could avoid Cologne by calling in at Zündorf, on the opposite bank, where their goods could be unloaded and then transported northwards along the so-called Mauspfad to Mülheim, and then loaded back onto a ship.

Zündorf today looks rather different, although there are numerous tangible reminders of the old village still to be seen. On Burgweg, for example, can be found the lovely Chapel of St. Michael (St.-Michael-

The pretty Chapel of St. Michael on Burgweg in Zündorf

Kapelle), and at Haupstrasse 43–47 stands the Church of St. Martin (St.-Martin-Kirche). With elements dating back a thousand years, these little buildings make a refreshing change to the great Romanesque churches of Cologne's Altstadt. Nearby, at Haupt-strasse 181 there stands the twenty metre high Zündorfer Wehrturm, a defensive structure dating back at least as far as 1380, making it the oldest existing secular building in Porz. In addition there are several charming old timber-framed buildings awaiting discovers along Enggasse, Markt-gasse, and Burgweg.

It's all change down at the former quayside, however, where the old market place (Am Markt) once faced the small offshore island of Groov, the intervening waterway forming Zündorf's harbour. As a result of repeated flooding the island was connected to the mainland during the nineteenth century, leaving only a pair of lakes where the river once ran freely.

The island of Groov is today given over to leisure activities, and is also the embarkation point for the ferry to Weiss. Called the KroKoLino because its ramp resembles the mouth of a crocodile the tiny ferry runs every twenty minutes or so from the middle of March to the middle of October, between 11 am and 7 pm on weekdays and between 10 am and 8 pm at weekends. If the ferry is moored on the opposite bank it is easy to get the ferryman's attention simply by sitting firmly on the quaint quayside seat; in doing so an armature raises a bright red board above the seat that is visible from the opposite bank – and the ferryman will come to collect you! Especially popular with walkers and cyclists the KroKoLino makes landfall in Weiss on Plaster-hofweg, from where the sand-fringed Naturpark Rheinland nature conservancy is easily accessible.

Weiss is first documented in 1130, when the Archbishop of Cologne bequeathed land here to the Canon of St. George's Church in Cologne, permitting him to establish a monastic vineyard. This has long since been erased by the numerous catastrophic floods suffered along this part of the Rhine. Like Zündorf, however, several traditional timber-framed buildings are still in evidence, and no visitor should miss the atmospheric little St. George's Chapel (St.-Georgs-Kapelle) on Georgstrasse, dating from the early fifteenth century, which contains seafaring frescoes and an old ship's wheel.

46 Wild in the Country

Porz (Borough 7), the Birds of Prey Conservation Centre
(Greifvogel-Schutzstation) at Gut Leidenhausen between
Grengeler Mauspfad, Hirschgraben and the A59
Bus 152 Eil/Heumarer Strasse, then walk along Hirschgraben

The Borough of Porz is the largest of Cologne's nine boroughs by size (78.87 kilometres square) and was incorporated into Cologne during the 1970s. Dividing it down the middle is the A59 Autobahn, to the west of which lie the majority of the borough's districts and thus most of its housing and industry. To the east it is a very different story, the area to the southeast being occupied by Köln/Bonn Airport, whilst that to the north-east is a nature conservancy *(Naturschutzgebiet)* comprising forests, open pastures, and streams.

At the heart of this surprisingly wild urban area is a former medieval estate called Gut Leidenhausen, which was established by a knight in 1329 on Hirschgraben, between the area occupied today by the A59 and Grengeler Mauspfad. It is remarkable how the short walk from the bus stop on Heumarer Strasse, eastwards along Hirschgraben, quickly leaves the roar of modern traffic behind and opens up an entirely natural world of bird song and rustling trees. The area is known accordingly as the Gut Leidenhausen Recreation Area (Naherholungsgebiet Gut Leidenhausen).

The visitor's first encounter with wild nature comes just beyond the car park, where a large fenced enclosure *(Wildgehege)* on the right-hand side contains some splendid deer and wild boar. At the end of the path stands a group of old brick estate buildings dating from the mid-eighteenth century; the imposing clock tower and gate were added in the early-nineteenth century.

Before exploring the buildings turn right to visit the Birds of Prey Conservation Centre (Greifvogel-Schutzstation). This bird sanctuary founded in the 1960s is run by volunteers, and is financed by donations, as well as the City of Cologne. It falls under the auspices of the Cologne German Forest Protection Agency (Kölner Schutzgemeinschaft Deutscher Wald). Since the 1970s the sanctuary has opened its doors to visitors each Sunday. In a series of twenty five or more large aviaries visitors can see some impressive specimens, including falcons, buzzards, and snowy and eagle owls, each one brought here because of sickness, injury, or abandonment. Less spectacular but equally important patients include pheasants, ravens, and even pigeons. After being treated (and where necessary reared) they are in most cases released back into the wild. Those that remain are either considered as having become too tame or else, as is the case with the non-indigenous Snowy Owl, would not receive legal protection if released into the skies over Cologne. A pleasant walk can be

An owl at the Birds of Prey Conservation Centre (Greifvogel-Schutzstation) in Porz

had by walking southwards from the sanctuary past the old horseracing track (Leidenhausener Pferderennbahn).

Return now to the estate buildings and enter the courtyard, where one of the buildings contains the Haus des Waldes, illustrating the history and technology of forest management down through the ages. This theme is continued in a final attraction for visitors, namely the open-air German Fruit Tree Museum (Deutsches Obstmuseum). Many old varieties of fruit trees can be seen growing in an orchard here, each one carefully documented (more old varieties can be found in Finkens Garten at Friedrich-Ebert-Strasse 49 (Rodenkirchen)). Plans are afoot to one day transform the estate buildings into a multimedia visitors' centre, with the emphasis on the contrast between urban and country landscapes.

Another knightly estate in Porz is Schloss Röttgen, one and a half kilometres north of Gut Leidenhausen, which it predates by several hundred years. The original seat was demolished in 1790 and replaced in the 1860s by the present castle. In 1909 it became the property of Peter Mülhens, the manufacturer of the 4711 perfume brand, and it remains with the family to this day. Between 1945 and 1953 the castle was occupied by the British military government of Cologne, and it was here in 1952 that Federal Chancellor Konrad Adenauer negotiated the Germany Treaty (Deutschlandvertrag) with the three Western occupying powers (England, France and the USA), ending in 1955 the occupation of West Germany and granting it the rights of a sovereign state (with certain restrictions that remained in place until German reunification).

47 At the Temple of the Afghan Hindus

Porz (Borough 7), the Hari Om Mandir Afghan-Hindu Temple
at Wikinger Strasse 62
Stadtbahn 9 Porzer Strasse; Bus 154

The region immediately south of Wikinger Strasse in the district of Rath/Heumar (Porz) is marked on the map as *Industriegebiet*, that is a hinterland of factories, railways, and other industrial concerns. For this reason the area rarely gets a mention in mainstream guidebooks. It therefore comes as a pleasant surprise to discover that Rath/Heumar is home to one of the city's most surprising places of religious worship: the Hari Om Mandir temple belonging to Cologne's Afghan Hindu community. The modest building which contains the temple at Wikinger Strasse 62 appears much like any other on this industrial estate, and gives little suggestion of the ornate idols and sacred atmosphere within.

Hindus have been living in Afghanistan for many centuries, forming a prosperous urban minority working mainly as traders in Kabul. From the 1980s onwards they were forced by civil war and the rule of the Taliban to flee. Many headed to Germany, a country with which Afghanistan had maintained a special bond since King Amanullah (1892–1960) visited Berlin in 1927. Of the approximately one hundred thousand Afghans now living in Germany, only a minority of around five thousand are Hindus.

Germany's first Afghan-Hindu temple opened in a rented property in Cologne's Mülheim district shortly after the founding of the Association of Afghan Hindus (Afghanische Hindus Gemeinde in Köln e.V.) in 1990. Other temples soon sprang up in Hamburg, Frankfurt, Stuttgart, Essen, and Kassel. In 2004 the Mülheim temple was replaced by the present purpose-built structure on Wikinger Strasse, which was opened by the London-based Pujya Shri Rambabaji, the so-called 'Saint of the Thames'. For the approximately two hundred and fifty Afghan Hindus currently residing in Cologne it provides a venue not only for worship but also social interaction. The temple also serves as a focus for the ongoing integration of Afghan Hindus into the wider German community, and for the dissemination of knowledge about Indian-Afghan culture.

The Hari Om Mandir temple is open daily to people of all religious persuasions. The best time to visit is on Monday, Tuesday, Wednesday, or Sunday, when Afghans congregate for prayer *(Puja)*. The proceedings take place in a carpeted prayer hall, where worshippers sound a bell upon entry (all visitors must remove their shoes and cover their heads out of respect). Directly ahead sits the priest and either side are the twenty

Hindu idols (Murtis) in the Hari Om Mandir Afghan-Hindu Temple in Porz

or so sacred marble statues of the Hindu deities *(Murtis)*, which are revered as living gods. They include, on the right-hand side, the supreme goddess Radha Krishna, and the monkey-headed Hanuman, who led an army to fight the demon king Ravana; on the left-hand side is the supreme God Vishnu, the elephant-headed Ganesha, and the mother goddess Maa Durga astride a lion (she is periodically worshipped throughout the night in a ceremony known as *Jagran*). Worshippers make invocations to the statues together with offerings and the burning of incense. In the far corner of the hall there is a small, marble-lined pool containing a stone *Lingam*. This is a potent symbol for the worship of the Hindu deity Shiva, husband of Durga and one of the three main male Hindu gods, to whom offerings of milk, flower petals, and fruit are made.

After prayers the festivities continue with hot sweet tea and *Langar* (free vegetarian food), which is served in the dining area to all people irrespective of their caste, creed, colour, or status. For everyone it is taken whilst sitting on the floor.

The temple is also the venue for important Hindu festivals, for example the spring festival of *Holi*, the ancient harvest festival of *Vaisakhi*, the *Diwali* festival of light, and the joyous nine-day festival of *Navratri*. It is worth noting, too, that the temple doubles as a *Gurudwara*, that is a place of worship for Sikhs.

48 On God's Green Acres

Kalk (Borough 8), the Old Kalk Cemetery (Alter Kalker Friedhof) on Kapellenstrasse
Stadtbahn 1, 9 Kalk Kapelle; Bus 159

The word *Gottesacker*, meaning literally God's Acre, is an Old German expression used to designate a burial ground. The use of the word *Acker* suggests that burial grounds were once small, intimate spaces, little more than the size of a farmer's field. As populations in Europe expanded so these original cemeteries were quickly filled to capacity, and encroached on by newly built suburbs. Deemed impractical and unhygienic many were eventually closed and replaced by much larger, planned cemeteries farther out.

There are two particularly interesting examples of these old cemeteries still extant in Cologne. The Old Kalk Cemetery (Alter Kalker Friedhof) occupies a wedge-shaped piece of land between Kapellenstrasse and the nearby railway line. It was founded in 1856, at a time when the Industrial Revolution caused a huge influx of workers into the suburbs of Kalk, so much so that by 1904 the last burial plot had been filled. No further burials could be accepted and on the 1st November (All Saints' Day) the cemetery was closed and then deconsecrated. A larger cemetery to replace it was opened on Kratzweg, farther east in the district of Merheim.

The Old Kalk Cemetery today has a melancholic air about it. Although the boundary walls, gateway, and paths are still intact, most of the gravestones are gone. In their place are overgrown trees and bushes, with an occasional headstone left as a reminder of what was once here. The most imposing monument stands in the centre of the cemetery and is neo-Classical in style. It commemorates those soldiers who fell in 1864, 1866, and 1870–71 whilst establishing the German Empire. All is not sadness though, since today the Old Kalk Cemetery is regarded by many as a green oasis, and a perfect place to relax or walk the dog.

After leaving the cemetery call in at the Kalker Kapelle on the corner of Kapellenstrasse and Kalker Hauptstrasse. Since the seventeenth century pilgrims have come here on the eighth of September (the official birthday of the Virgin Mary) to view a fifteenth century wooden *Pietà* depicting the Virgin Mary cradling the crucified body of Christ.

A much older cemetery is the Old Protestant Cemetery (Alter Evangelischer Friedhof) on Kerpenerstrasse (Lindenthal). The oldest Prot-

Only a few gravestones remain in the Old Kalk Cemetery (Alter Kalker Friedhof)

estant burial ground in the Rhineland it was established in 1576 beyond the Weyertor, a gate of the Free Imperial City of Cologne, where it was the only place a Protestant could receive a Christian burial during the time of the Catholic Counter Reformation. The cemetery's alterna-

An ornately carved gravestone in the Old Protestant Cemetery (Alter Evangelischer Friedhof) in Lindenthal

tive name of Geusenfriedhof is derived from the French word *Gueux*, meaning beggar, a word applied to the Dutch-speaking freedom fighters of the war against Catholic Spain (1568–1648), who arrived in Cologne as refugees.

Not until 1802 was Cologne's first Protestant church – the Antonite Church (Antoniterkirche) at Schildergasse 57 (Altstadt-Nord) – constructed as a result of the religious tolerance introduced by the French. Meanwhile Cologne's Lutheran and Reformed communities continued to be served by the Old Protestant cemetery until 1829, when it was finally allowed for them to be buried in Melaten Cemetery (Melaten Friedhof) (see no. 77).

Although the Old Protestant Cemetery was closed in 1876 it was never cleared, and very many of its old gravestones are still visible, standing proud like islands in a sea of green ivy. Now restored the cemetery is noteworthy for its abundance of ornately carved headstones from the sixteenth to the nineteenth centuries. Unlike Catholic gravestones, which are so often shaped in the form of standing crosses, these Protestant stones are usually flat slabs, adorned with coat-of-arms, as well as skulls and angels symbolising death and the transience of life (later stones take the form of stelae and obelisks).

An interesting cemetery that has never been abandoned is Cologne's Commonwealth Cemetery (Commonwealth-Ehrenfriedhof). It can be found in the city's Southern Cemetery (Südfriedhof), founded on Höninger Platz (Rodenkirchen) around 1900, and laid out on land acquired by the British during their occupation of Cologne in 1922. There are 2482 First World War servicemen buried here, and a further 132 Second World War graves.

Other places of interest nearby: 49

49 From Brewery to Beer Glass

Kalk (Borough 8), the Sünner Brewery (Sünner Brauerei) at
Kalker Hauptstrasse 262
Stadtbahn 1, 9 Kalk Kapelle; Bus 159

Beer is as much a part of Cologne's cultural heritage as it is Munich's, and just as the Bavarians are proud of their *Weissbier* (a top-fermented pale wheat beer), so the citizens of Cologne are very fond of their *Kölsch*, a clear hoppy beer with a straw-yellow hue. *Kölsch* is also the name of the local dialect, which has inevitably led to the joke that *Kölsch* is the only language one can drink!

The production of beer in Germany has been regulated since 1516 by the so-called *Reinheitsgebot*, a law which stipulates that only barley malt, yeast, hops, and water can be used in the brewing process. The brewing of *Kölsch* was further regulated by the Kölsch-Konvention of 1985, an agreement between the members of the Cologne Brewery Association (Kölner Brauerei-Verband) that strictly defines *Kölsch* as a pale, clear, highly attenuated, hoppy, top-fermenting beer, with an original gravity of between 11 and 16 degrees Plato. In 1997 the EU prohibited the brewing of *Kölsch*-type beers outside the Cologne region.

The term *Kölsch* was first used officially in 1918, to describe a type of beer brewed since 1906 by Cologne's Sünner Brewery (Sünner Brauerei). It had developed out of a similar but cloudier variant known as *Wiess* (meaning white in *Kölsch* dialect), although it didn't gain any great popularity during the first half of the twentieth century, when by far the most popular style of beer in Germany was bottom-fermented lager. Only during the 1960s did top-fermented *Kölsch* achieve hegemony in the Cologne beer market, reaching a production peak in 1980 of 370 million litres. Although price increases and changing drinking patterns have seen a subsequent decline in production, *Kölsch* is still enormously popular, and the best place to see it being brewed is where it was invented – at the Sünner Brewery at Kalker Hauptstrasse 262 (Kalk).

The Sünner Brewery celebrated its 180th anniversary in 2010, making it Cologne's oldest brewery still in existence. Founded in Deutz in 1830, at the eastern end of the old pontoon bridge across the Rhine, the brewery relocated to its current location in 1858 on land purchased from the owner of a failed coal mining enterprise (see no. 78). Tours of the superbly preserved complex of nineteenth century yellow-brick buildings are available by appointment and include the complete

production process for *Sünner Kölsch* (tel. 0049-2137-103786, www.
suenner-brauerei.de). First sweet barley is crushed and then water
added ('mashing'), during which starch is converted into sugar. The liquid is then pumped into the copper brewing vessels (the 'brewhouse'),
which can be seen from the street, where it is heated to 100 °C, and
hops added for refreshing bitterness. This unfermented liquid ('wort')
is then pumped into fermentation tanks, where the yeast is added, and
warm-fermented at a temperature of around 13–21 °C. The *Kölsch* is
then stored in cool cellars for up to four weeks, at which point it is ready
for consumption.

Tours of the Sünner Brewery include an obligatory tasting, and
more *Kölsch* is available in the public beer garden shaded by chestnut
trees, as well as in a vaulted cellar, constructed originally for the storage
of ice, which is now used as an events venue. However, perhaps now
is the time to see how *Kölsch* is drunk in the city's many historic bars
(Kölschkneipen) and brewery taverns. One of them is the Brauhaus Sünner im Walfisch at Salzgasse 13 (Altstadt-Nord), where *Sünner Kölsch*
is served at cellar temperature (around 10 °C) in thin, cylindrical, 0.2
litre glasses known as *Stangen* (meaning rod or pole). This preserves
the taste of the beer, which has no added carbonic acid, and is at its best
when drunk extremely fresh on draught (it's also worth remembering
that *Kölsch* waiters *(Köbes)* will replenish empty glasses unprompted
until a beer mat is placed on top!).

Brauhaus Sünner im Walfisch is Cologne's oldest brewery tavern,
which makes it also one of the most popular, and so to escape the
throng – and to try someone else's *Kölsch* – visit the Brauhaus Lommerzheim at Siegestrasse 18 in Deutz (Deutz). Opened in 1959 by Hans

The venerable Brauhaus Lommerzheim on Siegestrasse in Deutz

"Lommi" Lommerzheim this most original of brewery taverns has lost little of its original charm despite the death of its publican and a restoration by the Päffgen Brewery. The nicotine-stained walls are still peeling and the welcome is still warm.

Other authentic *Kölsch* brewery taverns include Brauerei zur Malzmühle at Heumarkt 6 and Brauhaus Päffgen at Friesenstrasse 64–66 (Altstadt-Nord), and Früh em Veedel at Chlodwigplatz 28 (Altstadt-Süd). The latter is known also as the Invalidendom since it was popular with wounded ex-servicemen after the First World War.

The experience of drinking *Kölsch* can be enhanced (and extended!) by accompanying it with some typical Cologne drinking food. This includes curious-sounding delights such as *Flönz* (blood sausage), *Kölsche Kaviar* (*Flönz* with onions and rye bread), *Himmel un Ääd* (*Flönz* with potato purée and apple sauce), *Hämche* (pork knuckle), and *Halvehahn* (rye bread with Gouda cheese and mustard).

Other places of interest nearby: 48

50 The Real Home of the Suspended Railway

Mülheim (Borough 9), the former railway carriage factory
of Van der Zypen & Charlier at Deutz-Mülheimer-Strasse 129
Stadtbahn 1, 3, 4, 9 Bahnhof Deutz/Messe

Everyone in Cologne knows the *Rheinseilbahn*, a cable car traversing the Rhine between the zoo and the Rheinpark in Deutz. The nine hundred and thirty metre long journey, which has entranced children and adults alike since 1957, takes just seven minutes, and affords some exciting views along the way. Few of those alighting in Deutz, however, will be aware that in an abandoned factory not far away another of Cologne's great technological achievements occurred: the testing and construction of the Wuppertal Suspended Railway (Wuppertaler Schwebebahn).

It was an English engineer, Henry Palmer (1795–1844), who in 1824 first proposed the notion of a railway in which carriages (horsedrawn at the time) were suspended from a single aerial rail. In 1826 a suitably impressed German industrialist called Friedrich Harkort (1793–1880) built a test track in Elberfeld on the River Wupper, a tributary of the Rhine, in the hope of generating public interest. In September of the same year Elberfeld's town councillors met to discuss the possible construction of such a railway, to bring cheap coal into the city from the Ruhr. The plan never came to anything, however, following disapproval from local mine owners, who believed the railway would undercut their business.

Despite this early setback the suspended railway did eventually come to the Wuppertal in 1898 when construction work began on a line to connect Elberfeld with Barmen, on the opposite side of the river. The railway was planned and tested in Cologne by Carl Eugen Langen (1833–1895), an entrepreneur, engineer, and inventor, who had initially intended to construct such a railway in Berlin. Langen, who had co-founded the world's first engine factory in Cologne in 1864 (see no. 43), was also co-owner of the Van der Zypen & Charlier Railway Carriage and Machine Works (Eisenbahnwagen- und Maschinenfabrik Van der Zypen & Charlier) on Deutz-Mülheimer-Strasse, and it was here in 1894 that the Wuppertal Suspended Railway went into development.

During its heyday the Van der Zypen & Charlier factory was huge,

Archive photograph and model of the Wuppertal Suspended Railway (Wuppertaler Schwebebahn) in the Cologne City Museum (Kölnisches Stadtmuseum)

filling a triangular site delineated by Deutz-Mülheimer-Strasse and Messeallee-Nord. As well as the suspended railway, the company also manufactured tram cars and locomotives, examples of which can be seen in the KVB Tramway Museum Thielenbruch (KVB-Strassen-bahn-Museum Thielenbruch) at Gemarkenstrasse 139 (Mülheim), as well as specialist vehicles used to clean the city's sewers (see nos. 25 & 53). A visit to the site today, however, reveals little of these past achievements. Most of the site has been cleared, leaving only a few isolated structures. All is not lost, however, since beyond the gateway at Deutz-Mülheimer-Strasse 129 can be made out a row of red-brick machine halls with pitched roofs. The tallest of these has three doorways, the right-hand side one of which has been adapted to only open at the top. It was through this opening that Langen's suspended railway carriages once ran along a three hundred metre-long test track (fifteen metres of track still survives and was identified as such in 2003). A model of the railway together with archive photographs can be seen in the Cologne City Museum (Kölnisches Stadtmuseum) at Zeughausstrasse 1–3 (Altstadt-Nord).

Construction on the actual Wuppertal Suspended Railway began

The former railway carriage factory of Van der Zypen & Charlier on Deutz-Mülheimer-Strasse

in 1898 and lasted for three years. On 24th October 1900 the German Emperor Wilhelm II (1888–1918) participated in a trial run – his personal carriage *(Kaiserwagen)* is still used on special occasions – and in 1901 the line was inaugurated under its full title of the Eugen Langen Monorail Suspension Railway (Einschienige Hängebahn System Eugen Langen). The oldest monorail system in the world it is still in use today and carries twenty five million passengers annually. One hopes that the forgotten corner of Cologne where it was pioneered will one day be marked for the benefit of those who would otherwise associate the suspended railway with Wuppertal alone.

The southern end of the former Van der Zypen & Charlier site is marked today by a car park, one side of which is a tall brick wall against which the roofs of machine halls were once built. The wall has been enlivened by a novel art installation in the form of a vertical car park, painted across the wall, replete with parking spaces and even a lamp post!

51 The Heart of Turkish Cologne

Mülheim (Borough 9), a tour of the Turkish Quarter on
Keupstrasse
Stadtbahn 4 Keupstrasse; Bus 151, 152, 153, 250, 260

The majority of Germany's 3.4 million Muslims are of Turkish origin, and a hundred and twenty thousand of them live in Cologne. They began arriving during the early 1960s, as part of the guest worker *(Gastarbeiter)* programme to help with the country's economic revival, making up for a manpower shortage that resulted not only from the Second World War but also the erection of the Berlin Wall, which blocked the flow of German migrant workers from the east. The plan was originally for them to return home but that idea was abandoned in the 1970s, when workers' families were permitted to join them. In 2005 the government acknowledged that Germany was officially no longer a migration country but rather a destination country.

For fifty years now multiculturalism has fared relatively well in Germany. This is in part due to its great size, allowing migrant communities to be better absorbed, and also because few of its urban areas are dominated by a single ethnic group. Unfortunately, many Germans still have little real contact with their Turkish neighbours, dissuaded in part by the presence of radical Islamists determined to prevent the integration of Turks into German society.

The heart of Turkish Cologne is Keupstrasse in Mülheim, a bustling little street that stretches between Schanzenstrasse and Holweider Strasse. Authentic Turkish sights and sounds have turned it into an unconventional tourist destination, which offers the intelligent explorer an opportunity to participate in, and perhaps even contribute to, Europe's elusive goal of multicultural integration.

Beginning with the odd numbers on the left-hand side of the street this tour starts with the grand Kervansaray Turkish Restaurant at Keupstrasse 25. It is identified by its ornate tiled frontage, which incorporates a trio of camels and four projecting porches, each topped with an Islamic crescent giving the impression of a row of mosques. Inside there is a counter selling takeaway Döner kebabs, the meat sliced from one of three colossal revolving spits, and a wooden rack in the window stacked with traditional Turkish flat bread. The restaurant proper is to the rear of the building.

After such grandeur it's easy to miss the tiny Terzi seamstress shop

Preparing a kebab in the Kervansaray Turkish Restaurant on Keupstrasse in Mülheim

at Keupstrasse 51, its window filled with a selection of Turkish antiques. Next door at number 53 the grandeur continues with Istanbul Gardinen, a glittering store selling gold-edged crockery, ornate curtain fittings, and frilly, silken bed linen. Kuaför Mustafa at number 57 is one of several Turkish men's' barbers on the street, which double as a meeting place for young Turkish men, who are usually happy to discuss the affairs of the city's Turkish community.

Urfa Antep Kilim at number 73 is one of numerous traditional confectioners, selling an array of Turkish sweets, including the world-famous *Baklava*, a sticky mix of phyllo pastry, honey and nuts that dates back to the time of the Ottoman Empire. This side of the street finishes at number 87 with the Kardeşler, a traditional café-cum-living room, where the television is always on and the coffee is always strong and sweet.

Returning down the opposite side of Keupstrasse, at number 106 is the Nargile Café, not easily missed thanks to the oversized water pipe outside its doorway. At number 94 is Sultan Hali, a shop selling carpets, scarves, silver filigree shoes, and dress jewellery, whilst Turkish wedding dresses and children's suits are available a few doors along at Öz Moda at number 86. Wedding cakes are available at Hasan Özdağ at number 84 and Öz Gaziantep at number 82.

For Turkish music and films there's the well-stocked Music Gala at number 78, and just about everything else for the home – light fittings, fancy goods and jewelled Koranic wall hangings – are available at Ayhun Export at number 76. Gold and other types of jewellery are sold next door at Ağirbaş Kuyumcusu at number 74. This tour of Keupstrasse ends at number 62 with the stylish Café Cengizhan, where everyone is welcome to take a rest and a well-earned non-alcoholic drink.

Germany's Muslims have long worshipped wherever they can, which means disused apartments, old factory buildings, and community centres. Hidden from public view such prayer halls have provoked little racial tension.

Cologne's new Central Mosque (Zentralmoschee Köln)

However, with the Turkish population now considered a permanent one, the community has understandably voiced the need for identifiable, purpose-built places of worship. If Keupstrasse is the heart of Turkish Cologne then its soul is the new Cologne Central Mosque (Zentralmoschee Köln; Markez-camii in Turkish) at the junction of Venloer Strasse and Innere Kanalstrasse (Ehrenfeld). The largest mosque in Europe it is a tourist attraction in its own right. Certainly the young Turks in the barbers' shop on Keupstrasse are enthusiastic about it, saying that it is something for them to be proud about. The new mosque has been built by the Turkish Islamic Union for Religious Affairs (Diyanet İşleri Türk Islam Birliği, or DITIB) and contains a bazaar and other secular areas intended for interfaith activities, where non-Muslims will be welcome as part of an outreach programme.

Mülheim is also home to the Mülheimer Gottestracht, the largest ship procession on the Rhine, which is part of the four-day festival of St. Sebastianus, Mülheim's patron saint. Celebrated since the fourteenth century the festival begins with the ship procession on Corpus Christi (Fronleichnam), and ends on the Sunday of the same week, with events focussed around the Mülheimer bridge.

52 Where Robber Knights Once Held Court

Mülheim (Borough 9), Schloss Isenburg at Johann-Bensberg-Strasse 49
Stadtbahn 3, 13, 18 Holweide Vischeringstrasse; Bus 157

Until a few years ago the Restaurant Isenburg at Johann-Bensberg-Strasse 49 in the far-away district of Holweide (Mülheim) was the most romantic and the most historic restaurant in all Cologne. It was located within the sturdy walls of Schloss Isenburg, a medieval cas-

tle surrounded by a dark, tree-fringed moat. In its stylish and elegant dining room the restaurant offered fine French cuisine, with a well-stocked wine cellar to match. As such it is was a favoured address for gourmet diners, including celebrities such as the actor Peter Ustinov. Today, however, it has reverted to being a private residence, and an idyllic one at that. But from what little is known of its history, Schloss Isenburg has not always been such a peaceful place.

The castle is approached today by means of a Chestnut tree-lined avenue. At the far end is the castle moat, which is formed by the serpentine course of the Strunder Bach, a small tributary of the River Rhine. The borough name Mülheim reflects the existence of numerous mills once powered by the waters of the

The sturdy gatehouse of Schloss Isenburg in Mülheim

The charming inner courtyard of Schloss Isenburg

Strunder, so many in fact that the stream was dubbed "the most indus-trious brook in Germany". Extant mills include the fourteenth century Wichheimer Mühle on Wichheimer Strasse, which served until 1961 as a meal and oil mill, the Herler Mühle, the waterwheel of which can be seen across the fields from Buchheimer Ring, and the beaut fully reno-vated Iddelsfelder Mühle at Dabringhauser Strasse 50.

The existence of various ponds and earthworks around the castle are evidence of its former defensive nature, since it was here during the Middle Ages that Cologne's robber knights held court. Historians be-lieve that the construction of Schloss Isenburg and the establishment of its knightly estate *(Rittergut)* dates back to the twelfth century. The first documentary evidence for the castle comes from 1345, when one Jutta von Ascheid received the property after the death of her husband, Johann von Isenburg, who was a knight (a gentleman soldier of noble birth). Her son and heir William then inherited the property, and he too is recorded as having been a knight.

The castle next enters the history books in 1397, when the new owner Dietrich von Elberfeld, together with his friend Wilhelm von Stammheim, are recorded as having ambushed two citizens of Cologne, stealing forty one oxen in the process. These they drove to Düsseldorf, where they were shared out amongst their fellow knights. This curious story is indicative of the turbulent history of North Rhine-Westphalia during the Middle Ages. At the time the region comprised a complex patchwork of German duchies, the borough of Mülheim falling within the powerful Duchy of Jülich-Cleves-Berg. The City of Cologne was a part of the Holy Roman Empire, whilst also remaining an independent clerical state under its archbishop. At the Battle of Worringen in 1288 Archbishop Siegfried II (1275–1297) lost to Count Adolf V of the Duchy of Berg, as a result of which the citizens of Cologne gained their independence from the archbishopric, and city rights were granted to Düsseldorf, making it the capital of Berg and a commercial competitor to Cologne. The knights' abduction of the oxen can therefore be seen as an example of the ongoing rivalry between Cologne and the duchies in the wake of the battle.

During the sixteenth century an imposing manor house *(Herrenhaus)* was built on a small hill alongside the castle, reached by a bridge from the castle's pretty courtyard. This building is also still standing and its turrets imbue the whole complex with a fairytale appearance. From 1600 onwards Schloss Isenburg passed through the hands of many owners, including in 1799 the then mayor Bertoldi of Mülheim, who regaled Napoleon in his official residence at Buchheimer Strasse 29. Eventually, in 1980 the castle became the property of the City of Cologne, and underwent a programme of restoration.

Here's hoping the new owners sleep well in their beds without the fear of being robbed!

Two other medieval moated castles exist just beyond the western border of Cologne, in the region of Bergheim. Schloss Paffendorf is noted for its extensive arboretum, whilst Wasserburg Geretzhoven is known for its convivial atmosphere and public rooms. Both make ideal destinations for an afternoon visit.

53   A Home For Old Trams

Mülheim (Borough 9), the KVB Tramway Museum Thielenbruch
(KVB-Strassenbahn-Museum Thielenbruch) at Gemarken-
strasse 139
Stadtbahn 18 Thielenbruch

Cologne's KVB Tramway Museum Thielenbruch (KVB-Strassenbahn-
Museum Thielenbruch) opened in 1997 at Gemarkenstrasse 139, deep
in the borough of Mülheim. It is located very suitably in the former
Thielenbruch tram depot, at the terminus of what is today Line 18 of
the city's *Stadtbahn* light rail network. The museum's monthly open
days (every second Sunday in the month from March to December)
provide transport enthusiasts with an opportunity to see the ongoing preservation work of the Cologne Historic Tramway Association
(Verein Historische Strassenbahn Köln e.V.); they provide everyone
else with the chance to appreciate the crucial role played by the Cologne Transport Authority (Kölner Verkehrs-Betriebe AG, KVB) in the
growth of modern Cologne over the last one hundred and thirty years.

Today's tram terminus at Thielenbruch is housed inside a tram depot built in 1906, alongside which there is a secondary tram shed added
in 1926 in which the museum is housed. Behind its walls is hidden a secret world, where more than twenty historic trams are displayed, from
late nineteenth century horse drawn carriages to electric trolley cars of
the 1960s. The collection is filled out with technical equipment such as
signals and switching gear, scale models, old photographs, maps, posters, uniforms, timetables, and tickets.

The story begins on 20th May 1877, when a Belgian company financed the first horsedrawn tramway between the independent muni-
cipalities of Deutz and Kalk, which at the time lay outside the city
boundary. Other independent suburbs followed suit, and in 1879 even
the narrow streets of Cologne's Altstadt received a tramway. To avoid
unnecessary competition the Cologne Tramway Company (Cölnische
Strassenbahn-Gesellschaft) was formed in 1882, and by 1899 seven
hundred and sixty five horses were at work in the city. One of the museum's most cherished exhibits is horsedrawn tram number 211, which
dates from 1894 and could carry a dozen sitting passengers.

Rising demand and technical improvements saw Cologne's first
electric tram put into service on 15th October 1901, after which horsedrawn trams were gradually phased out (a former horsedrawn tram de-

One of Cologne's first horsedrawn trams in the KVB Tramway Museum Thielenbruch (KVB-Strassenbahn-Museum Thielenbruch)

pot with sculpted horses' heads on its façade still exists on Mülheimer Freiheit). The museum illustrates the first phase of electric tramways in Cologne with tram 407, manufactured in the Deutz carriage factory of Van der Zypen & Charlier (see no. 50). The popularity of tram travel increased rapidly and by 1908 the city had three hundred and seventy one trams in service. Each car could now hold thirty people, albeit in close proximity to each other (a ruling from the time forbade ladies sporting unprotected hat pins to travel!).

The years leading up to the start of the First World War saw a rapid expansion of the tram network connecting Cologne with its outer suburbs. Trams 1285, 1257 and 1286 represent the larger capacity three-car units required at this time, each capable of carrying sixty four persons sitting and standing. In 1914 the network's thousand vehicles carried one hundred and twenty five million passengers! During the 1930s certain very popular lines warranted more luxuriously appointed cars, of which trams 1824 and 2825 are examples, featuring larger windows, padded seats, and a separate smoking compartment.

By contrast, tram 1732 from the time of the Second World War is of necessity an economy model, with few seats and no luxuries. Tram 1872

This streamlined 1950s-era tram was nicknamed 'Sputnik'

from the early 1950s, put together from old damaged and disused trams by Cologne's Westwaggon company, reflects the continuing austerity of the immediate post-war period. The rather more comfortable trams 1321 and 1363 represent a deliberate attempt to reinvent the service during the latter part of the decade (tram 3413 was dubbed 'Sputnik' because of its contemporary streamlined appearance).

Despite further modernisation Cologne's tram service came increasingly into conflict with the automobile, and from 1968 onwards trams were moved increasingly into tunnels, resulting in today's *Stadtbahn* system, a hybrid of underground and overground routes that exists in reasonable harmony with the road network.

54 Cologne's Earliest Inhabitants

Mülheim (Borough 9), prehistoric grave mounds in the park
between Pilzweg and Schilfweg
S11 Dellbrück, then walk

Cologne's urban history begins with the arrival of the Romans in the first century BC, as part of their conquest of Gaul (see no. 1). Caesar's legions thoroughly depopulated the left bank of the Rhine (at the time inhabited by hostile Germanic tribes) to make way for the re-settlement of the more Roman-friendly Ubii people from the right bank, and the establishment of a legionary camp. By 90 AD Colonia Agrippinensium had become the capital of the Roman province of Germania Inferior. It would be wrong, however, to assume that because the Romans left so much for archaeologists to dig up that man hadn't lived in Cologne long before they arrived. On the contrary, there is considerable evidence for the presence of prehistoric man in North Rhine-Westphalia, albeit of a far less imposing nature.

A little-known but important prehistoric site can be found in a tiny park in the district of Dellbrück (Mülheim), squeezed between a pair of leafy suburban streets called Pilzweg and Schilfweg. An inscribed stone at each entrance to the park – not to be confused with similar stones forbidding ball games, untethered dogs and the riding of bicycles – informs the unsuspecting passer-by that the tree-topped hillocks beyond are in fact prehistoric grave mounds *(Vorgeschichtliche Grabhügel)*.

Grave goods found within the mounds confirm they were constructed during the Early Iron Age (800–600 BC) by members of the Hallstatt Culture. Named after an eponymous type site in the Austrian Salzkammergut, Hallstatt was the predominant culture in Central Europe at the time. It has been identified across a thousand kilometre swath of territory from the Champagne-Ardenne in the west to the Vienna Basin in the east, and from Bohemia in the north down to Slovenia in the south.

Despite leaving no written records the former presence of Hallstatt peoples can be clearly demonstrated by their distinctive grave mounds. Elsewhere in Cologne these are found on the right bank of the Rhine along what is now Mauspfad, suggesting they had settled hereabouts as hunters and farmers. Unfortunately, by the early twentieth century grave robbers had excavated most of the mounds, drawn by local legends of buried treasure. One of these told of a heathen chieftain buried somewhere on the Thurner Heath (Thurner Heide) in a solid silver sarcophagus! The largest known grave field, consisting of over twelve hundred graves, was strung out along Iddelsfelder Hardt but was obliterated by the construction of Cologne's East Cemetery (Ostfriedhof) (Mülheim); a solitary example remains amongst the graves of Plot 43, close to the cemetery's funerary chapel.

A prehistoric grave mound in a park in Mülheim

To discover more about Cologne's prehistoric inhabitants visit the Romano-Germanic Museum (Römisch-Germanisches Museum) (Altstadt-Nord) (Borough 1) at Roncalliplatz 4. Although there is nothing from the Hallstatt period here, there are plenty of other ancient artefacts on display, in a series of display cabinets on the first floor. The majority of finds come from the Dellbrück and Fühlingen districts, to where prehistoric man was drawn by fertile soils, mineral resources, navigable waterways, and a mild climate. Some of the oldest artefacts are Stone Age implements, including a Lower and Middle Palaeolithic hand axe from Dellbrück (c. 35000 BC), and Upper Palaeolithic stone flakes (used as tools) from Fühlingen and Worringen (c. 35000–8000 BC). Of particular interest is a group of artefacts recovered from an Early Neolithic village site in Lindenthal (c. 5300 BC), including stone tools and the polished pottery that gave its name to this particular culture – *Linienbandkeramik*. Also notable is a Late Iron Age assemblage of iron spear, knife, bracelet, and key from Müngersdorf (c. 400 BC).

55 A Prussian Optical Telegraph Station

Mülheim (Borough 9), the Prussian Optical Telegraph station at Egonstrasse 152
Stadtbahn 4 Mülheim Berliner Strasse, then Bus 151, 152

Optical telegraphy (known also as semaphore) is the technique of communicating across long distances by means of an apparatus visible to the human eye. In ancient times this meant smoke signals and hilltop fire beacons. The first modern optical telegraph, using towers with mechanically operated signals, did not appear until 1794, when the engineer Claude Chappe unveiled a network of more than five hundred telegraph stations, stretching 4800 kilometres across France. Used to transmit both military and administrative communications the French signalling system was soon copied elsewhere in Europe, notably Sweden, Denmark, and England.

Throughout Germany, however, where the necessary centralised administration for such a project did not yet exist, couriers remained in use. Despite Napoleon having used telegraph technology successfully in his European campaigns, the German states remained resistant to the idea. Only when nobles and liberals in the Rhine region began opposing the administration in Berlin during the early 1830s did the Prussian military see value in constructing the Prussian Optical Telegraph (Preussischer Optischer Telegraf), to speed up communications between Berlin and Koblenz, the western headquarters of the Prussian army.

The Prussian Optical Telegraph was inaugurated in 1832, and covered a distance of 550 kilometres. It comprised sixty two stations, built on average eleven kilometres apart: fourteen stations between Berlin and Magdeburg, thirty eight between Magdeburg and Cologne, and ten between Cologne and Koblenz. The stations were located on hills or tall buildings, such as church towers, so as to ensure a clear line of sight, and were ideally set against an open sky so that the signals could be easily seen. Each station was equipped with a pair of telescopes enabling the station operator to copy down coded messages from one station and forward them on to the next. Originally, only the terminal stations in Berlin and Koblenz functioned as dispatch stations, where official telegrams were coded before sending, and then decoded upon receipt. This meant that messages could not be sent or received by the larger and economically more important city of Cologne, indeed messages arriving in Cologne from England or Belgium, and addressed to Berlin, had to be dispatched by courier to Koblenz and from there telegraphed back via Cologne to Berlin. The resulting delay prompted a third dispatch station to be opened in Cologne itself, on top of the Church of St. Pantaleon (St.-Pantaleons-Kirche) at Am Pantaleonsberg 8 (Altstadt-Süd).

Although Cologne's dispatch station no longer exists, its neighbouring station farther north does, indeed Telegraph Station 50 at Egonstrasse 152 in the district of Flittard (Mülheim) is one of only a handful of stations to survive. The observation room occupies the top storey of the building, and from its roof emerges a mast just over

One of the last Prussian Optical Telegraph stations is on Egonstrasse

six metres high. Attached to the mast are six hinged wooden signal arms, three on either side, operated by cables running down through the mast into the room below (the wires connecting the top of the mast to the corners of the roof are for stability only). The signal arms, which are almost two metres in length, are counterweighted to facilitate easy adjustment, using a system of levers. The position of each lever corresponds to the three-level alignment of the signal arms relative to the mast (45°, 90° and 135°). In good weather a message could be sent to Koblenz and back in under two minutes; all the way to Berlin took about two hours.

The Prussian Optical Telegraph was the only state-run system of its kind ever constructed on German soil but it remained in operation for less than two decades. Limited by both geography and weather it was superceded in 1849 by electrical telegraph lines, which were not only cheaper but also more secure.

Those with an interest in telescopes might also like to visit Cologne's astronomical observatory (Sternwarte Köln) at Blücherstrasse 15–17 (Nippes). Occupying the top storey of a school it was set up by former pupils during the early 1960s. As well as two telescopes there is also a planetarium.

56 An Unexpected Japanese Garden

Mülheim (Borough 9), the Japanese Garden on Kaiser-Wilhelm-Allee
Stadtbahn S6, Bus 152 Bayerwerk, then walk along Otto-Bayer-Strasse

It is a truism that industrial landscapes rarely co-exist with landscape gardens. It therefore comes as a pleasant surprise to find a rare and successful example in Cologne, on the right-hand bank of the Rhine. The large and beautiful Carl-Duisberg-Park straddles the districts of Flittard and Wiesdorf, and is surrounded on all sides by the vast CHEMPARK Leverkusen, an industrial facility dominated by the headquarters of the chemicals and pharmaceutical giant Bayer AG.

The presence of the chemicals industry in this part of Cologne goes back a long way. Bayer moved their offices into the area in 1912, after acquiring the dye factory of Carl Leverkus in Wiesdorf in 1891. In 1925 the CEO of Bayer, Carl Duisberg (1861–1935), together with Carl Bosch (1874–1940) of BASF, facilitated the merger of their dyemaking operations into a single company called the Interessengemeinschaft Farbenindustrie AG (or IG Farben, for short). This huge conglomerate, which soon included related industries such as explosives and fibres, became the biggest enterprise in Europe, and the fourth largest in the world (after General Motors, United States Steel, and Standard Oil of New Jersey). Despite suffering extensive damage during air raids in the Second World War, the Flittard-Wiesdorf site has continued to be a major force in the chemicals industry in Cologne, together with the CHEMPARK Dormagen on Neusser Landstrasse (Chorweiler) (known previously as Bayerwerk Dormagen). Lest anyone forget the contribution made by Bayer to the proceedings there is a towering red-brick chimney to remind them, which carries the name 'BAYER' painted in huge letters. Visible from afar the chimney makes a useful point of reference when visiting the Carl-Duisberg-Park, which is located on Kaiser-Wilhelm-Allee.

The park measures two hundred and twenty thousand square metres, and consists of rolling lawns, densely planted flower beds, and a great variety of specimen trees. A very special feature is its Japanese Garden, which by comparison covers a relatively intimate fifteen thousand square metres. On the initiative of Carl Duisberg both gardens

This Japanese garden was created for the workers of the Bayer factory in Mülheim

were established in 1912, as places where Bayer company employees might find peace and relaxation, and they are still maintained by Bayer to this day.

Authentic Japanese gardeners were employed to create the Japanese Garden, which is entered by means of a red-painted, Japanese-style gateway. This is situated at the end of a Japanese bridge, which transports the visitor from park to garden across a fish-filled moat. The transition works magically, as the visitor is immediately enveloped by an authentic East Asian landscape. Despite the garden's name it contains traditional elements of both Japanese and Chinese landscape gardens, including stone and bronze sculptures of the Buddha, stone lanterns, and a tea house in the style of a Chinese temple. On the steps of the tea house are a pair of Chinese bronze lions, given as a gift by the president of an Osaka-based pharmaceutical company to mark the centenary in 1988 of the founding of Bayer.

The garden also features three thousand square metres of water features, the most impressive of which is a tranquil, lily-strewn lake that can be crossed by means of a series of stepping stones. The lake is home to Mandarin ducks, turtles, goldfish, and Koi Carp. On the banks of the lake and elsewhere in the garden are planted flame-coloured Japanese maple trees and other plants popular in the gardens of East Asia.

Immediately alongside the Japanese garden is the BayKomm visitors' centre, where those wishing to learn more about the products of Bayer (including *Aspirin*) can take an afternoon guided tour by appointment (www.baykomm.bayer.de). Bayer reverted to an individual business in 1952 after the break-up of IG Farben, following its implication in Nazi war crimes during the Second World War.

57 On the Trail of Rare Creatures

Nippes (Borough 5), Cologne Zoo (Kölner Zoo) at Riehler
Strasse 173
Stadtbahn 18 Zoo/Flora; Bus 140

Cologne Zoo (Kölner Zoo) opened in 1860 making it Germany's third oldest zoo after Berlin and Frankfurt. Despite being badly damaged in the Second World War it reopened soon afterwards and today contains more than five hundred species, in modern enclosures spread across an area of twenty hectares. Most visitors, especially those with children, will probably head straight for the perennial favourites – Elephants, Gorillas, Giraffes, Hippos, big cats – and who can blame them! However, it should not be forgotten that Cologne Zoo is also home to many lesser-known endangered species, some of which contribute to important international breeding programmes. A great way to lost the crowds is to track down some of these rare creatures, noting what's left architecturally of the old zoo along the way.

This tour begins just inside the main entrance on Riehler Strasse, where the path to the right leads past the ever popular Meerkat paddock to a moated rockwork enclosure containing the Malayan Sun Bear *(Helarctos malayanus)*, so-named because of the yellow fur around its snout. A denizen of the rainforests of Southeast Asia it is the smallest of the bear family. Despite this the Sun Bear has few enemies except man, who has reduced its numbers considerably through poaching for the animal's fur, as well as its bile, which is prized in Chinese medicine.

Continuing on past the splendid old aviary of 1899, built in the style of a Russian Orthodox church, the path curves round past the lions and tigers to the tropical rainforest house, which contains the critically endangered Bali Starling *(Leucopsar rothschildi)*. White with distinctive bare blue skin around the eyes it is Bali's last surviving endemic vertebrate species. Despite only six birds being recorded in the wild in 2001, a concerted protection effort in conjunction with Cologne Zoo has subsequently seen numbers increase.

In the ape house beyond, alongside the ever popular Chimpanzees, Orang Utans, and Lowland Gorillas, there is an extremely rare breeding group of endangered Red-Shanked Douc Langurs *(Pygathrix nemaeus)*. These most colourful of primates, with red legs, white forearms, and a golden face, hail from Vietnam and Laos, where hunting and habitat destruction has driven them towards extinction.

A herd of Przewalski's Horses in Cologne Zoo (Kölner Zoo) in Nippes

Following the path around the huge elephant enclosure and the Sea Lion rock pool, constructed in 1887, there is a paddock containing a herd of Przewalski's Horse *(Equus ferus przewalski)* (pronounced '(p) she-vahl-skee'). Known also as the Asiatic or Mongolian Wild Horse it is named after General Nikolai Przhevalsky (1839–1888), an explorer and naturalist, dispatched in 1881 by the Tsar of Russia to capture a specimen. By 1900 over fifty foals had been acquired for aristocratic and zoo collections throughout Europe. During the 20th century the native population died out due to hunting, and grazing competition from domestic flocks. Consequently, today's global population of about two thousand horses, including the specimens seen in Cologne, have been bred from captive animals descended from those original imported foals.

Past the Musk Ox now, with their charming Swiss-style chalet stables, and on the left there is a paddock containing the graceful Bactrian Deer *(Cervus elaphus bactrianus)*. Native to central Asia there were only about four hundred of these animals left in 1999, their numbers reduced by warfare. An initiative by the WWF has seen numbers increasing again in the wild.

After passing the former Giraffe and Antelope House on the left,

A large Nile Monitor
relaxes in Cologne Zoo
(Kölner Zoo)

which was built in 1863 and is the zoo's oldest surviving structure, the main entrance is reached again, where a memorial stands to the founder of the zoo, Dr. Caspar Garthe (1796–1876), together with a monument topped by one of two statues of stags that originally graced the main entrance.

This adventure finishes in the aquarium at the main entrance, where the Nile Monitor *(Varanus niloticus)* can be seen. Not especially rare, as it is found throughout much of Africa, it is remarkable for its size, and can reach almost three metres in length. Although happy to spend much of the day basking on a flat rock, this member of the lizard family has a ferocious reputation, and is said to be every bit as dangerous as a crocodile of the same size.

South of the Zoo Bridge (Zoobrücke), on the east bank of the Rhine, lies the spacious Rheinpark, first laid out for a flower festival in 1957. It still retains its distinctive 1950s-style garden architecture and is also home to a flock (or more correctly a company) of escapee parrots from the zoo!

Other places of interest nearby: 58

58 Palm Trees and Giant Water Lilies

Nippes (Borough 5), the Flora and Botanical Garden
(Flora und Botanischer Garten) at Am Botanischen Garten 19
Stadtbahn 18 Zoo/Flora; Bus 140

The rare and wild creatures of Cologne Zoo (Kölner Zoo) find their botanical counterparts in Cologne's Flora and Botanical Garden (Flora und Botanischer Garten), which lies immediately west of the zoo at Am Botanischen Garten 19 (Nippes). The Flora arboretum was established in 1864 as an exclusive and exotic garden for Cologne's well-to-do citizens, although it has long since been merged with the city's botanical gardens, which were relocated here in 1914 after their original location had been cleared for the construction of the main railway station. Containing both recognisable and highly unusual plants from home and abroad the Flora and Botanical Garden today offers the possibility of an afternoon's adventure without ever leaving the city.

The gardens are entered by means of a grand gateway, which opens directly onto a lovely French *Parterre*, at the end of which is the Flora pavilion, a glasshouse erected during the late nineteenth century but seriously damaged during the Second World War. There are numerous signposts hereabouts detailing the various elements of the main garden beyond, including a well-stocked alpine garden (Alpinum), a scented garden for the blind, and a typical suburban Cologne garden, which visitors can enjoy as if it were their own. Watch out, too, for examples of the curious Gingko *(Gingko biloba)*, a unique species of tree with no close living relatives. With its distinctive, fan-shaped leaves it is one of the best examples of what is known as a 'living fossil', since the other members of its family appear only in fossilised form.

There's so much to see, smell, and feel in these gardens, and everyone will find a favourite corner. Two areas deserve special note, the first of which is the so-called Palm Alley (Palmenallee) planted in 2006. Germany's first avenue of palms it consists of around forty specimens of the Chinese Windmill Palm *(Trachycarpus fortunei)*, a species native to the region between central China and northern Burma (Myanmar), where its fibrous leaves have long been valued for making ropes, sacks, and coarse cloth. Although not the northernmost naturally occurring

The Palm Alley (Palmenallee) in the Flora and Botanical Garden (Flora und Botanischer Garten) in Nippes

palm it is certainly one of the hardiest, as it grows at altitudes of up to 2400 metres in the mountains of southern China, and is frost resistant down to –20 °C. This makes it a palm ideally suited to Germany, with its cold winters and cool, moist summers.

The Chinese Windmill Palm was first introduced into Europe from Japan in 1830 by the German physician Philipp Franz von Siebold, where it found favour as an ornamental plant. Despite this it is named after Robert Fortune, who was the first to observe cultivated specimens of the plant on Chusan (now Zhousan) Island, which accounts for the palm's other popular name, Chusan Palm.

Palms feature in the botanical garden's second area of special note, namely a series of hothouses erected before the First World War. Together with potted specimens of bamboo, olives, and bananas the palms are dotted around a beautiful outdoor pool containing an example of the huge *Victoria* genus of water lilies, first identified on a tributary of the Amazon by a Bohemian botanist in 1801. He died before being able to make a full report of it and it was eventually named by an English botanist in honour of Queen Victoria. The lily is famous for its night-blooming flowers and for being able to support the full weight of a child on its leaves, which can grow up to three metres in diameter.

Giant water lilies in the Flora and Botanical Garden (Flora und Botanischer Garten)

Inside the hothouses a series of narrow winding paths lead through a humid jungle of ferns, palms, climbers, orchids, and huge, antler-like epiphytes suspended from the ceiling. A separate hothouse contains a miniature desert planted with the most oddly-shaped succulents and cacti, all evidence of the astounding diversity of plant life on Earth.

Plant enthusiasts will enjoy two other unusual gardens in Cologne. One is an authentic olive grove at Widdersdorfer Landstrasse 103 (Lindenthal), which is part of the Baum-schule Belnatura, a nursery garden specialising in mediterranean plants. The other is a vineyard growing not on a hillside but rather on the sloping roof of the Kölner Weinde-pot Josef Wittling, a wine merchant and museum at Amsterdamer Strasse 1 (Nippes).

Other places of interest nearby: 57

59 Old Railroads of the Rhine

Nippes (Borough 5), the Rhineland Industrial Railway Museum (Rheinisches Industriebahn-Museum) at Longericher Strasse 249
Stadtbahn 15 Meerfeldstrasse, then walk along Paul-Humburg-Strasse, Lohmüllerstrasse and Longericher Strasse

The Rhineland Industrial Railway Museum (Rheinisches Industriebahn-Museum) occupies a former railway depot in Nippes

During the second half of the nineteenth century Cologne developed rapidly as a centre of industrial manufacturing. This success was facilitated in part by the arrival of the railway in 1839, when the Rhineland Railway Company (Rheinische Eisenbahn-Gesellschaft) inaugurated the Cologne-Aachen-Belgium line. The region's railway network expanded rapidly, and in 1850 the site of the old botanical gardens next to Cologne Cathedral (Kölner Dom) was cleared to allow for the construction of the city's main station (Hauptbahnhof). Opened in 1859 it initially serviced the lines of five different railway companies and is today Germany's largest railway interchange.

Although the station's steel and glass construction acts as a reminder of Cologne's great industrial age, there is another location in the city where the golden age of railways really comes back to life. This is the Rhineland Industrial Railway Museum (Rheinisches Industriebahn-Museum) at Longericher Strasse 249 (Nippes), which is located in the former Cöln-Nippes railway depot (for details of monthly open days between Easter and October visit www.rimkoeln.de). It is administered by the Rhineland Industrial Railway Museum Association (Rheinische Industriebahn Museum Köln e.V.), founded in 1987 by a group of enthusiastic railway workers determined to preserve for posterity the Rhineland's fast disappearing historic rolling stock.

The Cöln-Nippes railway depot is the largest industrial monument in the north of Cologne. Constructed in 1914 it was one of the last great building projects commissioned by the Prussian state in the Rhineland, at a time when the name Köln was still spelt with a letter 'C'. Steam locomotives were housed here until 1958, when the first diesel locomotives and tramcars began appearing. In the same year four Flying Hamburgers (Fliegende Hamburger), Germany's first high speed diesel train, passed through the sheds; travelling before the Second World War between Berlin and Hamburg they provided the fastest passenger service in the world at the time.

The engine sheds today provide the perfect backdrop for the museum's collection of locomotives and other rail vehicles. Some were manufactured in Cologne's own Deutz factories, whilst others were made elsewhere in North Rhine Westphalia (for example Hohenzollern in Düsseldorf and Arnold Jung in Kirchen (Sieg)). There are also locomotives from manufacturers elsewhere in Germany, including Henschel in Kassel and Orenstein & Koppel in Berlin. At the heart of the shed is a massive transporter *(Schiebebühne)*, used to move locomotives inside for repairs.

The collection includes many rarities too, including a narrow-gauge locomotive *(Feldbahn Lok)* from 1937, which was used to clear rubble from around Cologne Cathedral (Kölner Dom) during the Second World War, a 45-bed military hospital wagon from the years following the same conflict, two so-called fireless locomotives driven by steam alone *(Dampfspeicherlok)*, and the last surviving electric railcar of the Cologne-Bonn railway (Köln-Bonner Eisenbahn), which was closed in 1992. There are also several examples of the 123 000 wagons constructed before the First World War, which were used for the rest of the century to carry not only freight but also soldiers and, eventually, deportees during the Nazi regime. A normal gauge Henschel DH440 locomotive is used to transport visitors into the engine sheds upon their arrival at the museum.

All budding train drivers and railway enthusiasts are encouraged to join the museum association and to take an active part in the ongoing preservation, restoration, and demonstration of this fascinating collection.

The ruins in the centre of an artificial lake in the MediaPark on Hansaring (Neustadt-Nord), which could be mistaken for a Roman aqueduct, are in fact the remains of the Güterbahnhof Gereon, a freight station built in 1859.

60 Bunker World

Nippes (Borough 5), a tour of Second World War air raid shelters beginning with the *Winkelturm* at Neusser Landstrasse 2 Stadtbahn 12, 15 Wilhelm-Sollmann-Strasse, then Bus 120 or walk

In September 1940, Hitler's Luftwaffe attacked civilian targets in London and Coventry in an attempt to break British morale. It was a flagrant violation of the terms of the Hague Aerial War Convention of 1922, and British Bomber Command responded likewise. Two hundred and sixty two air raids were conducted against Cologne, an important industrial target, which had been designated by the Wehrmacht as the Military Area Command Headquarters (Militärbereichshauptkommandoquartier) for Military District (Wehrkreis) VI in Münster (see no. 28).

The commencement of the aerial war on Nazi Germany prompted a crash air raid shelter-building programme, in an effort to protect the civilian population and to shore up confidence in Germany's ability to win the war. Requiring an estimated two hundred million cubic metres of steel-reinforced concrete it would be the largest building project in history. By the end of the war, with Germany's cities in ruins, only the shelters remained intact. This tour of extant shelters in Cologne serves to illustrate the different forms taken by the shelters, whilst also acting as a sober reminder of their limitations, since twenty thousand people still perished in Cologne during the raids.

The air raid shelter at Neusser Landstrasse 2 (Nippes) is known as a *Winkelturm* and stands in the middle of an industrial estate. Taking the form of a slender cone, with walls that flare outwards to a reinforced base, it looks more like a rocket from a 1950s science fiction film. It was designed by the German engineer Leo Winkel (1885–1981) and patented by him in 1934. From 1936 onwards almost a hundred of them were erected in Germany, where they were nicknamed *Betonzigarre* (concrete cigar) or *Zuckerhut* (sugarloaf) on account of their shape. Up to ten metres wide and twenty nine meters high their concrete walls are one and a half metres thick. Despite this their main design strength comes from having a small footprint. The Cologne *Winkelturm* which was constructed in 1940 could hold more than six hundred industrial workers from the nearby Glanzstoff-Courtaulds-Werke, a rayon tire manufacturer vital to the Nazi war effort. The interior of the tower can be visited every third Saturday afternoon in the month.

A Winkelturm air raid shelter on Neusser Landstrasse in Nippes

The *Winkelturm* is classed as a *Hochbunker*, since it rises above the ground, as opposed to a *Tiefbunker*, which is subterranean. The usual form for a *Hochbunker* is a simple square or rectangular-shaped block of steel-reinforced concrete, containing numerous cell-like rooms, and a strengthened entrance, an example of which stands at Elsassstrasse

42–46 (Neustadt-Süd). With walls two and a half metres thick such shelters were promoted by the German authorities as being bombproof, and served to protect the civilian population in areas of high density housing. A five-storey, 210-room *Hochbunker* was erected in 1942 at Herthastrasse 43–47 (Rodenkirchen), and could shelter almost 2700 people (a similar number could be catered for in a Cold War-era civilian shelter in the U-Bahn station Kalk-Post). The shelter was ingeniously incorporated into an existing row of houses, and given a saddle roof with dormer windows, in an attempt to disguise it from the air (even more ingenious were those disguised as churches; see no. 41). Used to house the homeless until 1954 the Herthastrasse shelter has subsequently been converted into half a dozen stylish modern apartments. A similar conversion has been achieved with another large former *Hochbunker* at the junction of Siegburgerstrasse and Rolshoverstrasse (Porz), whilst another at Körnerstrasse 93 (Ehrenfeld) is used for occasional art events.

A well-known example of a *Tiefbunker* is the so-called Cathedral Bunker constructed in 1941 beneath Roncalliplatz (Altstadt-Nord) to safeguard the cathedral treasures. During excavations the magnificent Roman Dionysus mosaic was unearthed, which together with the incongruous concrete walls of the shelter can be viewed today in the basement of the Romano-Germanic Museum (Römisch-Germanisches Museum).

Little-known by comparison is the recently opened Museumsbunker Reichsbahn Ausbesserungswerk at Werkstattstrasse 106 (Nippes), constructed in 1941 to safeguard workers from the nearby railway workshops. The shelter still preserves its original ventilation and telephone system, gas-proof doors, medical room, and a display of contemporary artefacts. A smaller variant of the *Tiefbunker* is the tube-shaped *Röhrenbunker*, an example of which is situated beneath Reichenspergerplatz (Neustadt-Nord), its hand-cranked ventilator still in evidence.

Other places of interest nearby: 61

61 The Forty Millionth Ford is a Fiesta

Nippes (Borough 5), the Ford Works (Ford-Werke GmbH)
at Henry-Ford-Strasse 1
Stadtbahn 12 Geestemünder Strasse

Perched on top of Cologne City Museum (Kölnisches Stadtmuseum) at Zeughausstrasse 1–3 (Altstadt-Nord) is a gold-painted Ford Fiesta with wings! Known as the *Flügelauto (Flying Car)* it is the work of the German conceptual artist H.A. Schult (b. 1939), and has been there since 1991. It originally formed a part of his *Fetisch Auto* exhibition marking the sixtieth anniversary of the opening of the Ford Works (Ford-Werke GmbH) in Cologne. According to Schult the piece represents both the freedom, as well as the loss of it, bestowed on mankind by the car during the twentieth century. The controversy that surrounded the siting of such an outlandish piece of art on top of a listed historic building – a former seventeenth century arsenal – has since died down but the sight of it still serves as a timely reminder of Ford's continuing presence in the city.

The Ford Motor Company was founded in 1903 by Henry Ford (1863–1947) in a converted factory in Detroit, Michigan, using just $ 28 000 in cash from twelve investors. The company subsequently became one of the world's

Artist H. A. Schult's Flügelauto (Flying Car) on the roof of the Cologne City Museum (Kölnisches Stadtmuseum)

A Ford Taunus from the Ford Works (Ford-Werke GmbH) in Nippes

largest and most profitable, and remains amongst the top four car manufacturers worldwide. An important part of the company's success were the methods introduced by Ford for the large-scale manufacturing of cars using moving assembly lines.

It was Cologne's innovative mayor Konrad Adenauer (1876–1967) who promoted the establishment of a branch of the Ford German division in Cologne, emphasising the presence of the Rhine as the ideal means of transporting both materials and finished vehicles. On 2nd October 1930 Henry Ford personally laid the foundation stone of the new works on the riverside in the district of Niehl (Nippes), and on 4th May the following year the first car, a Ford Model A, left the production line. The official opening of the Ford Works (Ford-Werke AG) on 12th May 1931 attracted ten thousand visitors from across Germany.

From 1933 all Ford models produced in Germany received German names, in an attempt to maximise domestic sales. Accordingly, the Ford Model Y became the Ford Köln, a small family car designed specifically for the European market. With its four cylinder engine generating a maximum speed of 85 km/h it remained in production until 1936.

Hitler's preparations for war in Europe saw production in Ford's German division realigned for military purposes, and the factory in Cologne began manufacturing trucks. Other Ford branches produced jeeps, aircraft, and ships, and all were guilty of using forced labourers between 1941 and 1945. Defenders of the company argue that all Ford's German factories were commandeered by the Nazi government and therefore out of Ford's control, although detractors have cited evidence that Henry Ford may have been anti-Semitic. Whatever the case, the Ford Motor Company in America placed itself firmly at the disposal of the Allied war effort.

In 1948 the production line in Cologne started up again with domestic vehicles, and first off the production line was the Ford Taunus. It was the first European-made car to feature a curving windscreen and oval headlamps, and was known locally as the *Badewanne* (meaning bathtub) because of its revolutionary new streamlining. Almost 670 000 of them were manufactured between 1960 and 1964, and a splendid red-painted example is on display in the Cologne City Museum.

The Ford Works in Cologne have survived the highs and lows of the twentieth century; currently employing more than twenty thousand workers it remains one of the region's largest employers. Indeed on 5th February 2010 the forty millionth Ford to be manufactured in Germany – a Ford Fiesta – rolled off the production line in Cologne.

A two-hour tour of Cologne's Ford Works at Henry-Ford-Strasse 1 is possible by appointment (tel. 0049-(0)221-901-9991, www.ford.de). Those not able to visit can appreciate the size of the operation by using Google Earth, which shows clearly the four Stadtbahn stations required to service the site, and the Niehl II docks from where thousands of finished Fords are despatched by river.

Other places of interest nearby: 60

62 A Curious Lake

Chorweiler (Borough 6), the Fühlinger See on Stallagsbergweg
Stadtbahn 15 Heimersdorf, then Bus 122

Cologne's largest lake is the Fühlinger See in Chorweiler, and its waters are justifiably popular with bathers, divers, anglers, canoeists, sailors, and surfers. Over a hot summer's weekend up to eighty thousand people can visit the lake. With so much leisure activity it's all too easy to overlook the curious origin of the Fühlinger See, as well as the history of the area surrounding it.

Beginning in 1912 gravel quarrying started on the Fühlinger Heath (Fühlinger Heide), where the lake is now situated, to satisfy demand for ballast to support new railway tracks being laid between Cologne, Aachen, and Krefeld. An estimated thirty million cubic metres of material was removed from a series of pits reaching up to fourteen metres in depth. Due to the close proximity of the Rhine, and the existence of an old underground tributary of the river, the gravel pits soon began filling with groundwater, creating seven interconnected lakes as a result. Quite by accident the Fühlinger See had been created, and as early as the 1930s bathers began arriving to swim here. It is interesting to note that the water level of the new lake never drops below that of the Rhine, and indeed fluctuates with it by up to two metres.

In 1967 the Fühlinger See was officially recognised as a recreation area, each lake being designated for a different leisure activity: competitive swimming, fishing, surfing, three for bathing (notably the Naturfreibad Fühlinger See on Stallagsbergweg), and another for canoeing and sailing, the latter connected to a 2300 meter long, purpose-built regatta course (Regattastrecke).

The area surrounding the Fühlinger See has an interesting history, too. For a start, the name Fühlinger Heide is something of a misnomer, since the area prior to quarrying was in fact partially wooded, interspersed with areas of farmland; a ruined windmill on the Stallagsberg is testimony to past agricultural activity in the area. Long before that the Romans established brickyards hereabouts, and there is archaeological evidence for prehistoric man having sought high, dry ground here during the Stone Age (see no. 54). During the Middle Ages there were farms here, and in the nineteenth century the wealthy Oppenheim banking family established a racecourse and stud in Fühlingen, the proceeds from which financed a school and a church. The parish priest,

The Fühlinger See in Chorweiler is only a hundred years old

Joseph Frings, became archbishop of Cologne and is remembered for sanctioning the theft of coal after the Second World War.

In 1922 Fühlingen and the adjacent settlement of Worringen to the north were incorporated into Cologne. Approximately where the two meet, on the appropriately-named Blutberg, the Battle of Worringen occurred in 1288. The army of Cologne's Archbishop Siegfried II (1275–1297) confronted that of Count Adolf V of the Duchy of Berg, for control of the commercially important Duchy of Limburg. Both duchy and archbishopric were part of the Holy Roman Empire, although the archbishopric functioned as a powerful independent clerical state. This brought it into conflict with the surrounding German duchies, as well as the citizens of Cologne, who fought alongside the soldiers of Berg in an attempt to free themselves from Siegfried's yoke. Adolf was victorious, as a result of which the citizens of Cologne gained independence from the Archbishopric and took municipal control of their city, initially under a corporation of rich patrician families (a monument at St.-Tönnis-Strasse 33 in Worringen recalls the battle). With the passing of the *Verbundbrief* in 1396 (a form of urban democratic constitution) power was passed from the patricians to the city's trading guilds.

The tree-fringed shore
of the Fühlinger See

The style of dress and types of weapons used at the Battle of Worringen can be imagined when the Mittelalterlich Phantasie Spectaculum, the world's largest travelling medieval festival, sets down on the banks of the Fühlinger See for one weekend each summer.

Despite close proxity to chemical plants in Leverkusen and Dormagen, as well as an anti-aircraft battery, Fühlingen escaped the Second World War unscathed. In the 1950s it was selected as the location for a test track of the so-called *Alwegbahn*, an elevated monorail system, but the idea was never developed and the track dismantled in 1967. Around the same time a controversial proposal to transform Fühlingen into a green no-man's land between a new railway along the Rhine and a housing estate further west was dropped in the face of vociferous protests from established residents. Instead, Fühlingen was preserved along with its lake, where in 1998 the world rowing boat championships were staged. The lake has also played host to regular triathlon running events and open air concerts, as well as the 2006 Red Bull flying competition, much to the delight of 135 000 onlookers.

63 A Taste of the Country

Chorweiler (Borough 6), Auweiler village green between
Doktorshof, Pohlhofstrasse and Auweilerstrasse
Stadtbahn 15 Chorweiler, then Bus 126

It's difficult to imagine these days that Cologne's Altstadt, as defined by
its ring road (Kölner Ring) along which stood its medieval walls, ever
contained green fields. A visit to the Cologne City Museum (Kölnisches
Stadtmuseum) at Zeughausstrasse 1–3 (Altstadt-Nord) proves otherwise, with models and engravings clearly depicting farmers' fields and
market gardens, and even a trio of windmills built on top of the walls
themselves (see no. 35). Rapid industrialisation during the second half
of the nineteenth century, however, saw the disappearance of the fields,
and during the early 1880s even the walls themselves were demolished
to accommodate the growing city. One of the few reminders of the period is a tiny half-timbered building at Kettengasse 6 (Altstadt-Nord),
once a free-standing gardener's cottage. Today, it is hemmed in on all
sides by modern buildings.

To gain any sense of rural tranquillity in Cologne nowadays the explorer must travel far beyond the Altstadt, and out into the suburbs
that were not incorporated into the city until the twentieth century.
Of the many villages that once dotted this rich agricultural region few
retain their original charm and character. An exception is the village
of Auweiler, far to the north-west in the borough of Chorweiler, which
sits like an island amidst a sea of fields. Instead of high-rise apartment
blocks and busy road junctions there is a huddle of single- and two-
story red-brick farmhouses, set around a village green, which according
to historians was created by the infilling of a former lake. Each farm
has its own small yard, the name of one of them, the Pohlhof, thought
to reflect the presence of unclean, standing water, presumably a memory of the old lake. The Pohlhof today contains a restaurant inside its
charming cobblestoned courtyard, which is adorned with an old pump
and some antique agricultural machinery. Another farmyard at Auweilerstrasse 10 has a collection of old farm implements displayed on its
walls, as well as the date '1844' formed by the iron tie bars holdings its
old walls in place (this particular practice is also commonplace in the
medieval buildings of Cologne's Altstadt).

Auweiler's picturesque ensemble is completed by the presence of
a pavilion, in which village events are sometimes staged, and the two

An old farmhouse in the village of Auweiler

hundred year-old Chapel of Maria Virgo (Maria-Virgo-Kapelle), which has room for just a dozen worshippers. Auweiler during the medieval period belonged to the Herzogtum Berg and in the 1790s the French incorporated it into their Canton Dormagen, which was a part of the Arrondisement Cologne. The village was eventually incorporated into modern Cologne in 1975.

Another taste of the country is available on the opposite side of the Rhine, in the district of Dellbrück (Mülheim). At Mielenforster Strasse 1, on the banks of the Strunder Bach, there stands the Thurner Hof, a tall timber-framed house from the sixteenth century. It is named after a knight who used the building as a watchtower. Like Auweiler, Dellbrück was also a medieval possession of the Herzogtum Berg, its fields and forests used for hunting by the nobility. Later it passed through the hands of Napoleon and then the Prussians, and was incorporated into Cologne in 1914. The building has recently been enhanced by the addition of a charming organic farmer's garden, brimming with old-fashioned flowers, fruit trees, vegetables, and medieval medicinal plants (the garden is open to visitors during the summer months).

64 Where the Red Baron Learned to Fly

Ehrenfeld (Borough 4), the former Köln-Butzweilerhof Airport
at Butzweilerstrasse 35–39
Stadtbahn 5 Alter Flughafen Butzweilerhof

For aviation enthusiasts a journey out along Stadtbahn Line 5 to the district of Ossendorf (Ehrenfeld) represents an opportunity to see what's left of one of Germany's most historic airports. The history of the Köln-Butzweilerhof Airport starts in the late 1900s, when the Prussian Emperor Wilhelm II (1888–1918) bestowed upon Cologne the title 'Reichsluftschiffhafen Coeln' (Imperial Airship Port Cologne), and a thirty metre high airship hangar was constructed here. The arrival of the Zeppelin LZ5 at the hangar on 5th August 1909 drew thousands of spectators. At the end of the First World War, however, the hall was dismantled leaving only a solitary concrete airship anchor as a reminder at Mathias-Brüggen-Strasse 68.

Alongside the airships, however, were aircraft, and in 1911 a grass landing strip was created at Butzweilerhof together with several aircraft hangars. A flying school was established, and it was here that the legendary pilot Manfred von Richthofen (1892–1918) completed his training. Known as the Red Baron, because of his aristocratic background and trademark red-painted Fokker Dr. 1 triplane, Richthofen became Germany's most successful flying ace of the First World War, with eighty downed enemy aircraft to his name.

After the war, under the terms of the Treaty of Versailles, a ban was placed on Germany's air force, which remained in place until 1926. In the same year the Deutsche Lufthansa airline company was created, and Butzweilerhof emerged as Cologne's main civilian airport. Cologne became a key element in Germany's so-called "Luftkreuz des Westens" (Air Crossroads of the West), and by 1930 more than fifty aircraft were landing daily. New buildings were needed but plans were postponed due to the country's economic crisis. Everything changed, however, with the arrival of the Nazis, and in 1935 a new terminal was constructed in the pared-down Bauhaus style, using a workforce of unemployed labourers. Butzweilerhof soon became one of Nazi Germany's most important hubs for national and international air traffic, second only to Berlin-Tempelhof.

The arrivals hall of the former Köln-Butzweilerhof Airport

The new era of civilian air travel at Butzweilerhof Airport ended abruptly in 1939, when the facilities were turned over to the Luftwaffe. With little strategic importance the airport survived the war intact and in 1951 it was commandeered by the Royal Air Force, just as it had been after the First World War. The British remained until 1965, and in 1967 the airport was handed over to the German Federal Defence Force (Bundeswehr), who used a small part of it until the airport's complete closure in 2007. Shortly afterwards the northern part of the site was cleared and replaced with an assortment of retail, business, office, and residential units, creating more than ten thousand jobs in the process.

But what of the old airport terminal? Fortunately, at Butzweilerstrasse 35–39, the elegant, marble-lined arrivals hall is still standing, flanked by the control tower, hangars, airline offices, and a once glamorous restaurant. Together with Berlin-Tempelhof it is the only German airport to survive largely intact from the 1930s, and as such has been protected since 1988.

A foundation established in 1999 (Stiftung Butzweilerhof Köln) works to protect the remains, whilst also reminding visitors of how important the airport was during the 1920s and 30s. This is achieved through the foundation's Butzweilerhof Aviation Exhibition (Butzweilerhof Luftfahrt Ausstellung), a fascinating historical collection

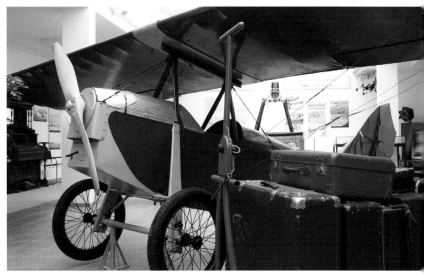

An aircraft on display in the Butzweilerhof Aviation Exhibition (Butzweilerhof Luftfahrt-Ausstellung)

opened in 1986 that tells the story of aviation in Cologne by means of more than five hundred artefacts, as well as old photographs, posters, and models. Tours of the collection and the airport buildings are available by appointment only (www.butzweilerhof.de).

Note also that some of the street names around Butzweilerhof recall famous aviators, including Günther von Hünefeld (1892–1929), who made the first east-west transatlantic flight in 1928, aircraft manufacturer Claudius Dornier (1884–1969), and the pioneering American aviator and polar explorer Richard Byrd (1888–1957). Those wishing to look behind the scenes of an operational airport can take a tour around Cologne/Bonn Airport "Konrad Adenauer" at Waldstrasse 147 (Porz). Tours depart from the airport visitor centre Monday to Friday at 10.00 am, 11.45 am, 1.30 pm and 3.15 pm by appointment only (www.koeln-bonn-airport.de).

65 The Jewish Stones Speak

Ehrenfeld (Borough 4), the Bocklemünd Jewish Cemetery
(Jüdischer Friedhof Bocklemünd) at Venloer Strasse 1152;
note: men must cover their heads when visiting the cemetery
Stadtbahn 3, 4 Bocklemünd; Bus 143

Despite Cologne being home to Germany's oldest Jewish community, until recently there was little left to see of it. Only in the last few years have archaeologists revealed the footings of the city's medieval synagogue beneath Rathausplatz, where the Cologne's Jews worshipped until their expulsion in 1423 (see no. 5). Of the handful of synagogues present in the city by the 1930s all were desecrated by the Nazis during their *Reichskristallnacht* pogrom of 1938. Except for the one at Roonstrasse 50 (Altstadt-Süd), which was rebuilt after the war on the initiative of Konrad Adenauer, the rest are remembered only by wall plaques (for example Glockengasse 7 (Altstadt-Nord), now the site of the Cologne Opera House (Oper Köln), where composer Jacques Offenbach's father was cantor).

The most tangible evidence of what Cologne has lost to anti-Semitism is provided by the city's six extant Jewish cemeteries (Bocklemünd, Deutz, Mülheim, Ehrenfeld, Deckstein, and Zündorf). The remains of Cologne's oldest Jewish cemetery on Bonner Strasse (Rodenkirchen) were only uncovered in 1922 during road widening. It was founded in 1143 and remained in use until 1695, although it was desecrated in 1349 during a pogrom prompted by those looking for ways to explain the arrival of the Black Death. In 1936, when the area was cleared for the construction of the Great Market Hall (Grossmarkthalle) at Marktstrasse 10, the remains were removed to Cologne's largest Jewish cemetery in Bocklemünd (Ehrenfeld) (see no. 79).

Before visiting Bocklemünd though it is perhaps better first to consider Cologne's second largest Jewish cemetery on Judenkirchhofsweg in Deutz (Jüdischer Friedhof Deutz). It was to Deutz on the east bank of the Rhine that the Jews were expelled in 1423, when years of prejudice against them came to a head. From this position of relative safety they continued trading with the merchants of Cologne. The oldest extant gravestone in the cemetery dates back to 1699, with the majority dating from the eighteenth and nineteenth centuries (the cemetery was closed in 1918, with a solitary burial made in 1941). Important graves include those of the cantor Isaac Offenbach (1779–1850), the philoso-

Gravestones in the Bocklemünd Jewish Cemetery (Jüdischer Friedhof Bocklemünd)

pher Moses Hess (1812–1875), the prominent Zionist David Wolffsohn (1856–1914), and members of the Oppenheim banking dynasty. As with most Jewish cemeteries the place has a wild aspect to it, arising from the fact that trees are only removed when they present a danger, and many of those who would normally attend the graves were murdered or else deported by the Nazis. Those who visit today often leave a pebble rather than flowers, reflecting the old Bedouin tradition of using stones to mark out a grave in the sand. Unlike Christian cemeteries where untended graves are eventually cleared and reused, Jewish families retain their grave plots forever, renewing them every fifteen years.

On 17th November 1797 Jews and Protestants were granted the same rights as Catholics by Cologne's French occupiers, and all were allowed to engage in trade and manufacturing regardless of origin or religion. Jewish burials continued in the community's existing cemeteries until 1918, when the new Bocklemünd Jewish Cemetery (Jüdischer Friedhof Bocklemünd) opened at Venloer Strasse 1152 (Ehrenfeld). Still used today this is an important cemetery both historically and artistically, reflecting many strands of Jewish society. Modest graves inscribed in both Hebrew and German dominate the central area, with motifs such as paired hands reflecting the priestly profession *(Kohen)* and water jugs representing those who washed the hands of the priest *(Levites).*

Detail of a gravestone in the Bocklemünd Jewish Cemetery (Jüdische Friedhof Bocklemünd)

Around the perimeter of the cemetery are the elaborate mausoleums of the well-to-do, including that of the department store king Leonhard Tietz (1849–1914), whose shop at Höhe Strasse 41–53 was "Aryanised" by the Nazis and renamed Westdeutsche Kaufhof AG (a name it retains to this day). The cemetery also includes three important monuments, the most imposing of which is architect Robert Stern's pyramid-shaped Monument for the Jewish Frontline Soldiers of the First World War (Denkmal für die jüdischen Frontsoldaten des Ersten Weltkriegs). Nearby is a sculpture comprising six Stars of David, which marks where precious objects from Cologne's destroyed synagogues were buried in 1939, and a tall pillar recalls the more than eleven thousand Cologne Jews murdered during the Holocaust. Faced with such memorials it is easy to overlook the tiny lapidarium *(Steinhaus)* in which the pitiful fragments of the old medieval cemetery on Bonner Strasse are now displayed.

66   In Search of the Real Cologne

Ehrenfeld (Borough 4), a tour of idiosyncratic bars, cafés
and restaurants beginning with Café Franck at Eichendorffstrasse 30
Stadtbahn 5, 13 Nussbaumerstrasse

Where should one go to find the real Cologne? There are probably as
many answers to this question as there are people asking it. It all de-
pends on what one is looking for. It is often said that Cologne is very
"human" for a German city, and that its inhabitants display a distinctly
Rhenish tolerance, the result perhaps of their city having been Germany's largest medieval trading metropolis. This is particularly true in the
city's suburbs, so perhaps it's there that the real Cologne lies.

Certainly the suburbs have a unique flavour all their own, one
which has often defied the official district borders, resulting in the creation of a number of distinct quarters. The fashion-conscious citizens
that frequent the boutiques of the Belgian Quarter (Belgisches Viertel),
for example, between Aachener Strasse and Hohenzollernring (Neustadt-Nord), differ considerably from the happy-go-lucky bar flies of
the Students' Quarter (Kwartier Lateng in Kölsch dialect), centred
around Zülpicher Platz (Neustadt-Süd). Similarly, the smart shoppers
seen along tree-lined Neusser Strasse in the Agnes Quarter (Agnesvier-
tel), between Ebertplatz and Kanalstrasse (Neustadt-Nord), differ sub-
tly from the more down-to-earth shoppers along Severinsstrasse in the
Severin Quarter (Vringsveedel).

The official district of Neu-Ehrenfeld is different yet again, with its
older native inhabitant living alongside the incoming moneyed middle
class in search of leafy, nineteenth century properties in which to raise
their families. Just over the border in Ehrenfeld proper is a broader-
based ethnic mix of Turks, artists, Africans, and working class, bringing
new life to the area's former industrial landscape.

A walk through both these districts, stopping off at some idiosyncratic cafés, bars and restaurants along the way, reveals much of the real
Cologne. First stop is Café Franck at Eichendorffstrasse 30, a genteel
café-cum-living room popular with all ages that surprisingly doubles
as a DJ venue in the evenings. Established in 1938 it was managed until
recently by one of its original proprietors, ninety-year-old 'Susi' Franck.
A couple of streets away, Früh im Haus Tutt at Fridolinstrasse 72 is
not only a decade older but also serves its drinks a little stronger: as

its name suggests it is an official purveyor of the locally-brewed Früh Kölsch, which is served fresh from the barrel.

A brisk stroll, or a couple of stops on the Stadtbahn, leads eastwards to Kölnerstrasse, a traditional residential street being turned over slowly to cafés, artists' studios, fashion boutiques, and antiques shops. Some of the old places remain, however, including Em höttche – Beim Aggi at number 41, a typical suburban bar *(Kneipe)*, permanently dark and smoky, where the conversation flows as freely as the Kölsch. By contrast Café Sehnsucht at number 67 is light and trendy, where the only thing smoking is the fashionable wood-burning stove!

At the end of Körnerstrasse is busy Venloer Strasse, where at number 236 is the solid Restaurant Haus Scholzen. In the hands of the same family since 1907 it consists of a wooden bar, where valued regulars can enjoy their *Kölsch* behind the privacy of an opaque glass window; a fine restaurant to the rear specialises in hearty local dishes such as Ehrenfeld mustard roast *(Ehrensenfrostbraten)*. Those wishing for a less formal dining experience should head back along Venloer Strasse to its junction with Ehrenfelder Gürtel, where the snack bar Strohhut's Eck serves *Currywurst* and *Reibekuchen*, the latter being a fried potato pattie served with apple puree. Farther out still at Christinastrasse 2 can be found the Braustelle, Cologne's smallest brewery. The modest promises contain half a dozen tables and chairs, where punters enjoy *Helios*-brand wheat beer and *Ehrenfelder Alt* dark beer, both of which are brewed at the back of the room.

This tour finishes not in Ehrenfeld but at Gladbacherstrasse 48,

The 1950s lives on in the Weisser Holunder on Gladbacherstrasse

just over the border in Neustadt-Nord. Here can be found Weisser
Holunder, a unique and welcoming tavern named after a 1950s film of
the same name. And the connection with the fifties doesn't end there
since the entire place is decked out in the distinctive style of that period, including tables, chairs, light fittings, posters, and a 1957 *Rockola*
jukebox that plays for free. Established in 1991, when such nostalgia
was hardly fashionable, the Weisser Holunder was and still is proprietor Karl Schieberg's anti-establishment statement. Anything goes here,
whether you're a local or a tourist. How about a game of pool or sitting
down and listening to a record by Edith Piaf? Or maybe a game of *Skat*
(similar to Bridge) or joining in for a Sunday-evening singsong? And
for those with an appetite why not try a plate of traditional *Halvehahn*?
Despite its name this is nothing to do with poultry but is rather a slice of
Röggelche (rye bread) served with Gouda cheese and mustard. Delicious!

Other places of interest nearby: 67, 68

67 Memorials to Human Suffering

Ehrenfeld (Borough 4), a memorial marking a Second World War execution site at the junction of Schönsteinstrasse and Bartholomäus-Schink-Strasse
Stadtbahn 13 Venloer Strasse/Gürtel; Bus 141, 142, 143

This mural in Ehrenfeld marks the site where the Edelweiss Pirates (Edelweisspiraten) were hung

Like all cities subject to the murderous rule of the Nazis between 1933 and 1945, Cologne has memorialised the sites where those atrocities occurred. So numerous are they – around seventy five in Cologne at the last count – that entire guidebooks have been written about them (most recently *Mahnmalführer Köln* by Hans Hesse and Elke Purpus, 2010).

The memorials take a variety of forms, from simple wall plaques and inscribed stones embedded in the pavement to small-scale memorials and ambitious sculptural installations. After seeing so many it is perhaps the more novel ones that stick in the mind. These include the open-air pavilion on Appellhofplatz (Altstadt-Nord), the roof of which carries a long inscription honouring deserters and peace activists sentenced to death by the Nazi courts, and a poignant bronze sculpture of two grieving parents in the Gremberg Woods (Gremberger Wäldchen) (Porz), where seventy four Russian forced labourers were massacred by German soldiers as the Americans approached.

An unusual memorial is inside a railway arch at the junction of Schönsteinstrasse and Bartholomäus-Schink-Strasse (Ehrenfeld). It recalls a series of public executions carried out by the Gestapo and SS as a means of deterring further opposition to their brutal activities.

On 25th October 1944 eleven Polish and Russian forced labourers were hung here on specially-erected gallows. The bodies were left on display until dusk and then removed for burial in the West Cemetery (Westfriedhof). On 10th November thirteen further hangings took place, including members of the so-called Edelweiss Pirates (Edelweisspiraten), an Ehrenfeld-based group of young resistance fighters opposed to the ideals of the Hitler Youth movement. The gruesome events are commemorated by a series of striking murals depicting the hanging men.

Unusual memorials can also be found at Cologne's two main railway stations, where they commemorate the millions of innocent men, women, and children deported to the death camps from similar stations across Nazi Germany. One of them, at the front of the Köln-Hauptbahnhof, consists of an old wooden railway sleeper to which several inscribed plaques have been attached, recalling not only the victims but also the involvement of the German Railways (Deutsche Reichsbahn) in expediting the deportations. More conventional is the sandstone wall tablet outside the Köln-Messe/Deutz station on Auenweg, stating that more than fifteen hundred Roma and Sinti were deported from here by the SS in 1940, and that eleven thousand Jews followed them between 1941 and 1944. In front is one of many brass strips in the pavements of Cologne marking the journey made by the Roma and Sinti, from an assembly point in Bickendorf to the railway station (see no. 4); alongside it is a simple stone inscribed "Nie Wieder" (Never Again).

Next to Deutz station is the vast Cologne Trade Fair (Kölnmesse), which was laid out during the 1920s. Its halls were used by the SS as an internment camp for prisoners of war, and as an assembly point for those awaiting deportation by train. In 1942 it became a satellite of the Buchenwald Concentration Camp, a fact that is recorded in a rather forlorn red-brick memorial in front of the Cologne Trade Fair Tower (Messeturm Köln) on Messeplatz. The memorial, which also details camps for prisoners of war, forced labourers, and a special Gestapo camp for German and foreign political detainees, sits rather uneasily with the endlessly upbeat nature of the trade fairs and shows staged nearby.

Cologne also has approximately sixty five memorials commemorating the military and civilian victims of both world wars, including single graves, grave fields, and monuments, many of which can be found in Cologne's main west bank cemeteries: Südfriedhof (Rodenkirchen), Nordfriedhof (Nippes) and Westfriedhof (Ehrenfeld). An especially affecting example to the fallen of the Second World War is located in the Sürther Strasse Cemetery (Friedhof Sürther Strasse) (Rodenkirchen).

A memorial to the victims of war in the Sürther Strasse Cemetery (Friedhof Sürther Strasse)

Lying to the left of the chapel at the main entrance, in the permanent shade of a grove of trees, it consists of a group of five life-sized stone figures called *Die Opfer (The Victims)*: a soldier, a mother and child, a youngster clutching a drum, a shackled prisoner, and a shrouded victim of starvation. The message is unambiguous: modern war knows no borders. The memorial is especially interesting because it is the work of the Cologne sculptor Willy Meller (1887–1974), who had a busy career during the 1930s creating neo-Classical figures for Third Reich building projects such as the Olympic Stadium (Olympiastadion) in Berlin.

Other places of interest nearby: 66, 68, 69, 70

68   A Lighthouse Far From the Sea

Ehrenfeld (Borough 4), the Helios lighthouse on Heliosstrasse
Stadtbahn 13 Venloer Strasse/Gürtel; Bus 141, 142, 143

Cologne's district of Ehrenfeld, which was incorporated into Cologne in 1888, lies a very long way from the nearest ocean, and is not even within sight of the Rhine. It therefore comes as quite a surprise to discover a forty four metre high lighthouse there!

Towering above Heliosstrasse (suitably named after Helios the Greek sun god), the lighthouse was constructed as a landmark for the Helios Electric Lighting and Telegraph Construction Company (Helios AG für elektrisches Licht und Telegraphenanlagenbau), which was founded here in 1882. The site was selected because of its proximity to the already existing Cologne-Aachen railway, as well as the Ehrenfeld-Cologne horsedrawn tramway. The lighthouse today is the focal point for one of Cologne's most important industrial-era ensembles.

Around two thousand workers were employed by the company, manufacturing electricity generators, as well as Germany's first transformers, dynamos, and alternators. The workshop contained Germany's first electrically-powered crane, and in the grounds there was a test track for electric tramcars. Casings and castings were made in an on-site foundry, and power was provided by a pair of 250 horsepower Helios generators. No less than twenty three complete power stations were manufactured here, as well as all the components for six German tramway networks. As such the Helios company made a significant contribution not only to the development of power station technology but also to the Europe-wide electrification of industry, public traffic, and lighting systems.

In 1891 the company exhibited at the prestigious International Electrotechnical Exhibition (Internationale Elektrotechnische Ausstellung) in Frankfurt. Among its range of products were navigational lights for use on the North Sea and Baltic Canal. In 1895 the company supplied twenty beacons to the Kaiser-Wilhelm-Kanal (today the Nord-Ostsee-Kanal). Despite these many successes, however, a decrease in orders and an unsuccessful venture into banking saw the company taken over by Siemens and AEG in 1905, and its doors were eventually closed in 1930.

The Helios lighthouse appears today much as it did when first erected. Located in the northwest corner of the old factory, it consists of a sturdy square stone base, on top of which is the tapering, red-brick

This lighthouse in Ehrenfeld once marked a factory manufacturing navigational lights

tower, topped with an iron and glass lantern. Although it is still illuminated at night the lantern no longer contains any optical elements.

In addition to the lighthouse, which was given a new lantern in 1996, the company's imposing former administration building, the Helios-Haus, is also still standing at Venloer Strasse 389. It contains a splendid cast-iron galleried staircase, natural light being admitted by means of a skylight. It is today occupied by several medical practices, and is occasionally used as a set by television companies. The name Cölner Industrie Welt, which runs across the façade, recalls the company that from 1907 let the building to various industrial concerns.

The factory's two work halls are also still standing and were originally used for the assembly of large machines. In 1911 one of the halls, the so-called Rheinlandhalle, was used for the manufacture of car engines. The company failed and in 1928 the hall was converted into a cycle racing track (a wall plaque commemorates the champion cyclist Albert Richter (1912–1940), who was murdered by the Gestapo for opposing Hitler). The track was the venue for the Cologne six-day bicycle race, as well as for boxing matches and also election rallies of the Nazi party, indeed for a while it was named after Adolf Hitler. Badly damaged during the Second World War, in 1957 the hall became home to Cologne's first supermarket, since when it has been used by various retail companies.

A related site just around the corner from the Helios factory is the Vulkanhalle at Lichtstrasse 43. This brick-built factory hall dating from the 1920s is where equipment for gas works and street lighting was once manufactured. The hall is today used to host art events, as well as for office space and apartments. A little further along Venloer Strasse at Christianstrasse 2 is the Braustelle, Cologne's smallest brewery tavern serving *Helios*-brand beer (see no. 66).

Other places of interest nearby: 66, 67, 69, 70

69 Rock Climbing in the City

Ehrenfeld (Borough 4), Kletterfabrik at Lichtstrasse 25
Stadtbahn 13 Venloer Strasse/Gürtel; Bus 141, 142, 143

Cologne straddles the River Rhine on land that is as flat as the proverbial pancake! In geographical terms the city lies on the eastern edge of the so-called Cologne Lowland or Bay (Kölner Bucht), which forms the southern conclusion of the Rhenish Lowlands, and marks the transition to the Rhenish Massif (Rheinisches Schiefergebirge). This means two things: Cologne is extremely prone to flooding (it is considered the most flood-prone city in Europe) and it offers nothing to those interested in rock climbing. Or does it? In reality the lack of hills has prompted the city's climbing enthusiasts to create an enviable selection of artificial climbing facilities. Even if you are not a climber it is worthwhile visiting one of these climbing halls *(Kletterhallen)*, if only to marvel at their unusual locations and to see some impressive climbing techniques in an urban environment.

Cologne's first climbing hall was opened in 2004 at Lichtstrasse 25 in the district of Ehrenfeld. Called Kletterfabrik it is housed inside a cavernous former machine hall of the Ostermann Works (Ostermann Werke), where huge ships' propellers up to fifteen metres in diameter were once manufactured. With the fall of the Berlin Wall, and the opening up of cheap markets to the east, the works quickly became uncompetitive and were closed in 1991 (the surrounding area is filled with former factory buildings, some converted to other uses and others left empty; see no. 68). The hall containing the Kletterfabrik contains 1200 square metres of climbing wall *(Kletterwand)*, offering visitors more than one hundred and eighty different routes of varying complexity, the longest being ninety metres. Beginners' courses are available for those new to the sport, whilst expert coaches are on hand to customise routes for the more experienced. School groups and even children's birthday parties are also catered for.

Cologne's second climbing hall, the Canyon Chorweiler on Weichselring 6a (Chorweiler), opened in 2006. Germany's first not-for-profit climbing hall, the building also contains dance, theatre, and music facilities. The climbing wall covers 1100 square metres as well as two climbing towers (12 and 16.5 meters in height), a 5-metre wide cliff overhang, and a bouldering zone. Some fifty different climbing routes are available. Again tuition for all levels is available, and children are

The Kletterfabrik climbing wall occupies a former machine hall on Lichtstrasse

encouraged to take part, especially during the summer holidays when an adventure camp is made available.

Cologne's third and smallest climbing hall can be found in the Abenteuerhallen Kalk, another cavernous former factory building, this time on Christian-Sunner-Strasse (Kalk), where it shares the premises with skateboarders, rollerbladers, BMX riders, basketball and soccer players. At certain times the climbing wall is reserved for children only, and at other times specifically for families. Tuition is available to all and the premises can be rented for conference and seminar purposes.

Cologne's highest natural point is actually a hill on Wolfsweg in Königsforst (Kalk), on the eastern boundary of the city. It is 118.04 metres above sea level and known as Monte Troodelöh. This unusual designation is an amalgam of the names of three city administrators, who placed a plaque on the summit in 1999.

Other places of interest nearby: 67, 68, 70

A *Jugendstil* Bathing Temple

Ehrenfeld (Borough 4), the Neptunbad at Neptunplatz 1
Stadtbahn 3, 4 Körnerstrasse; Bus 141, 142, 143

At the turn of the 20th century German artists responded boldly to the success of French *Art Nouveau* by creating their own variant known as *Jugendstil*. Revelling in the same new-found freedom of artistic expression, the movement boldly turned its back on the staid historicist trends that had dictated art and architecture during the previous decades. The centre of *Jugendstil* was undoubtedly Munich but the style is represented in several other German cities including Cologne, where, for example, there is a fine Jugendstil façade at Neusser Strasse 27–29 (Neustadt-Nord). More unusually, at the corner of Ostheimer Strasse and Frankfurter Strasse (Kalk), there is a *Jugendstil* power station constructed in 1904.

A statue of Neptune still adorns the former Neptunbad swimming hall

The best example of *Jugendstil* in Cologne is undoubtedly the Neptunbad at Neptunplatz 1 (Ehrenfeld), which is a must for architecture students and fitness fanatics alike. The first modern public bath house in the suburbs of Cologne it opened in 1912 and was designed by the Prussian architect Johannes Baptist Kleefisch (1862–1932). It continued in use as a public swimming pool until 1994, when running costs became prohibitive. It was then purchased privately and lovingly refurbished, to be re-opened in 2002 as a health club and spa.

The main door, which still bears the inscription 'Städtische Badeanstalt' (City Bath House), is beautifully carved with sea creatures and cherubs. Beyond, in the entrance hall, there are numerous *Jugendstil* flourishes, including curvilinear plasterwork, elegant light fittings, and sea-green Villeroy & Boch wall tiles. At the heart of the building there is a magnificent thirteen meter high, vaulted and galleried hall, adorned with a statue of Neptune. This was once the swimming pool, which has now been converted into a fitness centre (the diving board is still in place!). Elsewhere new Asian elements, including a Japanese garden and a Turkish *Hamam*, have been incorporated succesfully into the old building, notably in the sauna areas, demonstrating the innately eclectic and flexible nature of *Jugendstil* architecture.

Cologne once boasted another *Jugendstil* bath building, the Deutz-Kalker-Bad at Deutz-Kalker-Strasse 52 (Deutz). Opened in 1913 as the Kaiser-Wilhelm-Bad it was used by the military until the First World War. Between the wars it was opened to the public but then seriously damaged during the Second World War. The main pool was later cleared of rubble and filled with water transported from a hot mineral spring in the nearby Rheinpark. In 1996 the Claudiustherme at Sachsenbergstrasse 1 (Deutz) was opened above the spring, as a result of which the Deutz-Kalker-Bad was closed. In 2008 the abandoned bath building, which closely resembles the Neptunbad, was cleverly incorporated into the newly constructed Günnewig Hotel Stadtpalais.

The Claudiustherme, whilst of little architectural interest to the historian, is one of Europe's most beautiful thermal baths. Half inside and half outside it features a Finnish sauna, herbal steam bath, and hot mud bath, and the panorama sauna has a splendid view of the surrounding Rheinpark, with the cathedral beyond.

Another of Cologne's historic baths is the Agrippabad at Kämmergasse 1 (Altstadt-Süd), which has always been a public facility. With the focus squarely on leisure the bath offers a twenty five metre long wave pool, a one hundred and twenty seven metre long slide, and a rooftop garden with sauna and panorama restaurant.

Completely different are Cologne's open air pools, which are justifiably popular during the hot summer months. One of the most attractive is the Vingster Freibad on Vingster Ring (Kalk), a former quarry given added beauty by being surrounded with meadows and its own beach, which is used for volleyball, barbecues, and relaxing. The outskirts of Cologne have many such water-filled former quarries, a num-

The Neptunbad is now used as a health club and spa

ber of which lie on the southern edge of Rodenkirchen. The Kiesgrube Meschenich, for example, is a former gravel pit between Kerkrader Strasse and Am Engeldorfer Berg that is now a haven for wildlife. Quite different is a former basalt quarry on Luxemburger Strasse that provides an unusual backdrop for the Klettenbergpark established by the garden architect Fritz Encke (1861–1931) in 1907. Until 1986 the oldest open air pool in Cologne was the Riehler Bad on Niederländer Ufer (Nippes). Founded in 1902 it is now a beer garden.

Those wishing to escape entirely into nature might like to try the Dünnwalder Freibad at Peter-Baum-Weg 20 (Mülheim), nestled within a forest in the outskirts of northern Cologne. This nature lover's paradise is open all year round and offers fresh air and greenery in abundance, enhanced by the proximity of the Dünnwalder Wildpark on nearby Dünnwalder Mauspfad.

Other places of interest nearby: 67, 68, 69, 77

71 The European Capital of Carnival

Ehrenfeld (Borough 4), the Cologne Carnival Museum (Kölner
Karnevalsmuseum) at Maarweg 134–136
Stadtbahn 1 Maarweg, then walk; Bus 140, 141, 143

The celebration of Carnival in Cologne is probably as old as the city itself, since its origins appear to lie with the Romans, who prepared for the harvest and the arrival of Spring by honouring their gods Bacchus and Saturn. The Germanic tribes marked the winter solstice as a means of expelling the evil demons of winter, and Christians later adapted these pagan customs into their own period of fasting prior to Easter, known as Lent. That period is heralded with Carnival, a word derived from the Latin phrase *Carne Vale*, meaning "Farewell to meat"; in Germany *Karneval* is also known as *Fastnacht*.

Since 1341 Carnival in Cologne has taken the form of a spirited and boisterous street parade, extended during the eighteenth century to include Venetian-style masquerades known as *Redouten*, originally the preserve of the aristocracy and wealthy patricians. Despite French occupation and Prussian domination Carnival has continued to thrive in Cologne, and in 1823 a dedicated planning committee was founded (Festkomitee des Kölner Karnevals). The committee still organises Carnival from their headquarters at Maarweg 134–136 (Ehrenfeld), where they share the premises with the Cologne Carnival Museum (Kölner Karnevalsmuseum). Opened in 2005 the museum is the largest and most modern of its kind in the German-speaking world, and is well worth visiting to discover more about the origins and traditions of what is today one of the largest annual street festivals in Europe.

The museum is entered by means of a large foyer, which betrays its origins as a former machine hall. Centre stage is a full-size carnival float, which visitors can clamber around so as to get a feel for Carnival outside of the Carnival season itself. Since 1823 this has started officially "am elften elften elf Uhr elf" – 11th November at 11 minutes past 11am – with the proclamation of the new season, and continues until Ash Wednesday (Aschermittwoch). A lull in the preparations follows for the celebration of Advent and Christmas, after which the so-called Crazy Days *(Tolle Tage)* of Carnival commence on Alter Markt on the Thursday before Ash Wednesday – known as *Weiberfastnacht* (Women's Carnival). Around a million people take to the streets for the start of the celebrations, which reach their climax a few days later on Rose Monday *(Rosenmontag)*.

Also in the museum's foyer are numerous mannequins wearing the colourful uniforms and outfits of the hundred or more societies *(Gesellschaften)* that take part in Cologne's Carnival. Amongst them is a member of the *Rote Funken*, the red-uniformed city militia that Cologne was permitted to maintain during its time as a Free Imperial City from 1475 until 1794. The *Rote Funken* was one of the first Carnival societies to be established in 1823.

The Dreigestirn in the Cologne Carnival Museum (Kölner Karnevalsmuseum)

Moving into the museum proper there is a small display cabinet containing a fine Meissen porcelain clown, a *Lappenclown* so-called because of the coloured rags that make up his outfit. He represents Carnival for the people in much the same way that the Harlequin represented the masked ball for the nobility. This distinction is still felt today as Cologne's Carnival is celebrated democratically across the city, from the humblest of backstreet bars *(Kneipe)* and suburban schools to the Gürzenich, a splendid Gothic festival hall at Martinstrasse 29 (Altstadt-Nord).

The galleries beyond take the visitor on a journey down the ages – quite literally as many of the display cases take the form of carnival floats – from the time of Classical antiquity onwards. Themes include Shrovetide and Lent, the role of the Fool, the Baroque period in Europe and the influence of Italian *Commedia dell'Arte*, Carnival during the Third Reich and the years of Germany's Economic Miracle *(Wirtschaftswunder)*, as well as the medals, music, and shows *(Sitzungen)* that accompany the celebrations.

A few of the colourful uniforms worn during the Cologne Carnival

There are also samples of the one hundred and forty tons of sweets *(Kamelle)* tossed into the crowds along the six and a half kilometre-long route taken by the Rose Monday procession. At the end of it the onlookers are rewarded with the sight of the three stars of the show, the prince *(Prinz)*, the maiden *(Jungfrau)*, and the farmer *(Bauer)*, who also open the proceedings in Alter Markt. Known as the *Dreigestirn* they have been Carnival's three most important figures since the 1820s, and consequently are represented by a museum display case all of their own. With shield, keys, and a crenellated crown respectively they represent Cologne's continuing strength and independence.

A statue on one side of the Eigelsteintorburg depicts the *Köllsche Boor*, clutching the keys to Cologne in one hand and a shield bearing the crest of the German Empire in the other. He represents the steadfast protection of the city as well as loyalty to the Wilhelmine empire. With the prince and the maiden, he makes up the trio of characters at the heart of Cologne's Carnival (see no. 24).

72   A Hidden Roman Tomb

Lindenthal (Borough 3), the Roman Burial Chamber in Weiden
(Römische Grabkammer in Weiden) at Aachener Strasse 1328
Stadtbahn 1 Weiden Schulstrasse; Bus 141

Just as the urban sprawl of modern Cologne reaches into the coun-
tryside in all directions, so Roman Cologne (Colonia Agrippinensis)
was surrounded by suburbs and estates (see no. 1). There were also
numerous cemeteries beyond the Roman city walls, although most of
the surviving funerary monuments are now in museums. Far off the
tourist route, however, at Aachener Strasse 1328 in the borough of Weiden, there can be found a magnificent Roman tomb still in its original
state. A sensational find in 1843, the Roman Burial Chamber in Weiden
(Römische Grabkammer in Weiden) was opened to the public as early
as 1845. Restored during the 1970s it remains one of the most exciting
remnants of the Roman period in Cologne.

The tomb lies to the side of a normal suburban house, two blocks
west of the Weiden Schulstrasse Stadtbahn station, where its entrance
is covered by a sturdy modern structure inscribed "Roemergrab". Here
the householder directs visitors down a flight of stairs into a cool, brick-
vaulted, outer chamber which contains a handful of Roman artefacts,
and plans of the tomb. A further flight of stairs, past a portcullis-style
doorway, leads to the tomb proper, seemingly unaffected by the passage of almost two thousand years.

The tomb chamber measures twelve metres square, lies five and a
half metres beneath ground level, and has a floor made of stone slabs
(the lifting holes can still be seen). The focal point today is a damaged
white marble sarcophagus that once sat on top of the chamber's col-
lapsed vault. It is beautifully carved with reliefs of winged goddesses
flanking a portrait medallion, which presumably depicts the deceased.
Historians have suggested that in Roman times the tomb was located
on the private estate of a wealthy family, several generations of which
were laid to rest here.

According to the dates on coins found inside the tomb it was constructed sometime in the middle of the second century, originally as a
place in which to store funerary urns. These would have been placed
inside the twenty eight large and small niches cut into the chamber
walls. Two of the larger niches now contains portrait busts, again presumably of the deceased, including a distinctively moustachioed man

Inside the Roman Burial Chamber in Weiden (Römische Grabkammer in Weiden)

and a woman with a garment thrown over her shoulders. The tomb continued in use until the mid-fourth century, by which time bodies were probably also being interred in the tomb.

Either side of the doorway into the chamber are two limestone armchairs carved to look like wickerwork. It is thought that they might have been used by women at funerary feasts in honour of the dead; the men may have reclined on portable couches, or perhaps the stone bed-like arrangements inside the large niches.

The tomb is today administered by the Romano-Germanic Museum (Römisch-Germanisches Museum) at Roncalliplatz 4 (Altstadt-Nord), where further details about Roman funerary practice can be found in the basement. Although the names of those buried in the chamber are long lost, their memory lives on beneath the soil of suburban Weiden.

73 Historic Housing Estates

Lindenthal (Borough 3), the Gartenstadt Stadion housing
estate on Stadthalterhofallee, Frankenstrasse and
Paul-Finger-Strasse
Stadtbahn 1 Junkersdorf; Bus 143

During the 1920s and 30s the green belt beyond Cologne's Militärringstrasse, once the site of the city's outer line of Prussian-built defences (Äusserer Festungsgürtel), was targeted for development by
city planners. Partly to address Germany's post-war housing crisis, and
partly to fulfill the promise of Article 155 of the 1919 Weimar Constitution (which provided for "a healthy dwelling" for all Germans), single-
family homes and housing estates were erected in the fields of what
are today the boroughs of Lindenthal and Rodenkirchen. However, just
as the pared-down Modernist style of such architecture – the so-called
Neue Sachlichkeit (New Objectivity) – was beginning to transform the
landscape of cities such as Cologne, it was forcibly abandoned by the
Nazis in favour of more traditional forms.

A particularly interesting example of a *Neue Sachlichkeit* estate in
Cologne was constructed between 1930 and 1936 on a parcel of land
in the district of Junkersdorf (Lindenthal). Called the Gartenstadt Stadion after the Müngersdorf Stadium (the predecessor of today's Rhein-
EnergieStadion) it was originally slated to contain two hundred and
fifty buildings. By 1933, however, with the accession to power of the
Nazis and the global economic crisis, only thirty buildings had been
completed. These can be seen today on Frankenstrasse, Paul-Finger-
Strasse, and Stadthalterhofallee. Consisting of interlocked cubes with
plain white façades and flat roofs the single-family homes are the work
of an architectural partnership that comprised Ulrich Pohl, Heinrich
Reinhardt, Edmund Bolten, and H. Walter Reitz. In a direct reference
to the Weimar Constitution article a Cologne newspaper declared in
1931: "Gartenstadt Stadion – Erholungsurlaub im eigenen Haus" (Gartenstadt Stadion – A holiday in your own home). The article went on to
describe the advantages of modern architecture in a suburban location,
where sunlight and fresh air were available in abundance.

Despite such obvious benefits to the inhabitants of Cologne, conservative elements in German society feared the freedom of expression
contained within the *Neue Sachlichkeit* movement, and it was sup-
pressed. The result of this can be seen in the second building phase

A house with a flat roof in the Gartenstadt Stadion housing estate in Lindenthal

of the Gartenstadt Stadion, which commenced in 1935 under Wilhelm Wucherpfennig. At Frankenstrasse 54 he built a dwelling with a traditional sloping roof, in stark contrast to the modern-looking, flat-roofed houses of the first phase. A darkly comic episode ensued in which the owners of the flat-roofed properties complained that the introduction of sloping-roofed properties would disturb the original unified appearance of the estate, and that property prices might drop. In typical Nazi style the case was referred to the Reichskammer der Bildenden Künste (Reich Chamber of Applied Arts), which, not surprisingly, ruled in favour of the property with the sloping roof, and many more followed (the two styles can best be compared on Paul-Finger-Strasse, where they face each other across the street).

Needless to say the Nazi propaganda machine turned the situation to its favour by suggesting that the owners of flat-roofed properties were un-German. The ludicrous situation was summed up in a headline in the NSDAP weekly newspaper *Westdeutscher Beobachter*, which suggested that people living in flat-roofed houses lacked brains: "Häuser ohne Dach – Menschen ohne Kopf"! With the *Neue Sachlichkeit* in an early grave, the baton of Modernist architecture was taken up in America, where it gave rise to the International Style.

A housing estate with a very different history can be found not far away at the junction of Salzburger Weg and Dürener Strasse. This

This house with a pitched roof was favoured by the National Socialists

is the Stadtwaldviertel estate, which began life in 1936 as the Wehrmacht's Etzel Barracks (Etzelkaserne) (the name Etzel is German for Attila, the ruler of the Huns). After the Second World War the buildings were used as a holding centre for up to 2500 displaced Polish persons awaiting repatriation, mostly former prisoners of war and forced labourers. Despite severe overcrowding the British camp administration ensured that inmates' medical and spiritual requirements were adequately satisfied. Between 1949 and 1996 Belgian troops used the barracks as their Kwartier Haelen, named after a municipality in the south-eastern Netherlands. After their departure the barracks were transformed into the Stadtwaldviertel housing estate.

Other places of interest nearby: 74

74 A Kidnapping in Lindenthal

Lindenthal (Borough 3), the Hanns-Martin Schleyer Memorial at the junction of Friedrich-Schmidt-Strasse and Vincenz-Statz-Strasse
Stadtbahn 1 Eupener Strasse

The film *Deutschland im Herbst (Germany in Autumn)* released in 1978 mixes documentary footage with traditional staged scenes to impart a sense of the political and social mood in Germany during the late 1970s. The timeframe is a two month period during 1977, when the prominent businessman Hanns-Martin Schleyer (1915–1977) was kidnapped, and later murdered, by the RAF-Rote Armee Fraktion (Red Army Faction), a far left militant organisation known also as the Baader-Meinhof Gang. The kidnapping occurred at the junction of Friedrich-Schmidt-Strasse and Vincenz-Statz-Strasse, in Cologne's district of Braunsfeld (Lindenthal). The site is today marked by a modest wooden cross. A visit there is a reminder of the climax of the gang's bloody campaign, which has since been dubbed the German Autumn (Deutscher Herbst).

Hans-Martin Schleyer spent the Second World war as a fervent SS officer, for which he was afterwards sentenced to three years in prison. Repatriated in 1948 he joined the board of directors at Daimler-Benz, narrowly missing the post of chairman. Instead he became increasingly active amongst employers' associations and was simultaneously president of both the Confederation of German Employers' Associations and the Federation of German Industries. His uncompromising behaviour during industrial disputes, his Nazi past, and his aggressive appearance on television soon made him the ideal Conservative target for the left-wing student movements of the late sixties.

The German Autumn commenced on 30th July 1977 with the botched kidnapping and shooting of the banker Jürgen Ponto. Schleyer was kidnapped on September 5th after his Mercedes was stopped when members of the RAF reversed a vehicle into its path, and then opened fire on the car and police escort using semi-automatic weapons. Shleyer's driver and three police officers were killed during the gun battle. Schleyer himself escaped unscathed but was spirited away by the RAF to an anonymous rented apartment in Erftstadt, twenty five kilometres south-west of Cologne. Once in captivity Schleyer was forced into appealing directly to the centre-left West German government under

Helmut Schmidt: his life would be spared in exchange for the freeing of the RAF's imprisoned comrades. Schmidt refused to negotiate, stating bluntly that Germany would not be blackmailed by terrorists. Forty three days of stalemate followed during which Schleyer was moved across the Dutch border to Brussels.

The situation took a dramatic turn on 18th October, when German counterterrorism forces at Mogadishu Airport ended the RAF hijacking of Lufthansa Flight 181, with help from the Popular Front for the Liberation of Palestine (PFLP). The hijackers had again demanded the release of imprisoned members of the RAF, as well as two Palestinian compatriots held in Turkey, and fifteen

The Hanns-Martin Schleyer Memorial in Lindenthal

million US dollars. Within hours of the hostages being freed the three most prominent imprisoned members of the RAF (Andreas Baader, Gudrun Ensslin, and Jan-Carl Raspe) were found dead in their prison cells. Ruled officially as suicide it has subsequently become an article of faith for some members of the left-wing community that the three were murdered by the state.

After the kidnappers received news of the deaths they removed Schleyer from Brussels and on 18th October shot him dead on the road to Mulhouse in France, where his body was left in the trunk of an abandoned car. The vehicle's location was given to the Deutsche Presse-Agentur office in Stuttgart and Schleyer's body was recovered the next day. He was buried in Stuttgart's Ostfilderfriedhof in a ceremony attended by his widow Waltrude, who for the rest of her life campaigned vociferously against granting clemency to former members of the RAF. Alongside the cross today is a stone column dedicated to all victims of terrorism.

Other places of interest nearby: 71, 73, 75, 76, 77

75 Adenauer the Innovator

Lindenthal (Borough 3), the former home of Konrad Adenauer
at Max-Bruch-Strasse 4–6
Stadtbahn 7 Brahmsstrasse; Bus 136

The Lindenthal home of Konrad Adenauer who became the
Chancellor of Germany

Cologne-born Konrad Hermann Joseph Adenauer (1876–1967) is best remembered as the first Chancellor of the Federal Republic of Germany, who between 1949 and 1963 pulled his country out of the ruins of the Second World War and transformed it into one of the most powerful nations in Europe. As the founder and leader of the Christian Democratic Union (Christlich Demokratische Union), a coalition of Catholics and Protestants that since 1946 has generally dominated German politics, he displayed shrewd, unswerving dedication to a broad-based vision of western-style democracy, capitalism, European integration, and anti-Communism. He restored the economy of West Germany to dominance in Europe, rebuilt its army, reached terms with France, helped establish European unity, fought relentlessly against the Communists in rival East Germany, made his nation a pillar of NATO and a firm ally of the United States, and commenced the difficult process of reconciliation with the Jews and Israel after the Holocaust. In summation Adenauer may not have reunified Germany but he certainly created prosperity, democracy, stability, and respect.

It was as the hardworking Mayor of Cologne, however, that Konrad

Adenauer first cut his political teeth. From 1917 until 1933, when he was deposed by the Nazis and interned at the Trade Fair (Kölnmesse) concentration camp in Deutz, he lived in a comfortable house at Max-Bruch-Strasse 4–6 (Lindenthal). The house is still there, with its white-washed walls and green-painted shutters, and above the entrance a re-lief showing three owls, an emblem chosen by Adenauer himself. Owls have long been associated with wisdom in the West, the connection going back at least as far as Ancient Greece, where both Athens (a city noted for its art and scholarship) and Athena (the city's patron goddess of wisdom) took the owl as a symbol.

Wisdom was something Adenauer displayed repeatedly during his years as Mayor, an innate talent that had already borne fruit during his time as Vice Mayor of Cologne between 1909 and 1917. Not many people realise that during the privations of the First World War he set up kitchens in working class districts to supply two hundred thou-sand rations a day. He also established large warehouses of food that enabled most people to avoid the worst of the shortages, patented rye flour as 'Cologne Economy Bread', and even pioneered a soya sausage.

Adenauer as Mayor did much to improve the infrastructure of Co-logne, and his efforts can still be appreciated today, despite the destruc-tion of the Second World War. It was Adenauer, for example, who on May 19th 1919 signed a document for the reopening of Cologne Univer-sity (Universität zu Köln), following a successful petition by Cologne City Council to the Prussian government. Founded in 1388 the univer-sity had been abolished by the French in 1798 because its professors, wishing to preserve their university's independence, had refused to swear an oath of allegiance to the French Republic. It was also Ade-nauer who re-established Cologne's Trade Fair (Kölnmesse) in 1924, promoted the development of Cologne's Butzweiler Airport in 1926, and invited Henry Ford to set up a car factory in the city in 1931 (see nos. 61 & 64).

Other innovations were of a more practical nature. After the First World War, for example, Adenauer commissioned the city planner Fritz Schumacher (1869–1947) and the garden architect Fritz Encke (1861–1931) to convert land won back by the defortification of Co-logne, resulting in a much-loved pair of green belts (Grüngürtel) (see no. 82). Adenauer was also responsible for initiating the construction of the Müngersdorfer Stadium on Aachener Strasse in 1923 (today the RheinEnergieStadion), and of the Mülheim Bridge (Mülheimer Brücke) in 1929 (rebuilt 1951). In late 1945 he actively encouraged the

This statue of Konrad Adenauer stands on Apostelnstrasse

restoration of the Volkstheater Millowitsch at Aachener Strasse 5 (Altstadt-Süd) because he thought the people needed something to laugh about again. The same people were ecstatic when in 1955 Adenauer visited Moscow and arranged for the return of the last German prisoners of war.

An unwitting innovation during the 1920s was the change in colour of Cologne's trams, after Adenauer's chauffeur crashed into one of them causing Adenauer facial injury. As a result the trams were painted a pale cream to reduce the likelihood of similar accidents happening again. Both the wisdom and the scars can be imagined when one gazes at the modest bronze statue of Konrad Adenauer, given by the grateful citizens of Cologne, which has stood since 1995 on Apostelnstrasse, close to where he lived as a young man.

Other places of interest nearby: 74, 76

76 How Hitler Became Chancellor

Lindenthal (Borough 3), the Schröder Villa at Stadtwaldgürtel
35; note: the villa can only be viewed from outside
Stadtbahn 7, 13 Wüllnerstrasse

On 4th January 1933 the Cologne banker and Nazi Party supporter Baron
Kurt von Schröder (1889–1966) hosted a two-hour secret meeting between Adolf Hitler (1889–1945) and the former Chancellor of Germany
Franz von Papen (1879–1969), in his neo-Classical villa at Stadtwaldgürtel 35 (Lindenthal). They discussed ways in which the Nazi Party could
seize power with Hitler as chancellor, despite the objections of the ail-
ing President of Germany Paul von Hindenburg (1847–1934). A metal
plaque outside the villa today records the event, and the fact that Hitler
succeeded to the chancellorship just a few weeks later on 30th January.
The German historian Karl Dietrich Bracher (b. 1922) dubbed the fate-
ful meeting the "time of birth of the Third Reich".

The events surrounding the meeting illustrate well the disparate
political forces at work during the last years of the Weimar Republic. On
1st June 1932 the Catholic nobleman, monarchist, and diplomat Papen
was appointed Chancellor of Germany by Hindenburg. The cabinet he
formed, with the help of General Kurt von Schleicher (1882–1934), enjoyed little support in the Reichstag except from the German National
People's Party (Deutschnationale Volkspartei), the main nationalist
party in Weimar Germany. Despite this Papen sought to impose his authoritarian rule, and overthrow the democratic system established by
the Weimar constitution. Accordingly he worked on the increasingly
senile Hindenburg to grant him emergency powers in order to dismiss
the cabinet of the Free State of Prussia, which represented the most
powerful remaining republican force within Germany. He also repealed
his predecessor's ban on the SA, the paramilitary wing of the nascent
Nazi Party, as a sop to Hitler in the hope that he would support the new
government.

Papen then called for an election in July 1932 but failed to get the
Reichstag majority he hoped for. On the contrary, the Nazis gained
enough seats to become the largest party, and so once again Papen
worked on Hindenburg, this time to secure the power to dissolve the
new Reichstag as soon as it came into being. He was caught out, however, when the Nazis under newly elected Reichstag president Hermann Göring (1893–1946) supported a Communist motion of censure,

The Schröder Villa on Stadtwaldgürtel where Hitler attended a meeting in January 1933

forcing a new election in November. This time the Nazis lost seats, and Papen still couldn't secure a majority, as a result of which Schleicher pressured him to resign.

Hindenburg now appointed Schleicher as chancellor believing it possible for him to form a broad-based coalition with the support of both the Nazis and the Social Democrats. Papen worked to undermine him and in early January met Hitler in the villa in Lindenthal to discuss plans to replace Schleicher with a right-wing coalition of Hitler, Papen, and Alfred Hugenberg (1865–1951) of the German National People's Party. Papen believed Hindenburg would put aside his Prussian scruples in favour of Hitler, if he could convince him that Hitler could be controlled in a cabinet not under Nazi Party domination. In the event, he was right about Hindenburg but wrong about Hitler. Once Hitler assumed chancellorship he quickly marginalised Papen, who left the government in August 1934 after the Nazi purge known as the Night of the Long Knives in which Schleicher was gunned down in his own home.

But what of Kurt von Schröder, whose luxurious home had provided the backdrop to the now infamous meeting? Compared with Papen he enjoyed a charmed life during the years of the Third Reich. His right-wing political beliefs prompted him to join the Keppler Circle (Keppler-Kreis), a think tank of economists and industrialists whose members contributed large sums of money to Hitler and his party during the 1930s, in the hope that they would create a politically and economically stable Germany in which commerce would thrive. With Hitler in power, Schröder was rewarded with the chairmanship and board membership of many large German companies, as well as the presidency of the Rhineland Chamber of Commerce (Wirtschaftskammer Rheinland). An SS member, Cologne councillor, and trustee of Cologne University, Schröder was also instrumental in the 'Aryanisation' of the private banking system in Germany. At the end of the war he was discovered in a French prisoner of war camp and tried for crimes against humanity. He got off lightly with a fine and just three months' imprisonment, and it is difficult not to think that he took quite a few secrets with him to the grave.

Another building associated with Hitler is the former bank at An der Dominikanern 2 (Innenstadt), which from 1933 onwards served as the headquarters of the German Workers' Front under Cologne-born Robert Ley (1890–1945). The organisation replaced the unions dissolved by the National Socialists, and also included the Strength through Joy organisation (Kraft durch Freude), which was designed to offer organised leisure activities to the German work force.

Other places of interest nearby: 74, 75, 77

77 Napoleon's Cemetery

Lindenthal (Borough 3), the Melaten Cemetery
(Friedhof Melaten) on Aachener Strasse
Stadtbahn 1, 7 Melaten

In 1804 during the French occupation of the Rhineland Emperor Napoleon I (1769–1821) ordered that henceforth all burials in Cologne were to take place beyond the city walls. His edict was based on reasons of hygiene in accordance with the traditions of Ancient Rome. Although the walls have long since been demolished, the Melaten Cemetery (Friedhof Melaten) on Aachener Strasse, which opened on 29th June 1810, has remained Cologne's most important burial ground ever since.

The name Melaten is derived from the French word *malade*, meaning sick, since the cemetery was founded on the site of a former hospice for lepers, which had existed since the twelfth century. The location of

This statue marks the entrance to the Melaten Cemetery (Friedhof Melaten) in Lindenthal

the hospice beyond the city gates ensured that any risk of contagion was contained (a wall niche outside the main entrance contains the statue of a man carrying a rattle, used to warn people when he accompanied a leper on a temporary journey outside the hospice). Until the 1790s the site was also used for executions and witch burnings (see no. 17).

The Melaten Cemetery was laid out on a grid pattern in the style of the Père Lachaise Cemetery in Paris, which Napoleon had commissioned for identical reasons several years earlier. In both cemeteries the main paths are lined with the imposing tombs and mausoleums of the well-to-do, whereas the graves of the less well-off are relegated to the second row, and the poorest to the furthest reaches of the cemetery, where their graves were often reused after fifteen years. Any number of grave styles can be detected from neo-Classical, neo-Gothic and neo-

Baroque to Art Nouveau and Modernist. Rich or poor, the many and varied monuments are fascinating to visit today, especially on All Hallows Eve (October 31st), when the cemetery stays open a little later, and the graves are ablaze with candles.

Until 1829 only Catholics were permitted burial in the Melaten Cemetery, whilst Protestants were buried in the so-called Geusenfriedhof beyond the Weyertor gate; until 1918 Jews were buried in their own cemetery in Deutz (see nos. 48 & 65).

Many of Cologne's celebrated inhabitants have found a final resting place at Melaten, including the inventor of the four-stroke engine Nicolaus August Otto (1832–1891) (Group C), the creator of *Eau de Cologne* Johann Maria Farina (1658–1766) (Row 60), and the brave champion cyclist Albert Richter (1912–1940) (Group E8), who was murdered by the Gestapo for opposing the Hitler regime. More recent incumbents include Heinz G. Konsalik (1921–1999) (Row 69a), the bestselling author of *Der Arzt von Stalingrad (The Doctor of Stalingrad)* and post-war Germany's most successful novelist, and the phenomenally popular stage and television actor Willy Millowitsch (1909–1999) (Row 72a), who brought Cologne dialect performances to a pan-German audience.

Visiting the Melaten Cemetery in spring can be a delight, when the many trees and shrubs that grow between two centuries' worth of tombs, headstones, and sculptured angels, burst into life. At this time the cemetery feels more like a park than a place of mourning, with more than forty species of birds and mammals in attendance. In addition to the squirrels, bats, and foxes there are also wild parrots that for several decades have made their home here. Perhaps the most unusual inhabitants have been the living people of Cologne, some of whom used the larger mausoleums as temporary lodgings after their homes were destroyed during the Second World War.

Walking around Melaten Cemetery it is obvious that many of the older graves are now untended. In 1981, so as to prevent them from collapsing, a plan was drawn up *(Patenschaften)* whereby interested parties are now able to adopt a particular grave in order to restore and protect it, at their own expense. In return they are presented with a legal document, and the right to use the grave themselves if they so wish. In this way more than five hundred historic graves have been preserved for posterity.

Other places of interest nearby: 38, 70, 76

78 The University Coal Mine

Lindenthal (Borough 3), the Barbarastollen training mine
beneath the Main Building (Hauptgebäude) of the University
of Cologne (Universität zu Köln) on Albertus-Magnus-Platz
Stadtbahn 9 Universität

The University of Cologne (Universität zu Köln) was founded in 1388 as the fourth university of the Holy Roman Empire. Abolished by the French in 1798 it was re-established by Prussia in 1919, and is today one of the largest universities in Germany. Attached to the various faculties of the university are some of Cologne's least known museums. Open by appointment these specialist collections include the Egyptian Collection (Ägyptische Sammlung) at Meister-Ekkehart-Strasse 7, the Prehistoric Collection (Prähistorische Sammlung) at Weyertal 125, the GeoMuseum at Zülpicher Strasse 49, and the Musical Instrument Collection (Musikinstrumentensammlung) and Papyrus Collection (Papyrussammlung), both in the Main Building (Hauptgebäude) on Universitätstrasse.

The most unexpected university museum, however, lies entirely hidden from view. Just a few metres away from the students' cafeteria in the Main Building (Hauptgebäude) there is a doorway that gives access to several flights of stairs leading down to the so-called Barbarastollen. Visited by appointment only (tel. 0049-(0)221-478-4451) this forty metre long artificial coal mine is named after the patron saint of miners, the word *Stollen* being German for tunnel or adit.

The Barbarstollen was constructed in 1932 for training purposes, as

The Barbarastollen training mine beneath the University
of Cologne (Universität zu Köln)

part of the School of Economics and Social Sciences (Wirtschafts- und Sozialwissenschaften). Abandoned during the Second World War the entrance was not reopened until the 1980s, having been concealed behind a bookcase. Since 1984 the mine has been administered by the Institute for Industrial Medicine, Social Medicine and Social Hygiene (Institut für Arbeitsmedizin, Sozialmedizin und Sozialhygiene), who in conjunction with the company Ruhrkohle AG renovated it and now conduct the tours.

Upon entry visitors are equipped with a hard hat: the ceiling is low as in a real mine. The walls of the mine are made of stone and wooden props, supported by steel girders. The real coal, which was brought from a real mine in Aachen, is attached to the walls with tar. The machinery, including a cage lift, hoist, air drill, and cat's eye signal, were donated by various companies throughout Germany. Similarly with the track way running along the centre of the tunnel, along which runs a tractor hauling coal-filled wagons. So accurate is the reconstruction that it is easy to forget the university lies right above one's head!

The walls of the training mine are lined with real coal

As a part of the Institute for Industrial Medicine the Barbarastollen serves an important educational function, reminding visitors and students alike of the hardships and dangers of working in a coal mine during the 1920s and 30s. Although today's modern machinery is considerably improved, the miners themselves (including children in some countries) are still at risk from coal dust and noise, and these aspects of mining are illustrated during the tour. Upon leaving the mine the visitor might be fortunate in receiving a small glass of Schnapps, something that a real miner would certainly be grateful for after a long shift at the coal face.

It is interesting to note that a real coal seam was discovered in the Cologne borough of Kalk in the mid-nineteenth century. In 1856 a mining concession was granted to one Wilhelm Eckardt, who oversaw the excavation of a shaft more than a hundred feet deep. Unfortunately, the operation failed due to seeping groundwater, and in 1858 the land was sold to the Sünner Brewery (Sünner Brauerei) for the construction of their headquarters at Kalker Hauptstrasse 260 (see no. 49).

Other places of interest nearby: 36, 37, 38, 77

79 From Cemetery to Market Hall

Rodenkirchen (Borough 2), the Great Market Hall (Grossmarkt-halle) at Marktstrasse 10
Bus 132, 133 Mannsfeld
(From 2015: Nord-Süd-Stadtbahn Marktstrasse)

It is difficult today to imagine that the land now occupied by Cologne's Great Market Hall (Grossmarkthalle) at Marktstrasse 10 (Rodenkirchen) was once the site of a twelfth century Jewish cemetery. In 1348 the Black Death swept through Europe leaving an estimated thirty five million people dead in its wake. Oblivious to the fact that the spread of disease was facilitated by poor hygiene and sanitation, many Europeans turned to astrological alignments, earthquakes, and the poisoning of wells by the Jews in their bid to find an explanation. There were many attacks against Jewish communities including those in Mainz and Strasbourg, and in August 1349 Cologne's Jewish cemetery on Bonner Strasse (Rodenkirchen) was desecrated. Not until 1922 was evidence for the cemetery uncovered, and in 1936, when the land was cleared for construction of the new market hall, the human remains were transferred to the Jewish cemetery in Bocklemünd (see no. 65).

Cologne's original market hall stood on Heumarkt, where it was erected in 1904. When it became outdated a replacement was designed by the architect Theodor Teichen (1896–1963) for construction away from the city centre in the district of Raderberg (Rodenkirchen). The new wholesale market site consisted of numerous buildings, the most imposing of which was undoubtedly the Great Market Hall. Constructed between 1937 and 1940 it consists of a colossal vaulted cold storage cellar, over which is seated a 132 meter-long hall. This is in turn roofed with a parabolic arch of steel-reinforced concrete reaching fifty seven metres in height. So successful, sturdy, and capacious was the design that it was quickly taken up by the German Luftwaffe for their aircraft hangars! Although the Great Market Hall was damaged during the Second World War it was later rebuilt, and still continues in its original function to this day, turning over 1.2 million tons of produce annually.

Visiting the Great Market Hall today is an unusual experience. The main entrance facing the car park, where trucks and vans come and go continually, is marked by a huge clock. Beyond the swing

Inside the Great Market Hall (Grossmarkthalle) in Rodenkirchen

doors are row upon row of lockable kiosks, each belonging to a different trader, from where fruit, vegetables, fish, and meat is sold. Business is conducted from Monday to Friday between 2 am and 1 pm, and on Saturdays until 8 am. Outside of those hours the hall is all but empty.

All is not quite as it seems though. Just inside the main entrance there is a balcony, where a cafeteria once did brisk business with the market traders. It's all boarded up and gathering dust now. Similarly, the huge vaulted storage cellar, which can be reached via a ramp at the side of the hall, has been mostly abandoned, its eerie acoustics and myriad dark corners now frequented only by filmmakers. It seems that market trading has changed in recent years, and plans are afoot to relocate the market once again this time to the district of Marsdorf on the city boundary, where transport connections are better. This is scheduled to happen around 2020 at which time the Great Market Hall will be left empty. Fortunately, as a listed building on account of its stunning architecture, it is hoped the old hall will find a new lease of life as an unusual housing project.

Alongside the Great Market Hall there is a much smaller structure that was another element in the original architectural scheme for the

A warren of vaulted storerooms lie beneath the Great Market Hall

market. The Old Auction House (Alte Versteigerungshalle) is a Bauhaus-style building that provides an almost delicate counterpoint to the enormous market hall. Also a listed building it has already lost its original function and been transformed into an events venue.

Those who enjoy the bustle and colour of traditional streets markets will find several in Cologne. One of them, the Markt Altstadt-Nord, has taken place on Sudermanplatz every week since 1947 making it Cologne's oldest. What sets it apart is its down-to-earth atmosphere, as older locals rub shoulders with Turks and visitors.

Other places of interest nearby: 39

80 Controversy at the Martin Luther House

Rodenkirchen (Borough 2), the Martin Luther House
(Martin-Luther-Haus) at Mehlemer Strasse 27
Stadtbahn 16 Bayenthalgürtel; Bus 130
(From 2015: Nord-Süd-Stadtbahn Bonner Strasse Gürtel)

"Hier stehe ich, ich kann nicht anders" (Here I stand. I can do no other) reads an inscription on one side of the entrance to the Martin Luther House (Martin-Luther-Haus), a parish community centre at Mehlemer Strasse 27 (Rodenkirchen). The words are attributed to the German priest and theologian Martin Luther (1483–1546), who in 1521 at the Diet of Worms refused to retract a long list of Catholic heresies he had nailed to a church door in Wittenberg, thereby sparking the Protestant Reformation. Accompanying the inscription is a relief of Luther by the Cologne-born sculptor Willy Meller (1887–1974).

Directly opposite the inscription, on the other side of the entrance, is a second relief. Partially erased after the Second World War it depicts a member of the SA (Sturmabteilung), the paramilitary organisation that proved instrumental in Adolf Hitler's rise to power; alongside it is a Reich eagle clutching a wreath and a swastika. Flanking the relief is a quotation credited to Hitler: "Wenn so die Welt gegen uns steht dann müssen wir um so mehr zu einer Einheit werden" (If the world is against us we must be more united than ever)".

This seemingly curious mixture of images and words tells the on-looker much about Germany during the 1930s. The building was erected in 1933–1934 to a design by the Cologne architect Clemens Klotz (1886–1969), an architect favoured by the Nazi regime, who often worked in conjunction with Willy Meller (see no. 21). The reliefs were approved by the influential German banker and politician Robert Pferdmenges (1880–1962), in his capacity as a municipal leader, their purpose being to demonstrate the unswerving loyalty of German Christians to the Third Reich; in reality the National Socialists wanted faith in Christianity to be replaced by devotion to the Führer.

Does this mean that Pferdmenges was a Nazi? His former home around the corner at Pferdmengesstrasse 52 (a street named in his honour) is where a meeting took place after the First World War with his colleague and friend Konrad Adenauer (1876–1967), to discuss the composition of the first federal government. This, and the fact that after the

The partially erased relief in the Martin Luther House (Martin-Luther-Haus) in Rodenkirchen

Second World War he became active in the newly-formed Christian Democratic Union (Christlich Demokratische Union), suggests definitely not. However, to retain his status and freedom under the Nazi regime it was necessary for him to tread cautiously, and sometimes to kowtow to the regime. This would explain his approval of the reliefs, as well as facilitating the "voluntary" Aryanisation in 1936 of the Cologne-based bank of Salomon Oppenheim Junior (of which Pferdmenges was a partner) in order to preserve the German Jewish owners' assets. Pferdmenges' membership of Heinrich Himmler's Circle of Friends (Freundeskreis Heinrich Himmler) and involvement with the company German General Electric (AEG), which actively supported Hitler's war machine, are two other aspects of this highly politicised, well regarded, and controversial businessman's life.

And what of the inferred connection between the words of Martin Luther and the actions of the SA, who not only instigated street violence against Jews, Communists and Socialists, but also enforced boycotts against Jewish-owned businesses? The link is based upon anti-Jewish rhetoric found in Luther's later writings, which some historians believe contributed significantly to the development of anti-Semitism in Germany. Other historians disagree, seeing Luther's words as misguided but not racist. Whatever the truth, Luther's words were used by the Nazi regime to underpin its attacks on the Jews.

Visitors to the Martin-Luther-Haus today will find a modern information panel alongside the entrance explaining how the Nazi-controlled Protestant Church condoned a deliberate merging of Christian and National Socialist ideologies. In so doing the Church failed its congregation, as emphasised by a Biblical inscription added to the SA relief in 1984: "Gerechtigkeit erhöht ein Volk; aber die Sünde ist der Leute Verderben" (Righteousness exalts a nation; But sin is a disgrace to any people) (Proverbs 14:34).

Other places of interest nearby: 81

81 Building Towers for Bismarck

Rodenkirchen (Borough 2), the Bismarck Tower (Bismarckturm)
on Bayenthalgürtel
Stadtbahn 16 Bayenthalgürtel; Bus 130

Many things have been named after Otto Eduard Leopold von Bismarck (1815–1898), the Minister-President of the Kingdom of Prussia
(1862–1890), Federal Chancellor of the North German Confederation
(1867–1871), and first Chancellor of the newly-unified German Empire
(1871–1890). Schools, towns, mountains, ships, a coal mine, and even a
type of pickled herring have all borne his name. Such was the esteem
for the man responsible for creating the first German nation-state.

The most common and perhaps strangest symbol of Bismarck fa-
naticism that swept the young German nation was the Bismarck Tower
(Bismarckturm), a lofty monument erected with the sole purpose of
honouring the man's name, and reminding the onlooker that he or she
was a loyal German wherever they happened to live. Between 1869 and
1934 some two hundred and forty such towers were erected, across ten
different countries on four continents, with a further one hundred and
seventy planned but unrealised. Almost concealed today by a stand of
huge plane trees, Cologne's own Bismarck Tower overlooks the Rhine
at the end of Bayenthalgürtel (Rodenkirchen). Unveiled in 1903 it was
largely financed by the local chocolate manufacturer Ludwig Stollwerck (1857–1922).

The craze for building Bismarck Towers got off to something of a
slow start, with loyal followers initially favouring conventional wall
plaques, statues, and obelisks. It was only after Bismarck's resignation
as chancellor, at the insistence of German Emperor Wilhelm II, that
Bismarck hysteria really started to spread. Special committees were
established to decide how best to honour the 'Iron Chancellor', and
many planned traditional statues were abandoned in favour of the new
phenomenon of the Bismarck Tower. Fifteen were erected during Bismarck's lifetime, some in stone and others in wood, with most located
at prominent geographical positions.

Building towers for Bismarck really took off after his death in 1898.
In December of the same year the Deutsche Studentenschaft, a nationalist democratic students' organisation, announced an architectural design competition for Bismarck Towers under the motto "Flammen über
ganz Deutschland zu Ehren Bismarcks" (Flames over Germany to hon-

our Bismarck). The rules stipulated that the towers be constructed from durable German granite, that they be located on a highpoint away from other buildings, and that they have a brazier on top in which an eternal flame could be lit.

With a deadline of 1st April 1899 and a budget limit of twenty thousand Marks competition was strong. The titles of some of the designs, including *Deutsch bis ins Mark* (German to the core) and *Dem deutschesten Deutschen* (To the most German of Germans), sound rather ominous to modern ears. Letters were sent out to every German community of more than five thousand inhabitants, proposing the construction of a Bismarck Tower, and within six weeks every university town had signed up for the project. The eventual winner of the competition was the architect Wilhelm Kreis, whose entry *Götterdämmerung* took the form of an oversized column on a square base, with a viewing platform on the top.

The Bismarck Tower (Bismarckturm) on Bayenthalgürtel in Rodenkirchen

The imperial German government was never involved with the construction of the towers at anything more than a municipal level. Funds were raised from local donations rather than taxes, with each tower serving as an expression of a community's identity. Though based on a common ideal all the towers were different, the one in Cologne being fashioned in the colossal image of Bismarck himself. The times when the brazier was ignited differed, too, being either Bismarck's birthday, the date of his death, the anniversary of the Battle of Sedan, or simply during the town's own celebrations. Despite inflation during the 1920s putting pay to the lighting of the braziers, one hundred and seventy two Bismarck Towers are still standing and together they document an intriguing chapter in German history.

Other places of interest nearby: 80

82 Once Germany's Largest Fortress

Rodenkirchen (Borough 2), the Cologne Fortress Museum
(Kölner Festungsmuseum) at Militärringstrasse 10
Stadtbahn 16 Heinrich-Lübke-Ufer; Bus 130

Although Cologne survived the Reformation and the Counter Reformation largely unscathed, by the late seventeenth century its time as a booming medieval *Hanse* town was long over, reflected in the fact that work on the city's great Gothic cathedral had already ground to a halt in 1560 through lack of funds. In 1815 Cologne came under Prussian administration, and eventually in 1842 King Frederick William IV (1840–1861) allowed work on the cathedral to re-commence. This signalled a revival of Cologne's economic fortunes, which had been kick-started during the earlier French occupation of the city (see no. 17).

Under Prussian administration the Rhineland became a bastion of German liberty and independence, and Cologne was transformed into the country's largest fortress. Rather than a continuous wall, as the city's earlier Roman and medieval walls had been, the new Prussian fortifications consisted of two concentric rings of fortresses, each fortress self-contained with its own garrison. The Inner Fortification Ring (Innerer Festungsgürtel) was the first to be built, between 1816 and 1863, and was located just outside the line of the medieval wall (see no. 35).

It consisted of eleven forts interspersed with seven munitions depots known as *lunettes*. During the late nineteenth century, however, when many people arrived in Cologne to take advantage of the Industrial Revolution, the medieval wall was demolished and Forts III, IV, V, VI and VII of the Inner Fortification Ring were abandoned in order to create space for new houses and parks. There are still remains to be seen, including Fort IV on Eifelstrasse (Neus-

The Cologne Fortress Museum (Kölner Festungsmuseum)
on Militärringstrasse

tadt-Süd), which is now the centrepiece of the pretty Volksgarten (an adjacent *lunette* became an *orangerie*), and Fort V between Zülpicher Strasse and Otto-Fischer-Strasse, which is occupied today by the University of Cologne's Department of Geography and Nuclear Chemistry.

The Prussian military authorities would certainly not have agreed to the abandonment of the forts if they were not confident in the effectiveness of their Outer Fortification Ring (Äusserer Festungsgürtel), which was constructed between 1873 and 1881. This consisted of twelve forts interspersed with twenty three smaller forts known as *Zwischenwerke*. As its name suggests the Outer Fortification Ring was located well beyond the Inner Fortification Ring, and was a direct response to the increase in canon-firing distances. The forts were surrounded by barbed wire-filled ditches and serviced by almost two hundred ancillary buildings, many of which functioned as powder magazines. Movement between the forts was possible by a road called the Militärring, beyond which was a one kilometre-wide no-man's land, left clear to deprive enemies of cover. The Outer Fortification Ring remained fully operational until the end of the First World War, when the Rhineland was demilitarised under the terms of the Treaty of Versailles and the forts were rendered militarily useless.

Again there are still remains to be seen, most of which can be visited on Cologne's annual Day of the Forts (www.tag-der-forts.de). Of particular interest is Zwischenwerk VIIIb at Militärringstrasse 10 (Rodenkirchen), which now contains the Cologne Fortress Museum (Kölner Festungsmuseum). Displayed inside a series of authentic brick-vaulted casemates are many fascinating plans, photographs, and artefacts that help bring the Prussian defences back to life. After the Second World War the fortress was occupied for a time by the homeless.

It was Cologne's mayor, the ever innovative Konrad Adenauer (1876–1967), who during the 1920s decreed that where possible the remaining forts, together with their no-man's land, should serve as a recreational greenbelt *(Grüngürtel)*. This explains the origin of three oddities in Rodenkirchen: the pavilion in Raderthaler Volkspark at corner of Kardorfer Strasse and Pingsdorfer Strasse, which was originally a powder magazine; the large blocks of concrete rubble from Fort VI in woods near the Decksteiner Weiher; and similar rubble used to make a rhododendron rockery in the Forstbotanischer Garten at Schillingsrotter Strasse 100.

Other places of interest nearby: 83

83 The Legend of Bishop Maternus

Rodenkirchen (Borough 2), the Old Church of St. Maternus
(Alt-St.-Maternus-Kirche) on Steinstrasse
Stadtbahn 16 Rodenkirchen Bahnhof; Bus 130, 131

Perched on the left bank of the Rhine, on Steinstrasse in the district of Rodenkirchen, is a small whitewashed church dedicated to Saint Maternus (?–328), the first known bishop of Cologne. It was Maternus who founded a basilica on the site of a Roman temple in Cologne, out of which grew Cologne Cathedral (Kölner Dom) (see no. 11). A visit to the church, which couldn't be more different to the mighty cathedral, provides an opportunity to delve deeper into the story of one of Cologne's most important historical characters.

The Old Church of St. Maternus (Alt St. Maternus Kirche) stands on the banks of the Rhine

vHard facts are few when dealing with Maternus, and the truth can only be guessed at from a number of ancient legends concerning his life. As a sub-deacon it seems certain that he accompanied Deacon Valerius and Saint Eucharias to Gaul, whence they were sent by Saint Peter to preach the Gospel. However, when they arrived at Ehl (Gallo-Roman Ellelum) in Alsace, Maternus died unexpectedly. According to legend Valerius and Eucharius hastened quickly back to Rome, where they entreated Saint Peter to resurrect their dead companion. Saint Peter agreed and presented his pastoral staff to Eucharias, instructing him to touch Maternus with it, whereupon the dead man would return to life (the staff today resides in the cathedral's Treasury (Domschatzkammer)). Following this miracle the work of evangelisation continued apace, with many churches being founded along the way.

Legend relates how Eucharius selected Trier as his base, where he was bishop for twenty five years, being succeeded by Valerius, and eventually by Maternus, who had in the meantime established bishoprics in Cologne and Tongeren, the oldest city in Belgium. The earliest documentary evidence for Maternus dates from 313, when as Bishop of Cologne he was called to a synod in Rome by the Emperor Constantine I (272–337), to adjudicate on the Donatist Schism that was afflicting North Africa. In total Maternus served for forty years as a bishop and died in 328.

Legend steps in again now, wherein it is related how Trier, Cologne, and Tongeren argued over where Maternus should be laid to rest: after all he had been bishop to them all. Eventually it was agreed to leave it to the will of God, and his corpse was set adrift on a funeral barque on the Rhine. The citizens of Trier believed the vessel would naturally come to rest on their shores but it defied the river's current and made landfall in Rodenkirchen instead, where the body was taken ashore, buried, and a chapel erected on the site.

The story connecting Bishop Maternus with the little church in Rodenkirchen, which is numbered amongst thirteen Romanesque village churches beyond Cologne's old medieval walls, has never been verified. Those in favour suggest that the name 'Rodenkirchen' comes from 'Ruenkirchen', which is derived from the word 'Rauen', being dialect for the verb 'to mourn'. Against any connection is the long-held opinion that the building's oldest structural elements date only from the tenth century. In 1925, however, some dateable stones were uncovered during renovation work that push the foundation of the church back into early Christian times, suggesting that it might just be possible that the church seen today has its origins in the funerary chapel of legend. Despite this most historians now believe Maternus was buried in Trier after all.

Rodenkirchen's increasing population and a series of bad floods – the church contains flood markers from 1882, 1925–26, and 1993 – prompted the construction in 1867 of a new Church of St. Maternus, on higher ground at Hauptstrasse 19. Maternus has never been forgotten, however, and a statue of him outside the old church still looks out towards the Rhine.

The streets surrounding the church, namely Steinweg and Auf dem Brand, comprise what is known as Fischerdorf (Fishermen's Village). Worth visiting is the mid-sixteenth century Gaststätte zum Treppchen at Kirchstrasse 15, named after the steps leading down to the foreshore, and the half-timbered eighteenth century Restaurant Fährhaus, once a ferry boat terminal.

A window inside the church recalls the legend of Bishop Maternus

On the opposite side of the Rhine stands another small Romanesque place of worship, the Nikolauskapelle on Pfarrer-Nikolaus-Vogt-Weg (Porz). Older than Cologne Cathedral it was constructed during the twelfth century for use by the inhabitants of Westhoven, who until then travelled up to Deutz to celebrate the Catholic Mass. The chapel was probably also used by merchants who travelled this way to avoid Cologne's so-called *Stapelrecht*, whereby any goods passing through the city by road or river had to be offered in the city's markets for at least three days before proceeding (see no. 45).

Other places of interest nearby: 82

84 Gunpowder, Candles and Art

Rodenkirchen (Borough 2), the Kunstzentrum Wachsfabrik
at Industriestrasse 170
Stadtbahn 16 Michaelshoven, and then walk

The landscape of suburban Cologne, like that of so many European cities subject to industrialisation during the nineteenth century, is punctuated by chimneys and water towers, and many of them have a story to tell. In the car park of the KölnArkaden shopping centre in Kalk, for example, there stands a tall water tower that is all that remains of the once mighty Chemische Fabrik Kalk (CFK), a chemicals factory founded in 1858. Until its closure in 1993 the factory was one of Germany's largest producers of soda ash (used in the manufacture of glass and laundry powder) and also one of Cologne's largest employers. Different in function but no less interesting is a pair of brick-built chimneys in Ehrenfeld, one at Hospeltstrasse 32 marking a former brewery maltings opened in 1899 (now offices), and another at Hauptstrasse 14 in the village of Widdersdorf, erected in 1904 for a former Schnapps distillery (today apartments).

A particularly interesting story is recalled by a redundant red-brick chimney in the southern part of the Cologne at Industriestrasse 170 (Rodenkirchen). Old work halls clustered around the chimney are today the studios of the so-called Kunstzentrum Wachsfabrik (Wax Factory Art Centre), a vibrant and distinctive artists' colony.

A clue as to the origin of this former industrial site is in its name, since in 1930 it was the property of a wax company, the Rheinische Wachsindustrie Otto Josef Menden and Peter Pazen GmbH. Before this, however, it had served as a distillery and as a gunpowder and ammunition factory; the site had first been developed in 1812 by the company Henkel for the production of bleach and detergent. In 1935 the factory reverted to the production of ammunition in preparation for the Second World War, and it wasn't until afterwards that wax production was resumed once again. Candle production continued well into the 1970s, at which time the factory closed down for good.

In March 1979 the artist and teacher Michael teReh began to rent part of the abandoned site, and he advertised for other artists to join him there. Eight likeminded artists quickly signed up, and in September of the same year they exhibited their work at the official opening of what is today the Kunstzentrum Wachsfabrik. A varied cultural programme with exhibitions, concerts, and theatre performances has taken place on a regular basis ever since, supported by an active friends association (Freunde des Kunstzentrum Wachsfabrik e.V.). Even the City of Cologne has taken note of the activities at the old factory and rented space for their own cultural office there, as a result of which further premises were made available to budding artists. In 1982 the Cafe in der Wachsfabrik was opened for use by artists and visitors alike (each afternoon between Monday and Saturday), and part of the old factory has even been converted into very tasteful lofts for rental.

The Kunstzentrum Wachsfabrik on Industriestrasse in Rodenkirchen

In the thirty years since the centre was founded numerous artists, organisations, and art initiatives have passed through its doors, including dance troupes, youth theatres, and television companies. Today's artists in residence encompass many disciplines and include the photographer Sabine Burghardt, painters Josta Stapper and Jeannette de Payrebrune, and sculptors Wolfgang Heckmann and Sebastian Probst. Simone Neveling at Atelier 3 offers regular art workshops for children under the motto "Die Kunst ist frei" (Culture is free), and next door is the Barnes Crossing choreography group.

For open days when the twenty or so studios can be visited see www.kölner-wachsfabrik.de.

Standing in the sculpture park of the Wachsfabrik in Rodenkirchen is perhaps as good a place as any to finish this odyssey, during which some of the more unusual and unsung corners of Cologne have been explored. Looking back across the city gives the satisfied explorer the chance to reflect on the myriad peoples, personalities, powers, and pilgrims that have helped shape this most historic and storied of German cities.

Surprises await the visitor to the Kunstzentrum Wachsfabrik

Opening times

for museums and other places of interest (after each name is the borough, and its number, with district names in brackets for the Innenstadt only)
Correct at time of going to press but may be subject to change.

Abenteuerhallen Kalk, Kalk (Borough 8), Christian-Sunner-Strasse, Mon 6.30–10pm (children only 4–6pm), Tue & Thu 6.30–10pm, Fri 10am–2pm

Agrippabad, Innenstadt (Altstadt-Süd) (Borough 1), Kämmergasse 1, Mon–Fri 6.30am–10.30pm, Sat & Sun 9am–9pm

Antiquariat Stefan Kruger, Innenstadt (Altstadt-Nord) (Borough 1), Auf dem Berlich 26, Mon–Fri 10.30am–6.30pm, Sat 10am–5pm

Antonite Church (Antoniterkirche), Innenstadt (Altstadt-Nord), Schildergasse 57, Mon–Fri 11am–7pm, Sat 11am–5pm, Sun 11am–5.30pm

Archaeological Zone/Jewish Museum (Archäologische Zone/Jüdisches Museum), Innenstadt (Altstadt-Nord) (Borough 1), Rathausplatz, guided tours Fri 2pm by appointment only, tel. 0049-(0)221-221-33422

Barbarastollen, Lindenthal (Borough 3), Main Building (Hauptgebäude), University of Cologne (Universität zu Köln), Albertus-Magnus-Platz, guided tours by appointment only, tel. 0049-(0)221-478-4451

Baumschule Belnatura, Lindenthal (Borough 3), Widdersdorfer Landstrasse 103, Mon–Fri 9am–1pm, Sat 10am–2pm

Birds of Prey Conservation Centre (Greifvogel-Schutzstation), Porz (Borough 7), Gut Leidenhausen, between Grengeler Mauspfad, Hirschgraben and A59, Sun Apr–Sep 10am–6pm, Oct–Mar 10am–5pm

Bocklemünd Jewish Cemetery (Jüdischer Friedhof Bocklemünd), Ehrenfeld (Borough 4), Venloer Strasse 1152, Apr–Oct Mon–Thu 8.30am–6pm, Fri 8.30am–2pm, Sun 9am–6pm, Nov–Mar Mon–Thu 8.30am–5pm, Fri 8.30am–2pm, Sun 9am–5pm; men must cover their heads when visiting the cemetery

Brauerei zur Malzmühle, Innenstadt (Altstadt-Nord) (Borough 1), Heumarkt 6, Mon–Fri 11.30am–12pm, Sat & Sun 11.30am–11pm

Brauhaus Lommerzheim, Innenstadt (Deutz), Siegestrasse 18, Mon, Wed–Sun 11am–2pm, 4.30–12pm

Brauhaus Päffgen, Innenstadt (Altstadt-Nord), Friesenstrasse 64–66, Sun–Thu 10am–12pm, Fri & Sat 10am–12.30pm

Brauhaus Sünner im Walfisch, Innenstadt (Altstadt-Nord) (Borough 1), Salzgasse 13, Mon–Thu from 5pm, Fri from 3pm, Sat & Sun from 11am

Braustelle, Ehrenfeld (Borough 4), Christianstrasse 2, daily 6pm–1am

Butzweilerhof Aviation Exhibition (Butzweilerhof Luftfahrt Ausstellung), Ehrenfeld (Borough 4), Butzweilerstrasse 35–39, guided tours by appointment only, www.butzweilerhof.de

C&A, Innenstadt (Altstadt-Nord) (Borough 1), Schildergasse 60–68, Mon–Thu 9am–9pm, Fri & Sat 9am–10pm

Café Central, Innenstadt (Neustadt-Süd) (Borough 1), Jülicher Strasse 1, daily 7am–12pm

Cafe Franck, Ehrenfeld (Borough 4), Eichendorffstrasse 30, Tue–Sun 10am–7pm

Café Sehnsucht, Ehrenfeld (Borough 4), Körnerstrasse 67, Mon–Fri 8am–1am, Sat & Sun 9am–1am

Canyon Chorweiler, Chorweiler (Borough 6), Weichselring 6a, daily 10am–11pm

CCAA-Glasgalerie Köln, Innenstadt (Altstadt-Nord) (Borough 1), Auf dem Berlich 26, Tue–Fri 10am–1pm, 2–6pm, Sat 10am–4pm

Chandelier Hall (Kronleuchtersaal), Innenstadt (Neustadt-Nord) (Borough 1), corner of Theodor-Heuss-Ring and Clever Strasse, guided tours Mar–Sep on last Sat of the month by appointment only, tel. 0049-(0)221-221-26845, www.koelntourismus.de

Church of St. Andrew (St.-Andreas-Kirche), Innenstadt (Altstadt-Nord) (Borough 1), Komödienstrasse 6–8, Mon–Fri 7.30am–7pm, Sat & Sun 8am–6pm

Church of St. Aposteln (St.-Aposteln-Kirche), Innenstadt (Altstadt-Nord) (Borough 1), Apostelnkloster 10, Wed–Sun 10–12am, 3–5pm

Church of St. Cecilia (St.-Cäcilien-Kirche), Innenstadt (Altstadt-Süd), Cäcilienstrasse 29, Tue–Sun 10am–6pm (Thu 8pm)

Church of St. George (St.-Georgs-Kirche), Innenstadt (Altstadt-Süd) (Borough 1), Waidmarkt, daily 6.30am–6pm

Church of St. Gereon (St.-Gereons-Kirche), Innenstadt (Altstadt-Nord) (Borough 1), Gereonskloster, Tue–Fri 10–12am, 3–5pm, Sat 10–12am; crypt Wed 3–5pm, Sat 10–12am

Church of St. Heribert (St.-Heribert-Kirche), Innenstadt (Deutz) (Borough 1), Tempelstrasse 2, Tue 9–12am, Wed 4–5.30pm, Thu 9–12am, Fri 9–11am, 4–5.30pm

Church of St. Hubertus (St.-Hubertus-Kirche), Mülheim (Borough 9), Hubertusstrasse 3, Sun Mass 11.30am

Church of St. Kunibert (St.-Kuniberts-Kirche), Innenstadt (Altstadt-Nord) (Borough 1), Kunibertskloster 6, Mon–Sat 10am–1pm, 3–6pm, Sun 3–6pm

Church of St. Mariä-Himmelfahrt (St.-Mariä-Himmelfahrts-Kirche), Innenstadt (Altstadt-Nord), Marzellenstrasse 26, daily 9am–6pm

Church of St. Maria im Capitol (St.-Maria-im-Capitol-Kirche), Innenstadt (Altstadt-Süd) (Borough 1), Kasinostrasse 6, Mon–Sat 10am–6pm, Sun 12am–6pm

Church of St. Maria in der Kupfergasse (St.-Maria-in-der-Kupfergasse-Kirche), Innenstadt (Altstadt-Nord) (Borough 1), Schwalbengasse 1, daily 6.30am–7.30pm

Church of St. Maria in Lyskirchen (Kirche St. Maria in Lyskirchen), Innenstadt (Altstadt-Süd) (Borough 1), An Lyskirchen 8, Mon–Sat 10am–6pm, Sun 10am–4pm

Church of St. Martin the Great (Gross-St.-Martin-Kirche), Innenstadt (Altstadt-Nord) (Borough 1), An Gross St. Martin 9, Tue–Sat 8.30am–7.30pm, Sun 1–7.15pm

Church of St. Pantaleon (St.-Pantaleons-Kirche), Innenstadt (Itstadt-Süd) (Borough 1), Am Pantaleonsberg 8, Mon–Sat 9am–5pm, Sun 12am–5pm

Church of St. Severin (St.-Severins-Kirche), Innenstadt (Altstadt-Süd) (Borough 1), Severinskirchplatz, Mon–Sat 9am–6pm, Sun 9–12am, 3–5.30pm; guided tours of the crypt Fri 4pm

Church of St. Ursula (St.-Ursula-Kirche), Innenstadt (Altstadt-Nord) (Borough 1), Ursulaplatz 24, Mon, Tue, Thu & Fri 10–12am, 3–5pm, Wed & Sat 10–12am

Cigarette Lighter Museum (Feuerzeugmuseum), Porz (Borough 7), Bergerstrasse 136, Mon–Fri 10am–6.30pm

Claudiustherme, Innenstadt (Deutz) (Borough 1), Sachsenbergstrasse 1, daily 9am–12pm

Cologne Astronomical Observatory (Sternwarte Köln), Nippes (Borough 5), Blücherstrasse 15–17, demonstrations Sat 5.30pm, www.koelner-planetarium.de

Cologne/Bonn Airport "Konrad Adenauer", Porz (Borough 7), Waldstrasse 147, guided tours by appointment only Mon–Fri 8.30am, 10.00am, 10.30am, 11.45am, 12.45am, 1.30 pm and 3.15pm, www.koeln-bonn-airport.de

Cologne Carnival Museum (Kölner Karnevalsmuseum), Ehrenfeld (Borough 4), Maarweg 134–136, Thu 10am–8pm, Sat & Sun 11am–5pm; closed during August

Cologne Cathedral (Kölner Dom), Innenstadt (Altstadt-Nord) (Borough 1), Domkloster 4, May–Oct daily 6am–9pm, Nov–Apr 6am–7.30pm; Cathedral Treasury (Domschatzkammer), daily 10am–6pm

Cologne City Museum (Kölnisches Stadtmuseum), Innenstadt (Altstadt-Nord) (Borough 1), Zeughausstrasse 1–3, Tue 10am–8pm, Wed-Sun 10am–5pm, first Thu in the month 10am–10pm

Cologne Fortress Museum (Kölner Festungsmuseum), Rodenkirchen (Borough 2), Militärringstrasse 10, first Sat & third Sun in month, guided tours at 12am, 2pm and 4pm

Cologne Zoo (Kölner Zoo), Nippes (Borough 5), Riehler Strasse 173, Mar-Oct 9am–6pm, Oct–Mar 9am–5pm (aquarium until 6pm)

Commonwealth Cemetery (Commonwealth-Ehrenfriedhof), Rodenkirchen (Borough 2), Southern Cemetery (Südfriedhof), Höningerplatz, Nov–Feb 8am–5pm, Apr–Sep 7am–8pm, Oct 7am–7pm

Deutz Jewish Cemetery (Jüdischer Friedhof Deutz), Deutz (Borough 1), Judenkirchhofsweg, Apr–Oct Mon–Thu 8.30am–6pm, Fri 8.30am–2pm, Sun 9am–6pm, Nov–Mar Mon–Thu 8.30am–5pm, Fri 8.30am–2pm, Sun 9am–5pm; men must cover their heads when visiting the cemetery

District Heating Tunnel (Fernwärmetunnel), Innenstadt (Deutz) (Borough 1), corner of Messeplatz and Kennedyufer, guided tours by appointment only, tel. 0049-(0)221-178-4660, www.rheinenergie.de

Dünnwalder Freibad, Mülheim (Borough 9), Peter-Baum-Weg 20, summer daily 9am–8pm

Elendskirche St. Gregor, Innenstadt (Altstadt-Süd) (Borough 1), An St. Katharinen 5, mass Fri 7pm; other times by appointment only, tel. 0049-(0)221-31-42-75

Em höttche – Beim Aggi, Ehrenfeld (Borough 4), Körnerstrasse 41, daily 11am–12pm

English Shop, Innenstadt (Altstadt-Nord) (Borough 1), An St. Agatha 41, Mon–Sat 10am–8pm

Farina House Perfume Museum (Duftmuseum im Farina-Haus), Innenstadt (Altstadt-Nord) (Borough 1), Obenmarspforten 21 opposite Gülichplatz, Mon–Sat 10am–7pm, Sun 11am–4pm; guided tours available on request

Filz Gnoss, Innenstadt (Altstadt-Nord) (Borough 1), Apostelnstrasse 21, Mon–Fri 9.30am–6.30pm, Sat 10am–4pm

Finkens Garten, Rodenkirchen (Borough 2), Friedrich-Ebert-Strasse 49, Mon–Fri 9am–4pm, Sat & Sun 10am–4pm.

Flora and Botanical Garden (Flora und Botanischer Garten), Nippes (Borough 5), Am Botanischen Garten 19, daily 8am–9pm; hothouses Apr–Sep 10am–6pm, Oct–Mar 10am–4pm

Ford Works (Ford-Werke GmbH), Nippes (Borough 5), Henry-Ford-Strasse 1, guided tours by appointment only 9.30am & 1pm, tel. 0049-(0)221-901-9991, www.ford.de

Forstbotanischer Garten, Rodenkirchen (Borough 2), Schillingsrotter Strasse 100, Nov–Feb 9am–4pm, Mar, Sep & Oct 9am–6pm, Apr–Aug 9am–8pm

Früh em Veedel, Innenstadt (Altstadt-Süd) (Borough 1), Chlodwigplatz 28, Mon–Sat 11am–1am, Sun 10am–9pm

Früh im Haus Tutt, Ehrenfeld (Borough 4), Fridolinstrasse 72, Mon–Thu 11am–12pm, Fri & Sat 11am–1am

Glaub Besteckhaus, Innenstadt (Altstadt-Nord) (Borough 1), Komödienstrasse 101–113, Tue–Fri 10am–6pm, Sat 10am–2pm

Great Market Hall (Grossmarkthalle), Rodenkirchen (Borough 2), Marktstrasse 10, Mon–Sat 12pm–2pm

Gustav Brock, Innenstadt (Altstadt-Nord) (Borough 1), Apostelnstrasse 44, Tue–Fri 8am–6.30pm, Sat 8am–4pm

Hänneschen Puppet Theatre (Hänneschen Puppenspiele), Innenstadt (Altstadt-Nord) (Borough 1), Eisenmarkt 2–4, performances Wed–Sun, ticket office 3–6pm, www.haenneschen.de

Hari Om Mandir Afghan-Hindu Temple, Porz (Borough 7), Wikinger Strasse 62, Mon-Fri 8.30am–6.30pm, Sat 9am–5pm, Sun 9am–6.30pm

Honig Müngersdorff, Innenstadt (Altstadt-Nord) (Borough 1), An St. Agatha 37, Mon–Fri 8am–1pm, 2–5pm, Sat 8–12am

Hoss an der Oper, Innenstadt (Altstadt-Nord) (Borough 1), Breite Strasse 25–27, Tue & Wed 9.30am–6pm, Thu & Fri 9.30am–7pm, Sat 9am–4pm

Imhoff Chocolate Museum (Imhoff-Schokoladenmuseum), Innenstadt (Altstadt-Süd) (Borough 1), Am Schokoladenmuseum 1a, Tue–Fri 10am–6pm, Sat & Sun 11am–7pm

Japanese Garden, Mülheim (Borough 9), Kaiser-Wilhelm-Allee, May-Sep 9am–8pm, Oct–Apr 9am–dusk

Joyce Merlet's Museum of Puppet History (Museum der Puppengeschichte), Innenstadt (Altstadt-Nord) (Borough 1), Unter Goldschmied 3, Mon–Sat 9am–5pm

Jürgen Eifler, Innenstadt (Altstadt-Nord) (Borough 1), Friesenwall 102a, Mon-Fri 11am–6pm, Sat 11am–4pm

Käthe Kollwitz Museum, Innenstadt (Altstadt-Nord) (Borough 1), Neumarkt 18–24, Tue–Fri 10am–6pm, Sat & Sun 11am–6pm

Kervansaray Turkish Restaurant, Mülheim (Borough 9), Keupstrasse 25, daily 6am–3am

Kletterfabrik, Ehrenfeld (Borough 4), Lichtstrasse 25, Mon–Fri 9.30am–11.30pm, Sat & Sun 10am–10pm

Kölner Münzkabinett, Innenstadt (Altstadt-Nord) (Borough 1), Neven-DuMont-Strasse 15, Tue–Fri 10am–1pm, 3–6pm, Sat 10am–1pm

Kölner Weindepot Josef Wittling, Nippes (Borough 5), Amsterdamer Strasse 1, Tue–Fri 8am–7pm, Sat 8am–2pm

Kölnischer Kunstverein, Innenstadt (Altstadt-Nord) (Borough 1), Hahnenstrasse 6, Tue–Sun 11am–6pm

KölnTriangle Viewing Platform, Innenstadt (Deutz) (Borough 1), Ottoplatz 1, Oct–Apr Mon–Fri 12am–6pm, Sat & Sun 10am–6pm, May–Sep Mon–Fri 11am–10pm, Sat & Sun 10am–10pm

Kolumbamuseum, Innenstadt (Altstadt-Nord) (Borough 1), Kolumbastrasse 4, Wed–Mon 12am–5pm

KroKoLino Ferry, Porz (Borough 7), Zündorf, Groov quayside, every twenty minutes Mar–mid October Mon–Fri 11am–7pm, Sat & Sun 10am–8pm

KVB Tramway Museum Thielenbruch (KVB-Strassenbahn-Museum Thielenbruch), Mülheim (Borough 9), Gemarkenstrasse 139, Mar–Dec every second Sun in the month 11am–5pm

Melaten Cemetery (Friedhof Melaten), Lindenthal (Borough 3), Aachener Strasse, Apr–Sep 7am–8pm, Oct–Nov 8am–7pm, Dec–Mar 8am–5pm

Mikveh, Innenstadt (Altstadt-Nord) (Borough 1), Rathausplatz, Tue–Sun 10am–5pm; prior registration necessary in the Praetorium at Kleine Budengasse 2

Money History Museum (Geldge-schichtliches Museum), Innenstadt (Altstadt-Nord) (Borough 1), Neu-markt 18–24, Tue–Fri 9am–6.30pm, Sat 10am–2pm

Monika Nachbar Beauty Hair Acces-sories, Innenstadt (Altstadt-Nord) (Borough 1), Breite Strasse 161, Tue–Fri 9am–6pm, Sat 9am–4pm

Museum of East Asian Art (Museum für Ostasiatische Kunst), Innen-stadt (Neustadt-Süd) (Borough 1), Universitätsstrasse 100, Tue–Sun 11am–5pm; first Thu each month 11am–10pm

Museumsbunker Reichsbahn Aus-besserungswerk, Nippes (Borough 5), Werkstattstrasse 106, every sec-ond Sun in the month 10am–4pm

Musikhaus Tonger, Innenstadt (Altstadt-Nord) (Borough 1), Brücken-strasse 6, Mon-Fri 10am–7pm, Sat 10am–6pm

Mustard Museum (Senfmuseum), Innenstadt (Altstadt-Süd) (Bor-ough 1), Holzmarkt 79–83, Mon–Fri 10am–6pm, Sat & Sun 11am–7pm; demonstrations daily 11.15am, 12am, 1pm, 2pm, 3pm, 4pm

Naturfreibad Fühlinger See, Chor-weiler (Borough 6), Stallagsbergweg, Mon–Fri 10am–6pm, Sat & Sun 9am–6pm

Nazism Documentation Centre of Cologne (NS-Documentationsze-ntrum der Stadt Köln), Innenstadt (Altstadt-Nord) (Borough 1), EL-DE-Haus, Appellhofplatz 23–25, Tue–Fri 10am–6pm, Sat & Sun 11am–6pm; first Thu each month 10am–10pm

Neptunbad, Ehrenfeld (Borough 4), Neptunplatz 1, daily 9am–12pm

Old Church of St. Maternus (Alt-St.-Maternus-Kirche), Rodenkirchen (Borough 2), Steinstrasse, daily 9am–5pm

Old Protestant Cemetery (Alter Evangelischer Friedhof)/Geusen-friedhof, Lindenthal (Borough 3), Kerpenerstrasse, Apr–Sep 9am–7pm, Oct–Mar 10am–5pm

Papa Joe's Klimperkasten, Innen-stadt (Atstadt-Nord) (Borough 1), Alter Markt 50–52, daily 11am–3am

Peter Heinrichs, Innenstadt (Alt-stadt-Nord) (Borough 1), Hahnen-strasse 2–4, Mon–Fri 6am–8pm, Sat 7am–6pm

Praetorium/Roman Sewer (Römi-scher Abwasserkanal), Innenstadt (Altstadt-Nord) (Borough 1), Kleine Budengasse 2, Tue–Sun 10am–5pm

RadioMuseum Köln, Mülheim (Bor-ough 9), Waltherstrasse 49–51 Haus 32, second Sun each month 2–6pm

Rautenstrauch-Joest Museum – Cultures of the World, Innenstadt (Altstadt-Süd) (Borough 1), Cäcilien-strasse 29–33, Tue–Sun 10am–6pm, Thu 10am–8pm

Restaurant Haus Scholzen, Ehren-feld (Borough 4), Venloer Strasse 236, Wed–Sun 11.30am–3pm, 5–12pm

Rheinseilbahn, Nippes (Borough 5), Riehler Strasse 180, mid-Mar–mid-Nov10am–6pm

Rhineland Industrial Railway Museum (Rheinisches Industrie-bahn-Museum), Nippes (Borough 5), Longericher Strasse 249, monthly open days between Easter and October, www.rimkoeln.de

Roman Grave Chamber in Weiden (Römische Grabkammer in Weiden), Lindenthal (Borough 3), Aachener Strasse 1328, Tue–Thu 10am–1pm, Fri 10am–5pm, Sat & Sun 1–5pm; closed Summer and Christmas holidays

Romano-Germanic Museum (Römisch-Germanisches Museum), Innenstadt (Altstadt-Nord) (Bor-ough 1), Roncalliplatz 4, Tue–Sun 10am–5pm, Thu 10am–8pm; each first Thu in the month 10am–10pm

Schirm Bursch, Innenstadt (Altstadt-Nord) (Borough 1), Breite Strasse 104, Mon–Fri 10am–6.30pm, Sat 10am–3pm

Schnütgen Museum (Museum Schnütgen), Innenstadt (Altstadt-Süd) (Borough 1), Church of St. Cecilia (St.-Cäcilien-Kirche), Cäcili-enstrasse 29, Tue–Sun 10am–6pm (Thu 8pm)

Sterck Joh. Jos & Zoon, Innenstadt (Altstadt-Nord) (Borough 1), Neue Langgasse 4, Mon–Fri 9.30am–6pm, Sat 10am–6pm

Strohhut's Eck, Ehrenfeld (Bor-ough 4), Venloer Strasse/Ehrenfelder Gürtel, Mon–Fri 11am–7pm

Sünner Brewery (Sünner Brauerei), Kalk (Borough 8), Kalker Hauptstrasse 262, brewery tours and cellar by appointment only tel. 0049-2137-103786, www.suenner-brauerei.de; beer garden Apr–Sep Mon–Sat 12am–11pm, Sun 11am–11pm

Sürther Strasse Cemetery (Friedhof Sürther Strasse), Rodenkirchen (Borough 2), Sürther Strasse, Mar daily 8am–6pm, Apr–Sep daily 7am–8pm, Oct daily 7am–7pm, Nov–Feb 8am–5pm

Thurner Hof, Mülheim (Borough 9), Mielenforster Strasse 1, garden in summer months Sat from 12am, Wed from 4pm

Ubiermonument, Innenstadt (Altstadt-Süd) (Borough 1), An der Malzmühle 1, guided tours by appointment only, tel. 0049-(0)221-221-223-94

Vingster Freibad, Kalk (Borough 8), Vingster Ring, Summer Mon–Thu 10am–7pm, Fri–Sun 9am–7pm

Wallraf-Richartz Museum, Innen-stadt (Altstadt-Nord), Obenmarspfor-ten, Tue–Sun 10am–6pm (Thu 9pm)

Water Storage Tank Severin, Innen-stadt (Neustadt-Süd) (Borough 1), Zugweg 29–31, guided tours by appointment only, tel. 0049-(0)221-178-4660, www.rheinenergie.de

Weiler Waterworks (Wasserwerk Weiler), Chorweiler (Borough 6), Blockstrasse, guided tours by appointment only, tel. 0049-(0)221-178-4660, www.rheinenergie.de

Weisser Holunder, Innenstadt (Neu-stadt-Nord) (Borough 1), Gladbacher-strasse 48, Mon–Thu 4pm–1am, Fri 4pm–2am, Sat 11am–2am, Sun 11am–6pm

Winkelturm, Nippes (Borough 5), Neusser Landstrasse 2, every third Sat in the month 2–4pm

Jugendstil decoration at the Neptunbad in Ehrenfeld (see no. 70)

Bibliography

GUIDEBOOKS

DuMont direkt Köln (Marianne Bongartz & Stephanie Henseler), DuMont Reiseverlag, 2009

Köln City Guide (Kirsten Kabasci), Reise Know-How Verlag, 2009

Cologne: A Practical Guide (Kirsten Kabasci & Marcus Knupp), Emons, 2005

PastFinder ZikZak Cologne (Gregory Piatkowski), PastFinder Ltd, 2009

Marco Polo Köln (Jürgen Raap), Mairdumont, 2010

Der Kölner Museumsführer: Faszinierende, grosse und kleine, weltberühmte und versteckte Museen in Köln (Susanne Raupriche), Emons, 2010

DuMont Kunst Reiseführer Köln (Werner Schäfke), DuMont Reiseverlag, 2005

Cologne Photo Guide (Various), Monaco Books/Verlag Wolfgang Kunth, 2008

Cologne Baedecker Guide (Various), Karl Baedecker Verlag, 2009

SECRET COLOGNE

111 Kölner Orte, die man gesehen haben muss (Bernd Imgrund & Britta Schmitz), Emons, 2008

111 Kölner Orte, die man gesehen haben muss Band 2 (Bernd Imgrund & Britta Schmitz), Emons, 2009

Das unterirdische Köln: Spurensuche im Kölner Untergrund (Franz Jungeblodt & Csaba Peter Rakoczy), Bachem, 2008

Kölner Oasen: Bekannte und unbekannte Orte und Plätze der Beschaulichkeit und Ruhe (Franz Mathar), Greven 2001

Köln – Der andere Stadtführer (Martin Stankowski), Kiepenheuer & Witsch, 2003

Geheime Gärten im Kölner Süden – Eine Reise durch die schönsten privaten Hausgärten (Karola Waldek), Bachem, 2010

ILLUSTRATED BOOKS

Köln – Eine grosse Stadt in Bildern (Detlev Arens & Celia Cörber-Leupold), Greven, 2006

Köln Bilder: Ein Fotoalbum (Friedrich Riehl & Uwe Dettmar), Greven, 2007

Köln – Bilder und Geschichte (Elke Heidenreich & Stefan Worring), Kiepenheuer & Witsch, 2004

ARCHITECTURE AND MONUMENTS

Festungsstadt Köln: Preussens Bollwerk im Westen (Bernd von der Felsen), Emons, 2010

Romanische Kirchen in Köln (Werner Halmert), Kiepenheuer & Witsch, 2004

Mahnmalführer Köln: Ein Führer zu Kölner Denkmälern zur Erinnerung an Verfolgung und Widerstand im Nationalsozialismus (Hans Hesse & Elke Purpus), Klartext Verlag, 2010

Romanische Kirchen in Köln (Hiltrud Kier, Ute Chibidziura & Hans Georg Esch), Bachem, 2004

Kölns Romanische Kirchen (Clemens Kosch), Schnell & Steiner, 2005

Kölns Romanische Kirchen: Architektur, Kunst, Geschichte (Werner Schäfke), Emons, 2004

HISTORY

Das Mittelalterliche Köln: Der Historische Stadtführer (Carl Dietmar), Bachem Verlag, 2003

Das Neuzeitliche Köln: Der Historische Stadtführer (Werner Jung), Bachem Verlag, 2002

Das Moderne Köln: Der Historische Stadtführer (Werner Jung), Bachem Verlag, 2005

The Empire Stops Here – A Journey along the Frontiers of the Roman World (Philip Parker) Jonathan Cape, 2009

Mittelalter in Köln: Eine Auswahl aus den Beständen des Kölnischen Stadtmuseums (Werner Schäfke), Emons, 2010

WEBSITES

www.koelntourismus.de (official Tourist Board)

www.stadt-koeln.de (official website of the Mayor)

www.koeln.de (City Portal for Cologne)

www.stattreisen-koeln.de (City walks away from the tourist routes)

www.expedition-colonia.de (Expedition Colonia – The City Exploration Festival, an annual three-week event offering tours with unusual topics)

www.romanische-kirchen-koeln.de (Friends of the Romanesque Churches of Cologne)

www.bilderbuch-koeln.de (extensive online archive of modern and old images of Cologne)

www.kvb-koeln.de (Cologne Transport Authority)

www.germany.travel (German Tourist Office)

The DuMont Fountain (DuMont-Brunnen) on Breite Strasse (see no. 3)

Acknowledgements

First and foremost I would like to thank my Viennese publisher, Christian Brandstätter Verlag, for realising the first edition of this book, especially Elisabeth Stein (commissioning editor), Else Rieger (editor), Ekke Wolf (design), Walter Goidinger (German translation), and Helmut Maurer (maps).

For kind permission to take photographs, as well as for arranging access and the provision of information, the following people and institutions are most gratefully acknowledged:

Sabine Abraham and Inga Malgady (Römische Grabkammer in Wieden); Gabriela Adams (Universitätsklinikum Köln); Franziska Bartz (Universität Köln); Rose and Mike Blackadder; Frank Blaeser and Gregor Jaeger (Kletterfabrik); Braustelle; Ralf Bröcker and Heinrich Spechtmeyer (Stadtentwässerungsbetriebe Köln); Hinnerick Bröskamp (intune-performance/DE CAMPO FILM); Kishor Chabra (Afghanische Hindus Gemeinde in Köln e.V.); Bettina Clever (Museum für Ostasiatische Kunst); Rifat Dumrum (Kervansaray Turkish Restaurant); Levent Ekiz; Jürgen Eifler; Monika Flick (Sterck Joh. Jos & Zoon); Robert Förster; Dr. Marianne Gechter (Stadt Köln, Archäologische Zone/Jüdisches Museum); Anita Glaub (Besteckhaus); Jane Hale, Dr. Klaus Hardering (Dombauverwaltung Köln); Hans Christian Hartmann and Dr. Rudolf Schmidt (KVB-Strassenbahn-Museum Thielenbruch); Haus Scholzen; Brigitta Hommelsheim (Marktverwaltung Stadt Köln); Dr. Patrick Honecker (University of Cologne); Hopper Hotel et cetera; Dr. Paul Kluitmann; Stefanie Kursawe (Museum der Puppengeschichte); Holger Lang; Daniel Lemberg (Bocklemünd Jewish Cemetery); Oliver Lueb and Ursula Metz (Rautenstrauch-Joest-Museum); Kölner Zoo; Prof. Dr. Herwig Maehler; Heribert Malchers and Stefanie Brands (Hänneschen Puppenspiele der Stadt Köln); Dr. Edgar Mayer (Stiftung Butzweilerhof Köln); A. Michael Marx; Monika Moik and Henning von Dombois (Duftmuseum im Farina-Haus); Andy Mossack; Volker Müller; Kathinka Pasveer (Stockhausen Stiftung für Musik); Michael Paukner (EL-DE-Haus); Marek Pryjomko; Brigitte Rollersbroich (Tyll Kroha Kölner Münzkabinett); Cornelia Römer; Jaime F. Rubio; Sönke Schacht (Neptunbad Premium Sports & Spa); Karl Schiesberg (Weisser Holunder); Rudolf Schmutz; Robert Schwienbacher (Kölner Forschungs-Institut für Festungsarchitektur); Joerg Seidel and Uwe Müller (Rheinisches Industriebahn-Museum); Andrea Seinen (Hotel Chelsea); Arne Seringer (Flora und Botanischer Garten Köln); Adrian Smith; Mary Smith; Wolfgang and Eva Steffens (Senfmuseum); Michael Strassburger (Odeon Kino); Frank Straube and Jörg Schmitter (RheinEnergie AG); Claudia Teichner (Kölner Karnevalsmuseum); Prof. Dr. Renate Thomas, Prof. Dr. Hansgerd Hellenkemper and Dr. Friederike Naumann-Steckner (Römisch-Germanisches-Museum Köln); Angelika Wied (Violin Expo Cologne); Heike Wester; Raphael Wissing, Tim Hamacher and Rita Wagner (Kölnisches Stadtmuseum); and Rosi Zander (Barbarastollen).

For accommodation, the staff at Hotel Star am Dom and Hotel Elite an der Universität, especially Wei Ying Chen.

For translations and moral support, Roswitha Reisinger.

For help with picture selection, Bob Barber, Andreas Eberhart, Tav Falco, and Simon Laffoley.

For website and technical support, Richard Tinkler.

Thanks also to my great cousin James Dickinson, whose boundless enthusiasm for my work has been both inspirational and infectious.

Last but not least I would like to thank the people of Cologne, who without exception were friendly and of great assistance to me during the time I spent in their fascinating and historic city.

2nd Revised Edition published by The Urban Explorer, 2014
A division of Duncan J. D. Smith
contact@duncanjdsmith.com
www.onlyinguides.com
www.duncanjdsmith.com

First published by Christian Brandstätter Verlag, 2011

Graphic design: Stefan Fuhrer
Typesetting and picture editing: Ekke Wolf
Revision typesetting and picture editing: Franz Hanns
Maps: APA, Vienna
Printed and bound by GraphyCems, Spain

ISBN 978-3-9503662-2-8

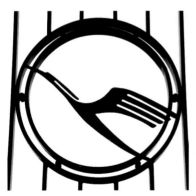

The familiar Lufthansa logo at the former
Köln-Butzweilerhof Airport (see no. 64)